the UBI-QUITOUS PER-SUADERS

A fifty year update of Vance Packard's book *The Hidden Persuaders*

WORDS by george PARKER / COVER and BOOK DESIGN by chris PARKER

ACKNOWLEDGEments

I won't go into the usual litany of groveling praise to everyone I've ever worked alongside, got drunk with, or woken up next to in the morning. However, a few special mentions. Jerry Calmes of Entrepreneur Press for the original idea of updating the Vance Packard classic. My agent, Bob Diforio for attempting to sell it to retarded publishers. Jeff Goodby for the Foreword. Jonah Bloom of AdAge for putting up with my frequent gaffes. Piers Fawkes of psfk, for giving me a platform to spout shit. My wife Maureen for putting up with the rest of my shit all these years... But most of all, to my Art Director Extraordinaire son, Chris Parker, for his superb cover and internal design. Which makes other business books look like the abysmal turds they invariably are.

CONtents

chapter EIGHT / get 'em while THEY'RE YOUNG / 105

Why the Adverati are hell bent on persuading children they should eat crap and play with things that might kill them. Most advertising aimed at children under the age of twelve is for junk food, plastic toys and electronic gizmos that invariably break before the batteries run out. Teens must have everything "cool" and Madison Avenue will make sure they do.

chapter NINE / is the PURPLE PILL making you SEE RED? / 119

Having persuaded us to smoke, drink, and eat our brains out for years, the Adverati have now discovered medicine, and are committed to having us all lead a healthier life. Well, as long as Big Pharma, hospitals, and insurance companies are ready to foot the bill!

chapter TEN / the FUTURE was/is/will be TECHNOLOGY / 138

In *The Graduate*, Dustin Hoffman was advised the future would be plastics. Sorry, close, but no cigar. They should have said technology. Because billions are spent annually persuading companies to buy hardware, software, and information systems that are obsolete before they're even paid for. No wonder BDAs love technology clients and their accounts, even though they invariably end up being a giant pain in the ass.

chapter ELEVEN / all POLITICS are AS ADVERTISED / 155

Fifty years ago, Vance Packard wrote about the ever increasing influence and effect of advertising on the political process. Today, its expense and impact is many times greater than it was back then. We explore the current state of political advertising and what awfulness we can expect in the future.

fore-WORD

by jeff GOODBY

If there were an emperor of advertising, I like to think he'd say things like, "Bring me George Parker's head, braised first to seal the juices, then roasted in a nice medley of root vegetables."

Yeah, George is a little controversial. He is, after all, the man who regularly refers to Martin Sorrell, probably the most powerful guy in advertising, as the "Poisoned Dwarf." He calls out big international clients in unflattering terms that often involve genitalia or bottom-feeding fish. And he's probably said some upsetting things about me that I've somehow managed to miss.

Yet here I am writing the preface of his Goddamn book. Because the thing is, the guy is so often, well, right.

There is still more Georgian rightness in what you're about to read between these covers. But what he has to say in here is not just right, it's hugely inspirational. How?

My first advertising job was at J. Walter Thompson/ San Francisco in 1977. One day, a woman in the media department, one of their more senior buyers, asked whether I had been requested to "airbrush female breasts into the ice cube photos" yet.

I laughed. "That's a myth, Joanne. One of those paranoia's people like Vance Packard have perpetuated."

She pitied my quaint naïveté. "You wait," she smiled, and walked off.

Thirty years later I have yet to review my first nude female ice cube separation job. Nor have I inserted "HAVE SEX NOW" flash frames into Bud TV ads or layered subliminal cereal buying suggestions into the Muzak soundtrack at a grocery store. I have, however, learned that there is something much more insidiously dangerous in advertising than these bogus, distracting worries — and that is the aggressive and cynical acceptance of – indeed, even celebration of – dumbing down.

Dumbing down is treating people like less intelligent sheep to be manipulated. It presumes they won't notice ham-fisted logic, irritating repetition, or the vulgar appropriation of culture and symbols dear to them. It blithely assumes that they don't know the difference between funny enough and truly funny, between beautiful enough and truly beautiful.

Ninety-nine per cent of advertising has always been about dumbing down. Advertising people, in fact, are unrepentant about this, even proud of it. People like David Ogilvy himself were fond of saying that advertising is, after all, not art. A creative director I worked with in the seventies was fond of putting down people who loathed one of his commercials by saying, "Yeah, but you noticed it."

There is a big hairy redemptive animal coming for such Luddites and it's called the Internet. Suddenly, people are developing the freedom to do away with insulting ads, even before they're exposed to them. Suddenly, more and more advertising people are being forced to wonder whether their messages are truly welcome.

George relishes the public flaying of the dumbing down forces. He has taken up a pike herein and is climbing over the crowd to finish the job. He knows that advertising may be a business that now turns out only one per cent goodness, but that letting the world devolve into dreary mercantilism and mere information gathering would be a sad fate for all of us. Because when advertising is done right, it changes commerce into magic, humor, even delight.

George will keep toiling until it all could be described that way. I think he has his work cut out for him. But this book is a great start.

Jeff Goodby
Co-Chairman
Goodby, Silverstein & Partners

INTRO-
duction

Fifty years ago, the publication of The Hidden Persuaders confirmed the American public's suspicion that the advertising business was engaging in devious practices, manipulating the buying habits of consumers through the use of subliminal messaging and thought control. How have things changed in the fifty years since, if indeed they have changed? That's what we shall explore.

Perhaps the best movie ever made about the advertising business starts with a helicopter shot of Manhattan. The film is photographed in black and white, high contrast, and somewhat grainy. The helicopter lands at the east river heliport. Waiting is a black stretch limo. A black suited chauffeur wearing dark aviator glasses stands by its open door. The door of the helicopter opens and out steps a tall, gaunt figure. He has long grey hair in a scraggy ponytail, is dressed in black leather motorcycle gear and boots, and is carrying a black attaché case chained to his wrist. The camera follows him as he stomps over to the limo. We notice on the back of his motorcycle jacket are a set of metal studs spelling out the letters… MENSA.

The limo pulls up outside a multi-story building on Madison Avenue and the MENSA guy enters through the revolving doors. We cut to the boardroom on the upper floor. Various members of the board of directors of a famous ad agency are awaiting the MENSA guy's arrival. The door bursts open and he strides in. Banging his case on the hundred-foot long, six-inch thick, mahogany table, he unlocks it and takes out a single piece of flimsy, translucent, onionskin paper. This is the moment they have all been waiting for. This is the world renowned guru of "motivational insights" they've paid hundreds of thousands of dollars to in order to benefit from his expertise on how they should advertise the "Schmucks Beer" account.

He speaks.

"Beer is peepy-dicky."

He puts the sheet of paper back in the case, locks it, and departs the room leaving behind a somewhat stunned and ashen faced bunch of Madison Avenue heavies.

The film was *Putney Swope*. A long forgotten, little known, but extraordinarily insightful cult movie made and directed by Robert Downey Sr., in 1969. Sadly, today Mr. Downey is remembered primarily for being the father of my all time favorite hell raiser, Robert Downey Jr.

The great thing about *Putney Swope* was that it confirmed the American public's worst suspicions of what the ad biz was really about. Even though it was an outrageous piece of satire, it did it far more believably than the saccharine laden, big hat wearing Doris Day, and martini swilling Rock Hudson epics, such as *Pillow Talk*; a film that unfailingly portrayed the ad biz as a glamorous world full of glamorous people who's main objective in life was to help corporate America convince millions of American consumers of the unquestioned benefits of leviathan sized cars, ever more powerful detergents, headache cures, and increasingly potent booze and cigarettes.

But in truth, even though when it comes to ethical standards, advertising people had always been placed lower down the totem pole than used car salesmen, the real disenchantment had begun to gather pace twelve years earlier in 1957 with the publication of a best selling book, *The Hidden Persuaders* by Vance Packard. This enormously successful book served to confirm the public's nagging suspicion that they were somehow being manipulated by a sinister combination of sharkskin suited Madison Avenue hucksters, and pseudo-psychiatrists with hard to pronounce European names and Transylvanian University credentials.

Yet, ironically enough, it was actually the hucksters of Madison Avenue who were being manipulated by the pseudo-psychiatrists, to the tune of tens of thousands of dollars a year in consulting fees. Because, as was demonstrated in the opening minutes of *Putney Swope*, even the largest ad agency never fails to clutch at the most ridiculous of straws if it believes it will help them arrive at a more effective way to influence the consumer and, in turn, liposuction more money out of their clients.

As *The Hidden Persuaders* pointed out, because of the lure of the heretofore uncharted waters of motivational research, even the most conservative ad agencies were ready to swoon when Dr. Shnitzlegruber delivered such mind-numbing insights as, "A sedan is a wife, but a convertible is a mistress." Or in the case of the MENSA guy in *Putney Swope*, "Beer is peepy-dicky."

Although *The Hidden Persuaders* was immensely popular and sold more than a million copies, it was criticized, not only by the advertising profession who felt it would unduly alarm the public by exposing some of the methodologies they were prepared to use on behalf of their clients, but also by psychologists and others in the social sciences who described it as light on facts and high on sensationalism. To be honest, there is a certain amount of truth in that accusation. But it did serve to open the American public's eyes to some of the strange and, indeed what many perceived as, perverse methodologies manufacturers of goods, providers of services, and the agencies they employed relied on to develop advertising that would persuade the American public to buy ever increasing amounts of stuff that they didn't really need.

In the fifty years that have passed since the publication of Packard's book, a great many things about how advertising is created and disseminated have changed. And yet, a surprisingly large number haven't. So, the purpose of this book is not merely to update the ideas, myths, and misconceptions that made up so much of *The Hidden Persuaders*, but to address the fact that as advertising has become so much more pervasive, if not ubiquitous in our lives. Ad agencies are still no nearer to understanding what drives people to make their buying decisions, let alone being able to influence them in making those decisions, than they were fifty years ago.

Conflating this puzzle is the fact that when Packard wrote his book fifty years ago, 95 percent of the viewing public watched television on only three networks, and you could reach the vast majority of Americans by buying ad space in just three magazines: the *Saturday Evening Post, Life,* and *Look.* Today, with the advent of the Internet, cable, satellite, ever increasing methods of broadband content distribution, and the upsurge of "alternative media," such as digital, online, guerrilla, viral, wireless, word-of-mouth, product placement, and other rapidly proliferating choices, a client now has many, many more ways to blow dumpster loads of money on advertising campaigns that still offer no guarantee of success. At the same time consumers now have multiple ways to screen out unwanted advertising through the use of electronic devices which allow them to skip TV commercials and ignore spam, text, and those annoying calls that always happen as you are about to sit down to your gourmet macaroni and cheese.

So, it isn't really surprising that many observers are increasingly of the opinion the days of the advertising agency as we have always known it are numbered. And even though agencies pay enthusiastic lip service to the notion they need to reinvent themselves, the vast majority are doing a remarkably poor job of going about it.

This book will look at how we got where we are today, how we should evaluate (wherever possible) the effectiveness of what is currently offered, and finally what we can only guess about the future of advertising and how it will continue to affect us, or perhaps not.

Hopefully this will be of interest and use to those who

continue to rely on advertising as a part of their marketing endeavors. There may even be a few morsels of advice, encouragement, and reassurance for the Armani-suited, weekends-at-the-Hamptons, Soho-loft living, limo-chauffeured Adverati of Madison Avenue, who—in spite of a constant gnawing in the pit of their stomach that is telling them all is not well back at the agency ranch—don't have a clue as to what the hell they should do about it.

chapter ONE. *relax...*

YOU'RE FEELING DROWSY

Imagine the mindset of midfifties America, which combined the suburban ideal of a Levittown paradise with Red Menace paranoia to create a fertile ground for the likes of motivational researchers, Dr. Dichter and Lois Cheskin, whose legacy continues today through twenty-first century practitioners of the snake oil arts.

In *The Hidden Persuaders*, Packard talks about "the large-scale efforts being made, often with impressive success to channel our unthinking habits, our purchasing decisions, and our thought processes by the use of insights gleaned from psychiatry." Unfortunately, with most of the examples he referred to, few were actually identified by name, with Packard relying on such generic descriptions as "a leading brand of toothpaste." Yet, these were presented as irrefutable illustrations of the success of these methods. So, it all came across as pretty scary. Particularly when you consider the fifties were rife with rumors of the dangers of the Red Menace and Manchurian-Candidate-like mind manipulation. As the book was published in the aftermath of the Korean War and with the added sensationalism engendered by the McCarthy congressional hearings, the media was more than happy to ride this rewarding wave of paranoia. And the timing certainly helped Packard hit a receptive chord with the anxious American public and sell a large number of books.

It also helped that the advertising business was always looked at with a somewhat jaundiced eye. Long perceived as snake oil salesmen who relied on smoke and mirrors to sell their clients wares, the industry's image was not helped by such derogatory films as *The Hucksters,* released in 1947, ten years before Packard wrote *The Hidden Persuaders.* Perhaps the title of an autobiographical book written in the seventies by Jacques Seguela, a famous French ad man and principal of a large international agency, best sums up the feelings, not just of the general public, but of many of those who actually made a living in advertising: *"Please don't tell my mother I work in advertising. Tell her I play the piano in a brothel."*

Throughout his book, Packard relentlessly gives example after example of how psychologists at "America's largest advertising agencies are probing humans in an attempt to beam messages to people of high anxiety, body consciousness, and hostility." He even talks of how a major Chicago agency is using psychiatric probing techniques on little girls. All pretty strong stuff, particularly in his choice of language, but as is usual throughout the book, with few specifics. As a further demonstration of how all forms of marketing and selling are being motivationally driven, he cites an unnamed "community of tomorrow" in Florida where the management provides newly signed-up tenants with a set of brand new friends along with clean linens when you move in. Unfortunately, my extensive research failed to come up with any reference of this hellish Shangri-La.

As a catch-all throughout the book, Packard uses two terms: "depth Interviews" and motivational research. Although the latter had been around since the thirties, motivational research, as he referred to it, really took off in the fifties. This was primarily because of the efforts of two men, Louis Cheskin and Ernst Dichter, and in no small measure to the notoriety Packard bestowed on both of them via his book.

Ernst Dichter was the archetypical European-looking "shrink," with tweedy suits and jelly-jar-bottom spectacles. He was the founder of The Institute of Motivational Research, where he and his staff of twenty or so, working out of a Gothic pile on a hill overlooking the Hudson River, studied such esoteric subjects as the effects of TV cartoons on the toilet habits of children at different times of the day, and why women buy different kinds of ketchup during their menstrual cycles. He insisted on always being referred to by all and sundry as doctor, even though there is some doubt he ever received a bachelor's degree, let alone a doctorate. According to Dichter's theories, humans were immature with lots of irrational insecurities and insatiable, erotic desires. This played nicely into the hands of Madison Avenue by providing titillating and easy to understand explanations for hard to comprehend consumer behavior. Plus, liberal helpings of sexual innuendo dressed up as science never hurt anyone.

Even though through the fifties Dichter's star was shining brightly and in his heyday he could command five hundred dollars a day in consulting fees, which was a considerable sum of money for the times, by the time the sixties rolled around he quickly fell from favor and soon disappeared from view.

Louis Cheskin, however, lasted much longer, and even though he died several years ago, his company still survives. This is no doubt because Cheskin considered that relying primarily on Freudian psychology, as Dichter did, was not always the way to go when poking around in the human psyche. A great example of this is when both men worked on cigarettes. Dichter claimed that women smoked more when ads showed "erect" cigarettes in the hands and mouths of other women because they suffered from "penis envy." Cheskin considered this to be a load of old tripe, explaining, logically, that women smoked more when they saw pictures of other women smoking. I must confess, even though Dichter's theory is more titillating, I'm with Cheskin on this one.

Cheskin's work was based on logic rather than bullshit. He looked for elements in behavior that signified acceptance and positive sensation. He would not commit to a recommendation until those triggers could be tested against real people. It's no surprise that Cheskin is remembered for many successes, including the creation of the Marlboro Man, the Gerber Baby, and the research responsible for the Ford Mustang and Lincoln Continental. Interestingly enough, months before the launch of the Edsel, Cheskin wrote a famous article forecasting it would be a bomb. Ford management told him he was full of crap. When after the launch he was proved to be absolutely correct, they immediately hired him as a consultant.

The only thing that Dichter is remembered for is telling the management of Mattel to make Barbie's boobs bigger prior to the launch of the doll - no surprises there.

It's obvious, however, when reading *The Hidden Persuaders* that Packard was much more taken with Dichter than Cheskin. Throughout its two hundred and thirty pages, Dichter, who is always referred to as Dr. Dichter, is mentioned more than fifty times, whereas Cheskin, who has to make do with a simple mister, gets a mere fifteen mentions. No doubt Packard was convinced Dr. Dichter's more sensational brand of motivational research would sell a hell of a lot more books than Mr. Cheskin's. He was absolutely right.

While it lasted, motivational research was a big deal. Even those who thought it was pure bullshit kept their mouths shut as far too many of their bosses, who should have known better, fell for it hook, line, and sinker. Remember the MENSA guy's "peepy-dicky" revelation from the opening scene of *Putney Swope?* As someone who has bounced around the rancid tar pits of Madison Avenue for far more years than was good for my liver, I can assure you that ad agency management will grab on to anything, no matter how outrageous, if they think it will help them win new business, save an existing account, or liposuction extra income from an unfortunate client before the day arrives—and believe me, it always does—when the long-suffering client begins thinking the grass might be greener somewhere else.

But in reality, Motivational Research never went away.

Over fifty years have passed since it was featured so prominently, and scarily, in Packard's book, but it has been constantly reinvented and repositioned in a less threatening guise. We now have an ever increasing proliferation of psycho/marketing/branding companies that claim, once again, an ability to delve into the inner depths of the consumer's mind and deliver to their clients a series of magic triggers that will reduce the waste of ineffective advertising and help them create messages that bring on an insatiable desire for their products.

Today, much of it is data driven, relying on masses of information that, through the miraculous manipulations of digital technology, allow its practitioners to forecast what advertising messages will influence a single welfare mother of three, living in a trailer park in Georgia, to buy a certain brand of cornflakes.

Often referred to as psychometrics, this new interpretation of motivational research relies on such awe inspiring and exciting sounding techniques as "factor analysis, multidimensional scaling, and data clustering." Very impressive, but still primarily bullshit.

A New York–based consultancy, Psychologics, claims through its proprietary technique, the "Psychological Probe," that it can reveal the core unconscious drivers of consumer behavior. The company's president, Dr. Sam Cohen, blithely sprinkles his conversations with words such as "dreamwork," "archetype insight technique," "covert imagery," "personification," and so on. He loftily claims that if companies don't realize they must own a piece of the consumers mind, they won't make it in business today. As he puts it, "I go where Freud would have gone if he were alive today." Ah yes, it never takes these guys long to get back to Freud.

Another outfit riding the crest of the rediscovered motivational research wave is Archetype Discoveries. The company is run out of Palm Beach, Florida, by Dr. Clothaire Rapaille, a long-haired, Beau Brummell-esque dressing Frenchman. Dr. Rapaille's major claim to fame seems to be that when working with Chrysler, he informed them that the code (he prepares "codes" for his clients) for their Jeep vehicle was "Horse." He said that it should be positioned as a go-anywhere vehicle, and because of this, they should not hesitate to replace the square headlights with round ones for the stunningly simple reason that horses have round eyes.

Inspection of the Archetype Discoveries Web site and literature shows how "Discoveries" are conducted in a step-by-step series of phases. A brief sample of the mind-numbing text on the site would be: "Phase Three: Following the lasting imprinting session, the third meeting with the Archetype Team is held. The results of the second-phase imprinting sessions are analyzed, and a new orientation is established. Then the Archetype Team Leader meets with the Core Team. We begin to understand the archetype, and to break the code." Pretty heavy stuff and no doubt worth the hundreds of thousands of dollars many clients are prepared to pay for it. Or, as one of the agency board members put it so well in *Putney Swope* after hearing the MENSA guy deliver his "peepy-dicky," "Well, it must be true; we paid a shit-load of money for it."

The funny thing is, if you go to the Web sites of both companies, they are equally badly designed and written, with the Archetype Discoveries site being particularly unfortunate. The site consists of juvenile graphics surrounded by hard to read, reversed out typography, accompanied by the obligatory picture of the erudite doctor in studious poses. Truly an "archetype" for bad Web site design.

Fifty years ago when Vance Packard wrote his book, there were no Web sites because there was no Internet, desktop computers, cell phones, PDA's, or Blackberries. There weren't even fax machines, and the first Xerox dry copier wasn't destined to revolutionize office productivity for another two years. And even though by today's standards we would probably think of fifties business technology and marketing/selling methodology as somewhat primitive, at the time, many were perplexed and worried by the pace with which things were changing. Packard's book played upon and reinforced those fears. As with all those who seek to justify their sensational revelations as a concern for the common good, at the end of his first chapter, Packard states: "These depth manipulators are, in their operations beneath the surface of American life, starting to acquire a power of persuasion that is becoming a matter of justifiable public scrutiny and concern. It is hoped that this book may contribute to the process of public scrutiny." Wow, if that isn't going to scare the bejesus out of you and make

you want to read the rest of the book, I don't know what will. I'd better think up something comparably scary for the end of this chapter!

Other practitioners of the dark arts of motivational research
are sprinkled throughout *The Hidden Persuaders*—all with subtle and
sometimes not so subtle references to their great expertise in mass
manipulation. Burleigh Gardener, the president of an outfit with the
somewhat innocuous name of Social Research, makes constant references to such "classic authorities" as Korzybski on semantics,
Whitehead on symbolic logic, and Durkhelm on sociology. All very
impressive, and all of which I am sure meant absolutely nothing to
Vance Packard, let alone his readers.

My favorite character though is the research director of a
major ad agency Packard makes mention of. A tense, tweedy man,
who when asked if he had a previous interest in psychology, replied
that his mother was a psychoanalyst and that he himself had once
worked as an aide in an insane asylum. Based on virtually every
agency I have ever worked in, I would say this guy was perfectly suited for his chosen profession.

One of the few truly valid points Packard does make early on
in the book is the fact that 99 percent of all the products we buy are
virtually the same. Even today, with rare exception, all fast moving
consumer goods (FCMG's) are homogenous. Seemingly, the only
exceptions are the ones that might end up killing you. As I write this,
the "scare du jour" is the news that prepackaged spinach, which is
thought to be infected with E. coli, has just reduced the population of
the western United States by half a dozen people. Apart from this
odd, extreme example, which will probably require the expenditure of
billons of dollars by the spinach growers of America to bring the buying public back, the similarity of most products has meant that ad
agencies have hammered clients over the head for years with the
"brand mantra" as the primary reason why they need to keep spending enormous sums of money on continuing ad campaigns. If everything about a product is the same, the only difference must be the
name on the package, i.e., the brand. Hence promoting the brand,
rather than the actual product itself becomes the primary function of
advertising. This is something I will go into in greater depth later in

the book. For now, suffice it to say that more wool, soft soap, snake oil, and general bullshit has been pulled over more clients eyes, while more money has been burned on the flaming pyres of "Building Brand Awareness" than any other single endeavor in the history of advertising.

Still, I have to admit, it's provided people like me with a very good living.

As with most businesses, advertising agencies go through cycles. Not just in the way they work, the quality of the work they produce, and how they are recompensed, but also in how they are perceived and respected by their clients and the general public. In spite of Mr. Seguela's desire to keep his mother in the dark regarding his preferred profession, choosing to build a career in an advertising agency has always been held in higher regard in Europe than in America, in spite of the fact that modern advertising as we know it originated in the U.S. This is perhaps partially due to the fact that there has always been tighter regulation on the content (if not quality) of advertising in Europe than in the U.S. However, the primary reason must surely be because commercial broadcast (TV and radio) advertising didn't take off until much later there than it did here. In virtually all of Europe, broadcasting was funded by each countries respective government and so didn't have to rely on the income from advertising to pay the bills. Consequently, when commercial TV and radio started in these virgin territories, the commercials were much less in your face than those the American audience had become accustomed to. There were no hammers in the head and flaming stomachs, let alone animated cartoons of razors slicing away magnified whiskers as Jake Dumbrowski, defensive end of the Metro Maulers droned on and on about how Whizo shaving foam lets you shave close, shave fast, without irritation. Then, to be absolutely sure the message had been hammered into your aching brain, he would repeat it at least another half dozen times, accompanied by big titles flashing the words "Fast," "Close," "Without Irritation" on the screen yet another half dozen times. Subtle was not a word lightly bandied about on Madison Avenue in those days. Whereas in Europe there was a more conscious effort to make commercials that would be perceived as entertaining and interesting, otherwise, the viewer would go to the kitchen and put the kettle on, or dash to the loo for a quick pee before the second half of the Benny Hill Show came on.

Sad to say, this generalization no longer holds true. Whenever I check into a hotel in London, Paris, Stockholm, Rome— or whatever other exotic location I have managed to convince a client it's essential for me to visit while staying in a multiple star, outrageously priced hotel so I can bust my chops on their behalf whilst wallowing in profligate luxury—the first thing I do is turn on the TV. Now and again I am pleasantly surprised and titillated by the quality and entertainment value of some of the commercials I view through my jet-lagged eyes as I rapidly empty the contents of the twenty-dollar-a-pop minibar."

Increasingly, I am not. But that's not to say there isn't hope that we'll get through the tunnel of mediocrity a great deal of today's advertising seems to be trapped in and eventually come out the other side able to enjoy work that doesn't treat us like a bunch of morons.

Strangely enough, this unfortunate state of affairs hasn't come about because of a lack of money to throw at the problem; in fact, I sometimes think it's happened because we have too much money at our disposal. As Howard Gossage, a famous, long dead ad man I love to quote, once said, "Most advertising is the application of a ten thousand dollar hammer to drive in a five cent thumbtack."

Right now, the average production cost of a network–ready, thirty-second TV commercial is getting close to six hundred thousand dollars, and that's just to make it. Buying the air time to run it with a decent amount of frequency and exposure will cost you millions more. Compounding the felony is the fact that many of the commercials we see today are masterpieces of cinematographic art, often layered with massive amounts of CGI (computer graphics) that enable cars to fly through the air and land on enormous ice floes in the Arctic sea, or causes housewives to be in such orgasmic raptures over the pineapple scent of their furniture polish, they are transported via a magic carpet to a beach in Tahiti. Unfortunately, in spite of advertising agencies spending more than the gross national product of a small African nation to produce these epics, when it comes to the vast majority of today's advertising, I can only echo the words of Gertrude Stein: "There's no there, there."

But as I said, it's a cyclical business, and in the next chapter we'll explore how we went from the hard sell of the fifties to the creative revolution of the sixties, then back to the even harder sell in the seventies. The thing that makes this current cycle different is that we seem to have become caught up in an accelerating technological revolution that in some ways seems to have passed and left us behind. While methods of delivery are proliferating, the quality of what we are delivering is declining. Without being able to rely on the crutch of ever more sophisticated production values and seemingly limitless budgets, it is doubtful that much of today's advertising would have any impact at all.

Compounding the problem is the fact that back in the days of *The Hidden Persuaders*, ad agencies simply created press, radio, and TV ads. Their media departments then bought the time and space to run the ads, the agency collected its 15 percent commission from the media, and everyone got fat and happy. Today's agencies are facing a veritable maelstrom of media and other communication choices. Everything from sponsorship, to guerilla marketing, to product placement, to consumer generated content, to the latest "buzz du jour," social networking. All of these contribute to the so-called "new-media-marketing" tsunami that's overtaken the ad biz in the last few years. Suffice to say that by the time you're reading this, the viral virus will have metastasized into a veritable bubonic plague of even more infantile, and most probably ineffective, marketing options. But without a doubt, every agency worth its salt will have jumped on the bandwagon and be promoting its own particular version of whatever is "hot."

No matter what bandwagon they do choose to jump on, most agencies have paid lip service for years to the concept of "Totally Integrated Marketing." With this concept, agencies can promise to offer clients the full Chinese restaurant menu of services: such as media planning and buying from column A, with a little direct marketing from column C, and how about some "teaser" ads from column D to start off with as an appetizer tonight? But, the way many agencies are structured today actually works against this, because in most cases, all these different services are not only usually run as separate profit centers, but very often there is little interaction between the people working in the different divisions. Consequently, the very concept of total integration is virtually impossible to achieve, and the work produced by each division often bears little resemblance to the others.

Back in the days of *The Hidden Persuaders*, just about every agency was independent. Now, virtually every major agency is part of one of four giant conglomerates whose slimy tentacles stretch around the known universe, strangling the breath, vitality, and guts out of most of the agencies they've swallowed up.

I shall be dealing with these "Dark Princes of Commerce" in a later chapter, suffice it to say at this stage that all these multinational conglomerates are run by bean counters anxious to make the next quarters numbers look good, because all are publicly traded. The bottom line is simply about making the bottom line. Or, as the financial director of one of Madison Avenue's largest agencies was reputed to have said upon hearing they had just picked up a prestigious national account that would allow the agency to do some high quality work, "Fuck the work. What about the money?"

And there's the rub. Even though the conglomerates have tried to sell the existing clients of agencies they have acquired on the benefits of consolidation and the ensuing economies of scale that will come from having all these wonderful services under one roof, it hasn't worked out like that. Now the member agencies are answerable to the conglomerate's bean counter who, more often than not, is based on a different continent with the single task of meeting the stringent financial goals dictated by the conglomerate's board of directors. The result is that agencies have become increasingly risk averse when it comes to carrying out what should be their primary function, producing great advertising for their clients. This is why so much of today's advertising is bad. Yes, on the surface a lot of it is flashy, particularly in execution, as I mentioned earlier, but far too much of it lacks substance and smells of fear. The fear that comes from not taking risks, of relying on research that always encourages the expected, and of bending over backwards to give the client what they want, rather than what they need.

But as anyone who's been in advertising for any length of time knows, it is quite possibly the dumbest business in the world. The average profit margin of most agencies is less than that of an ice cream vendor. And while it's true that many of them take in substantial fees, and large numbers of their senior agency people live like potentates, it's a sad fact that even the biggest of these agencies are run like an eighteenth century Opera Buffo. At the time of writing, the Interpublic Group, which is the third largest agency conglomerate in the world with hundreds of offices in dozens of countries, is mired up to its armpits in debt and has had to restate its earnings for the past four years. So what did they do at a recent Cannes International Advertising Film Festival when all the chit-chat of the Adverati as they sipped their twenty-dollar mimosas on La Croisette was about how deep in the financial mire they were? Interpublic went out and chartered the *Christina O*, the late Aristotle Onassis's battle-ship-sized yacht, and invited several hundred people to a multi-thousand-dollar party.

That takes balls, not to mention a large dash of hubris.

But to prove how some things seemingly haven't changed over the last fifty years, Vance Packard quotes a motivational research evangelist addressing a meeting of senior ad execs at a luncheon in Philadelphia all those years ago and warning, "Some of you will find it hard to change because literally I am pulling the rug out from under the notion that logic and purpose direct the things that you do." Unsurprisingly, the admiring crowd burst into rapturous applause.

Can you honestly think of any other business where the listeners would have listened to such a statement without bombarding the speaker with rotten eggs?

I think dear old David Ogilvy put it best in the final chapter of his first book written in 1963, *Confessions of an Advertising Man*. His sister, Lady Hendy, asked David—who was the most outrageous snob and loved to drop the names of friends and acquaintances from Winston Churchill to Her Majesty the Queen—"Should advertising be abolished?" He answered with the last two lines of the book: "No, my darling sister, advertising should not be abolished. But it must be reformed."

And that was forty five years ago!

In the rest of this book I will briefly dwell on how we got to the present state of things on Madison Avenue and then move on to how we might either go about reforming them, as David suggests, or simply have a jolly (and expensive) party on the *Christina O* as we continue to steam blithely towards the glistening icebergs ahead.

chapter TWO. *it's déjà vu* **ALL OVER AGAIN**

How advertising went from insidious mind manipulation and hitting the consumer over the head with a two-by-four, hard sell of the fifties, to the creative revolution of the sixties, then back to the hard sell of the seventies, and why it continues to do all of the above in never ending, repetitive cycles.

Even though he wrote the hugely successful *How to Succeed in Business without Really Trying*, whilst working as a copywriter in a Madison Avenue ad agency, Shepherd Mead's first published book after leaving the advertising profession was *The Admen*. This long forgotten epic appeared in 1958, just one year after Vance Packard wrote *The Hidden Persuaders*, and even though today *The Admen* might be considered a somewhat melodramatic potboiler, it was at the time, a surprisingly accurate snapshot of what the advertising agency world was like in the fifties. It is probably still a pretty accurate insight into the insanity and paranoia of the day to day workings of your average Big Dumb Agency today. Rereading it after nearly fifty years is still a salutary experience for those of us attempting to earn a crust in the business, not just in terms of what would be considered by today's standards the very un-politically correct attitudes and habits of 1950s Americans. I mean, what with everyone smoking about three packs of cigarettes a day in the office, bar, restaurant, car, on the train, in the theater, and cinema, plus drinking copious amounts of alcohol before lunch, during lunch, and after lunch. Then going through the whole cycle again during the pre/during/après dinner cycle. Fortunately, the beverage selection for breakfast seemed to be limited to juice and coffee. And why the hell not, I have to ask myself. A great many of the major ad accounts in those days were tobacco and booze companies, and as David Ogilvy once proudly claimed, "I have always believed in using my client's products." Amen to that David. Mine's a large gin and tonic. Cheers!

What also comes across strongly in *The Admen* is the difference in scale between the agencies of fifty years ago and those of today. Torrey Inc., the agency which serves as the centerpiece of the story, is described as a medium-sized Madison Avenue shop with billings in the range of twelve to fifteen million dollars. The big agencies they aspired to join the ranks of one day had billings in the range of fifty to one hundred million. Today this would be regarded as very small beer, with major agencies such as BBD&O, JWT, O&M, and others boasting billings well in excess of a billion dollars.

Another aspect of advertising in those days we've since forgotten about in this age of globalization was just how parochial the agency business was. Virtually all the accounts and the vast majority of the billings were concentrated in the U.S., and most of those were handled by either New York or Chicago agencies. And even though several of the larger agencies maintained offices in various capitols of Europe and South America, you could count them on the fingers of one hand, with most being little more than lightly staffed service offices to ensure clients with international operations could feel they were being looked after when they blew into town for a meeting.

Until the early sixties, the nature of the end product, i.e., the advertising that the agencies produced, had changed little from the nineteenth century. Print ads relied on the heavy handed and repetitious pounding away of perceived product benefits through clunky, hard-selling layouts featuring big, bold headlines, lots of repetitious copy. They would hammer away about how smoking Chesterfields was good for your throat and was indeed highly recommended by doctors. Others would explain how those clanging hammers in your head or that flaming acid in your stomach could be cured instantly through the application of miracle Pepto-Wizzo. Another product recommended by the American medical profession, or at least by a distinguished looking man - yes, it was always a man - wearing a white coat with a stethoscope draped around his neck. The visuals usually featured happy users, big pack shots and, wherever possible, more doctors. Illustration, rather than photography was very much in vogue, particularly in car ads, because through the miracle of heavily airbrushed and perspective distorted artwork, the artist could make those mighty Detroit chariots look even longer than they actually were. They were also guaranteed to have headlights big enough to stand atop the Pharos of Alexandria accompanied by mighty phalically engineered tailfins, which wouldn't have looked out of place on the pubescently throbbing flagship of Emperor Ming's battle fleet. When families were portrayed in ads, they consisted of an always grinning, forever pipe smoking, sports-coat-wearing dad in his mid-thirties, a slightly younger mum who rarely wore anything but full skirts and sensible twin sets, obviously with the finishing touch of a string of pearls. Two happy smiling kids, one boy, one girl, both preteen with copious freckles, and the mandatory family pet, usually a goofy looking Old English Sheep dog.

All of these elements summed up the picture of mid-1950s connubial bliss. This archetypal family lived in a Levittown suburban paradise and drove around in a humungous station wagon that the "little lady," along with the kids and the dog, would patiently wait in every evening at the nearest Long Island RR station. All for that happy moment when the 5:52 from Penn station would roll in and the "bread winner" would stagger off the train, having smashed down a trio of martinis in the bar car as he swapped war stories with the rest of his Manhattan warrior buddies.

It goes without saying that everyone in the ads was white.

Even with the growth of broadcast advertising, the formula remained pretty much the same. And though radio advertising had been around since the early twenties, with some making the claim that the first commercial radio station actually went on air in New Zealand at a time when the human population of that far off verdant land was outnumbered ten to one by its sheep population, the first paid-for radio commercial that we actually know about aired on WEAF New York in August of 1922. We should also remember that for many years, radio was listened to strictly in the home, unlike today when the vast majority of the radio audience listens to it while driving. Although car radios became available in the early thirties, their cost was prohibitive, and the audio quality pretty pathetic. As in the early days of television, most of the programming content was sponsored by a single company, rather than having individual adver-tisers buying thirty- or sixty-second spots as is the case today. Meaning that one of the very first soap operas, *The Ma Perkins Show*, was brought to you in its entirety by Oxydol detergent. Just as the *Life and Love of Dr. Susan* was a production of the Lux Radio Theater. So now you know why they're called soaps! But, to be fair, other major manufacturers of consumer products aimed particularly at a day time audience of housewives quickly got into the act, and the first nationally syndicated radio serial, *Today's Children,* was sponsored by the Pillsbury baking company. Even today, Proctor & Gamble, the world's largest manufacturer of soaps and detergents, is still the biggest single sponsor of soap operas. Only now these wonderful examples of the thespian art and craft are polluting the airwaves of daytime TV.

And so we come to TV. Even though the first recorded instance of a paid-for commercial airing on television was on July 1, 1941 with the broadcast of a ten-second spot for the Bulova Watch Company during a Brooklyn Dodgers, Philadelphia Phillies baseball game, for which they paid the mighty sum of nine dollars. Full-blown commercial TV did not take off until the post World War II era with the formation of the first nationwide TV network, NBC in 1947. Playing catch-up, CBS established its own nationwide network in 1950 by buying and building stations all over the country. They also poached away many of NBC's major stars, including Lucille Ball, who only agreed to come if she could bring along her husband, Desi Arnaz, to not only star in the show, but also to be responsible for financial control of the production. Now you know how the Desilu Empire was born! And even though it was calling itself a network in 1948, in truth, ABC merely consisted of a handful of individual stations in a few major cities, and didn't became the third network in actuality until 1953.

And so, at the time *The Hidden Persuaders* was written, if you wanted to advertise on television with a national campaign, those were your three choices. Yes, there were many individual stations scattered around the country, which you could use for regional campaigns and test markets, but for national TV, you had to talk to NBC, CBS, and ABC. Even in those early days it was becoming recognized that television was the single most powerful way for advertisers to reach the consumer, and with just three choices to cost effectively reach a national audience, it wasn't rocket science working out how to do it. I am sure there are many BDAs who today look back at those simple and highly profitable days with a great deal of envy.

The actual mechanics of creating and airing TV commercials was also much simpler in those days. Virtually all the programming, and obviously the commercials, were shot in black and white. Extensive use of color didn't happen until the late sixties and early seventies. The cinemaphotography, lighting, and set design were Spartan, sometimes almost primitive. Most of the TV spots were sixty seconds in length, and many of them used the stars appearing in the show the client was sponsoring. One of the best-known examples is Ronald Regan, who not only hosted the *General Electric Theatre* and *Death Valley Days*, but was also a leading spokesman for Chesterfield cigarettes for many years. In fact, what is now described as product placement was rampant in TV programming in the fifties and sixties, with once again the tobacco companies being the leading protagonists. For instance, when *I Love Lucy* was sponsored by Philip Morris, both Lucy and Desi would be seen smoking through the introductory credits. And believe it or not, at the end of *The Flintstones*, Fred, Wilma, Betty, and Barnie would sit around in their "rock-recliners" and light up a Winston. And remember, this was a cartoon show with a substantial proportion of the viewing audience being kids!

But even with only three national networks, the advertising component of the broadcast airtime was not as pervasive as it is today. Viewers were only subjected to an average of eight or nine minutes of commercials in every hour of programming. Today, twenty minutes is not unusual, with half a dozen program promos (which in reality is advertising for the station) thrown in for good measure. As for shopping channels, infomercials, and the unceasing bombardment of political advertising we are subjected to on an almost year round basis; I shall deal with these in a later chapter.

Print media at the time consisted of local and regional newspapers, Even those we consider as national today, such as the *New York Times, Washington Post, Wall Street Journal, USA Today*, and others, didn't have the national distribution so many of them enjoy today through the luxury of regional printing centers linked to their main editorial offices via satellite. And as I mentioned in the introduction, there were far fewer magazines than there are today, so you could reach the vast majority of Americans by buying ad space in just three magazines, the *Saturday Evening Post, Life*, and *Look*. Meaning that for advertising agencies in the fifties, life was much simpler and far more profitable than it is today. You could literally work out media schedules on the back of an envelope. Place a few ads, run a couple of TV spots, then sit back and wait for the media commissions to roll in. No wonder the three-martini lunch was the way to go!

Even in the sixties when I first arrived in the U.S. and managed to finagle myself a job at Benton & Bowles - yet another of the grand old agencies which no longer exist - I was quickly inducted into a "luncheon group." We gathered daily in the bar of the Gotham Hotel - which also no longer exists - just around the corner from B&B's offices on Fifth Avenue. Here I was introduced to the sybaritic pleasures of the martini. Being from Britain and somewhat wet behind the ears, I naturally assumed that this was a glass of either dry or sweet vermouth. I very quickly learned that the extra dry martinis the luncheon group slammed back in prodigious quantities over a three hour lunch had never been within a hundred miles of a vermouth bottle.

The lunchtime habits of the Adverati have certainly changed since then, and not necessarily to the good, in my opinion, particularly when you look at the pathetic output of these increasingly dour and uncheeringly sober captains of commerce.

But looking at the actual end product of the agencies of the fifties doesn't exactly lift the spirits either. "Hard sell" reigned and most advertising came via a belief that to be effective you had to be obvious, unsophisticated, and repetitious. There were a few tasteful exceptions, but most of it was pretty awful. The approach clients and their agencies took was probably best illustrated in the 1947 movie *The Hucksters*, when during its most famous scene, Evan Llewellyn Evans "The Soap King," superbly acted by Sidney Greenstreet, spits on the boardroom table as an example of how to go about catching the consumers attention. Adolphe Menjou, playing the ulcer-driven head of the agency which handles all of "The Soap King's" dreadful advertising, does a fine piece of ass kissing to demonstrate how much he is in agreement with Greenstreet and his grotesque demonstration. This is a scene I have seen repeated innumerable times in innumerable presentations during my long and somewhat checkered career - the ass kissing, I hasten to add, not the spitting. It is proof of something I have always believed: the vast majority of people earning their crust in advertising agencies will prostitute their wives and sell their children into slavery if it will keep the client happy.

Things took a dramatic turn for the better in the late sixties with the rise of agencies such as Doyle, Dane, Bernbach; Ogilvy & Mather; Young & Rubicam; Wells, Rich, Greene, Carl Ally and Papert, Koenig & Lois. There are others, but these six were the prime agents in a radical shift taking place in the way advertising agencies thought about the audiences they wanted to address on behalf of their clients.

They achieved this breakthrough in communications by doing one simple thing: by giving their audience credit for having brains. Or, as David Ogilvy so succinctly put it, "The consumer isn't stupid, she's your wife." A radical thought at the time when you consider the soporific imagery and language which had been used up until then by the vast majority of advertising agencies.

In many respects, the sixties are still considered as the golden age of advertising, which isn't surprising when you consider the long lasting quality of work that was produced: campaigns from Y&R for Eastern Airlines; Ogilvy for Rolls Royce, and Schweppes and Hathaway shirts; Braniff and Benson & Hedges from Wells, Rich, Greene; Carl Ally for Volvo; Papert, Koenig & Lois for Xerox, Coty, and Wolfschmidt's Vodka. All announcing to both the industry, as well as the public, that from now on there was going to be a different, more intelligent way of doing things.

Without a doubt, the single biggest influence on advertising in the entire twentieth century was the Doyle, Dane & Bernbach agency. This iconic and most unlikely melting pot of Jewish, Irish, Italian, and German ethnicity, all of whom were equally single- minded, principled, and stubborn about their work and the way they produced it. This resulted in advertising campaigns that are still recognized and acknowledged around the world as some of the best ever produced: "Think Small" for Volkswagen; "When you're Number Two, You Try Harder" for Avis; "You don't have to be Jewish" for Levy's bread; and on and on for clients such as Chivas Regal, Polaroid, El Al, and many others. Over a period of about ten years, DDB could do no wrong, producing advertising that was not only a pleasure to read or watch; it also sold tons of stuff. And it did it by relying on intelligence, logic, superb craftsmanship, and lots of hard work. Most agencies at that time relied heavily on research to test and fine-tune their campaigns, as indeed many agencies still do today.

Bill Bernbach, who was in essence the soul of DDB, was very much against an overreliance on research, considering it a major factor in dragging down work to a level of mediocrity that ultimately rendered it useless. As he put it, people in focus groups (which are still today the BDAs favorite crutch) always react negatively to something different, and yet it is the campaign, which is intrinsically "different," that gets their attention and triggers a favorable reaction; because it stands out from the mass of mediocre advertising they are increasingly exposed to. When Avis insisted on testing the "Try Harder" campaign, it bombed badly, because, as expected, people in the groups declared there was no way they would be inclined to rent a car from a rental company that acknowledged it was second best . Bill persuaded the CEO of Avis to trust him on this and run the campaign. The rest is history. In a very much watered-down version, the campaign still exists forty years later. But if it was presented today in its original form, there is no question it would never see the light of day in the current advertising environment. Why? Because there isn't a single person in the advertising business who would have the balls to go out on a limb the way Bill frequently did to sell the advertising that he truly believed in. Not to mention, there isn't a single client who would have the balls to give it the go-ahead.

So successful was this new form of advertising that toward the end of the sixties many of the large, established, and conservative agencies decided they should perhaps jump on the creative bandwagon that everyone, including many of their clients, were starting to talk about. So, in inimical BDA fashion, they went out and hired "hot" creatives from "hot" agencies for outrageous salaries, invariably giving them impressive titles and large corner offices. It rarely worked of course, because there was absolutely no change in the mindset of the BDA management. As someone far more erudite than I once described it, this was like putting lipstick on a pig. At the end of the day, the unfortunate pig is still a pig.

At the BDAs, the "hot" creatives would produce "hot" campaigns that the "suits" (a derogatory term the creatives use to describe agency account executives) would fail to sell because they would unhesitatingly backpedal at the first sign of client resistance or unease with the work being presented. The suits would return to the agency and ask the creatives to do something perhaps a little less "edgy." After throwing many hissy fits and drinking several gallons of "writer fluid," while contemplating the fact that he had already spent half his "signing-on" bonus on that cherry red sports car he drove to the

Hamptons on the weekend, while shoving the other half of the cash windfall up his "septum degenerating" nose, the "hot" creative would begrudgingly produce something a little less "out there." When this dumbing down procedure started happening more and more frequently, the agency would quickly realize this new creative experiment wasn't working very well, so the 'hot new" creative would be gradually sidelined, eventually coming to the realization that it was time to move on before his previous reputation for being "hot" had entirely dissipated. Back at the BDA, this temporary aberration would quickly be swept under the rug and things would settle back to normal, meaning the usual output of crap would unceasingly flow through the sausage-making machine of BDA mediocrity. Which is actually the way it's always been and probably always will be in the never-changing world of the BDA.

By the midseventies, the "creative revolution" was starting to run out of steam, and the reality of harder economic times was beginning to set in. Hence, as one well known ad man put it, "We now require hard advertising for hard times!" Once again, creative originality was forced to take a backseat to what agency management perceived as the tried and true methods that had always seen them through lean times.

This meant producing advertising that concentrated on the incessant hammering away of multiple product features, rather than benefits. An emphasis on price, rather than value, and the acceptance by those creating the ads that the consumer is really stupid, so you must not only talk to them as if they are cretins. You must repeat everything as often, and as annoyingly as you can.

This was best demonstrated in the TV commercials of the period. Even though enhanced production techniques allowed agencies to be far more visually interesting than the commercials produced in the fifties and sixties, particularly with the increasing penetration of color television throughout American households, the vast majority of spots fell into three categories:

Talking Head: Very much what was done in the early days, where a stand-up presenter would deliver his/her spiel to a "locked-off" camera (this means the camera is static and does not move either from side to side, or in and out). The presenter would hold the product up to the camera (always holding it in a very unnatural fashion to leave the label clear so the viewer could see it throughout the commercial, as they still do today). The presenter would then deliver the script while large "supers" (ad-speak for titles) would flash on-screen to make sure the viewing audience did not miss a single feature of the wonderful product they were being mercilessly persuaded to buy. For my sins, in my early days in this business, I made quite a few of these. The worst examples would be those for men's toiletries - as they still are today. Often I would be forced to use some sports-jock as a personality spokesman (they were all men in those days, because this was well before the gymnastics/golf/tennis nymphet scene happened). Always shot in a pseudo-locker room, Karl Dumbrowski of the New York Bombers would wax eloquently about the unmatched benefits of a very inferior shaving lather, deodorant, athlete's foot cream, or something equally obnoxious, whilst innumerable titles would flash on-screen repeating everything Ace had just said. The most egregious of these commercials would also have lots of cutaways to animated sequences showing the deep, epidermal action of whatever this particular marvel of modern chemistry was doing to your body. The clients loved them, because as sponsors of the programming they got box seats for all the games, which is the primary reason so many businesses sponsor tournaments and sports personalities still. Hey, if the CEO of the company gets to play golf with Tiger once a year, that's worth a hundred million of the shareholders money...fucking right, right?

Demos: Meaning a product demonstration, showing the wonderful results you can achieve by using "Miracle Whizo." Still very much in use today for detergents, bleaches, polishes, paper towels, in fact just about everything used in the home. The format has remained unchanged for years. If you worked on Procter & Gamble, Colgate, Palmolive, S.C Johnson, or any of the big package goods companies, the mantra was simple - problem–solution–resolution. In the incredibly short space of thirty seconds, a mini-drama worthy of Ibsen would take place. A housewife is faced with a problem, a really big problem. Her laundry detergent is not working properly. Her whites are not coming out white, and her colors are looking faded. She discovers "Miracle Whizo, now with added blue speckles." She uses it. The whites look like driven snow and the colors resemble a Picasso canvas. Her husband loves her more than ever and wants to ravish her night after night. The once bratty children turn into cherubs. Even the dog stops peeing on the carpet. And all this is thanks to "Miracle Whizo with added blue sparkles." Sound familiar?

<u>Slice of Life:</u> This one truly has been around forever, and will no doubt outlive us all. As its name implies, it's based on some supposedly normal situation that could happen in everyday life whereby a product is casually introduced into the drone-like existence of the protagonist. In reality, it is obviously contrived and usually ridiculous. The vast majority of these scenarios take place at the kitchen table. Usually the action is between the woman of the house and a visiting friend. They are having coffee when suddenly the visiting lady wrinkles her nose and says something terribly subtle like, "What is that smell?" The uber/embarrassed lady of the house explains she's having trouble with the drains/sink/toilet/garbage disposal/whatever. Her friend immediately produces a five gallon drum of "Miracle DrainoClean" from her purse and places it on the kitchen table, making sure the label is front and center. She then goes into a detailed technical explanation of how "Miracle DrainoClean" uses subatomic plutonium particles to scrub away offensive odors. We cut to a later period; they are back at the kitchen table drinking coffee. The visitor tells the lady of the house how wonderful everything smells now. The lady, all smiles, says, "Thanks to you." The visitor blushes and lovingly caresses the five gallon drum, which now seems to have become a permanent fixture on the kitchen table, and replies, "No, thanks to Miracle DrainoClean." Camera pulls into the label and an announcer voice over exclaims, "Miracle DrainoClean, now with added subatomic plutonium particles to turn your slum-like kitchen into a palace!"

And don't tell me you haven't seen a million variations of that particular scene.

There are many subdivisions of these three basic categories, but even today the great majority of the many thousands of TV spots the average viewer will see over the course of a year will undoubtedly fit into one of these painful executions.

Most of the print advertising the public was subjected to over this period reflected the crassness of the TV, in as much as it also was usually heavy handed with little attempt at subtlety and style. Having said that, I must admit that it wasn't 100 percent crap. There were some exceptions to the rule, as there must be over any ten-year period.

Through the seventies, the creative torch was kept aflame by a small number of agencies doing great work for clients such as American Express, Volvo, Purdue, FedEx, and others. But unfortunately, other than these isolated examples, most of the advertising the American public was exposed to during the decline of Elvis and the rise of the spaghetti western, had regressed to the awfulness of the mind-numbing stuff which had ushered in the sixties.

The same could not be said, however, of the rest of the world. Creativity was rearing its un-ugly head in other parts of the world. European agencies, particularly in the UK and France, were starting to do things the Madison Avenue crowd should have been doing if they hadn't been so obsessed with protecting their ass rather than creating good work. Thanks to agencies in London such as the cerebral Collett, Dickenson, Pearce, and Abbott, Meade, Vickers, plus the outrageous Ronnie Kirkwood, and the soon to be millionaires, Saatchi Brothers, British advertising was starting to develop a somewhat droll, but totally unique style. In Paris, a quartet of wandering ad men combined the national characteristics of France, Germany, Switzerland, and the U.S. to create TBWA, an agency which still exists and has created the outstanding Absolut Vodka advertising almost from day one. Even on the other side of the globe, Australia, with the opening of The Campaign Palace, was beginning to acquire a hot reputation, as well as Batey Ads in Singapore. At the same time, the seventies saw the prohibition of cigarette advertising on TV, and one of the giant cash cows of advertising bit the dust, only to be replaced twenty years later by the bonanza of prescription drug advertising we are now subjected to on a regular basis.

It's also worth noting that the seventies saw the creation of one of the most internationally recognized corporate symbols in marketing history: the Nike "Swoosh." Now seen on everything sporting from Tiger Woods hat to Maria Sharapova's panties. It's a rather sad piece of advertising trivia that the starving art student who designed it received the princely sum of thirty-five dollars for something which must now be worth many billions of dollars.

In the eighties, things began to improve again with the ascendancy of such agencies as Chiat Day, Wieden & Kennedy, Fallon McElligott, and Goodby Silverstein, to name just four amongst a host of other startups who were primarily breakaways of two or three people from large established agencies. Interestingly though, none of these now famous agencies were based in New York or Chicago.

Most of the founders of these new agencies worked previously in traditional agencies that operated in a strict hierarchical fashion, offering few opportunities to break the mold in terms of the kind of advertising they produced. Now these guys were running their own shops and determined to grow through the creation of work that not only treated their audiences with respect, but also allowed the principals to look at themselves in the mirror every morning and not have to question the value of what they were doing.

Eventually most of them have grown to become major agencies with impressive client lists, and virtually all have become a part of one of the four conglomerates I shall deal with in the next chapter (except Wieden & Kennedy, which has remained stubbornly independent). They have also managed, for the most part, to retain their high creative standards. When he first teamed up with Guy Day to form what was to become one of the world's great agencies, Jay Chiat is reputed to have said, "I want to see how big we can get before we get bad!" Unfortunately, Jay is no longer with us, but Chiat Day, which subsequently merged with TBWA, has indeed grown extremely big, but has also managed to remain very good.

The late eighties and early nineties saw tremendous growth and consolidation in the advertising industry with many agencies becoming part of the four international conglomerates I shall talk about in the next chapter. It also saw the invasion of the American market by many European agencies, initially to service clients who were doing business in the Americas, but eventually as part of the true internationalism which was increasingly taking place throughout the business. Large clients with overseas operations, irrespective of where their corporate headquarters happened to be, expected their agency to provide a full range of services globally.

Today the advertising business is truly ubiquitous in a geographic sense. At the time of writing this book, JWT has opened an office in Kabul, Afghanistan. And the chairman of the WPP Group has gone on record as stating that he fully expects its greatest future growth will be in the Chinese and Indian markets.

By its very nature, advertising is cyclical. Not just as a reflection of economic issues, which invariably dictate that when the economy shrinks clients obviously devote less money to advertising and marketing operations, but also as a reflection of societal issues. Just as at the time *The Hidden Persuaders* was published fifty years ago, the nature of the media, particularly the existing broadcast media, was going through a tremendous state of flux. The same is true today. Not just because of the proliferation of cable and satellite vehicles that can carry and deliver content, or the increasing availability of high-speed broadband connections that allow people to access content, but because the very nature of the content itself is constantly changing.

Just as a reader of *The Hidden Persuaders* fifty years ago could have no concept of the informational, educational, and entertainment choices that are available to a consumer today, we, in turn, cannot begin to imagine what will be available to consumers five years from now, let alone fifty. If we then couple that with the many ways consumers of the future will expect to access this content, we start to recognize the communications landscape is changing at an exponentially increasing rate.

This means it is more than possible many of the functions and services agencies have traditionally offered clients will increasingly become available elsewhere. You have only to look at the growth of companies such as Google, which is increasingly moving into areas that have traditionally been the purview of ad agencies. It's no secret that many agencies are increasingly being forced to convince their clients of their relevance.

This will not necessarily mean the end of the ad agency, but it might mean the end of the ad agency as we have always known it. This will require a fundamental rethinking by ad agencies as to exactly what their role will be in the marketing mix of the future. No doubt, some will adapt, but many will not. Remember the dinosaurs I talked about at the beginning of this book? Some adapted, which is why we have birds. Many did not, and that's why we have museums.

We'll get into this later.

chapter THREE.   *the*

CONQUEST *of the*
CONGLOMERATES

More than 90 percent of the advertising accounts of the world's major brands are handled by a very small number of very large agencies that, in turn, belong to one of four international juggernauts run by a bunch of bean counters whose only interest is making each quarter's numbers and boosting the bottom line. Which is why 90 percent of the advertising they produce, sucks.

In today's wired, and increasingly WiFi'd world, because of VCRs, iPods, DVDs, broadband Internet connections, Tivo, Blackberries, cell phones, iPhones and many other technological breakthroughs that are likely to appear in the next few years, the number of ways consumers are able to receive both information and entertainment content seems to be growing exponentially. At the same time, the ability of consumers to reject annoying advertising and filter out unwanted content will become increasingly easier.

Right now, 80 percent of America's teenagers use at least seven electronic devices for an average of three hours every day. Yet, less than 5 percent of that time is spent watching television. This is why we can look forward to the nonstop expenditure of massive amounts of money by advertisers as they continue to search for new ways to break through this increasing barrier of teen-consumer disinterest. A disinterest they will undoubtedly maintain as they grow older.

What is particularly interesting is that even though we constantly hear about all the wonderful new media choices and forms of communication, and how today's advertising agencies are in a maniacal rush to jump on the new media wave by setting up dedicated divisions to exploit them, there is in actuality, a basic dichotomy at work here.

Because even as the technologies that drive many of these new media choices have been developed by the visionaries of Silicon Valley, or the variations thereof, now scattered around the globe, they must, of necessity, become commercialized. How else are the founders of these companies and the venture capitalists who funded them as startups going to afford their next Ferrari and ocean-going yacht? At the same time, only by being commercialized can these technologies become affordable. Think of your first brick-sized cell phone which was the price of a small car. Now they give you phones for free with built in cameras, blenders, and garbage disposal units. All you have to do is sign up for a non-breakable, lifetime wireless contract. Unless you absolutely, definitely must have an iPhone, in which case you are back to the small car analogy. However, if you're an Apple freak, money is no object and you've probably got your name down for an iCar.

The thing that makes all this increasingly an exercise in futility is that all these breakthroughs are being adopted and utilized, often in ways their creators could not have envisioned, by an end-user generation increasingly divorced and alienated from the crass commercialism of most traditional forms of advertising.

This means consumers often use the very technologies and

media options that are ostensibly the channels advertisers are told will help them reach these highly desirable demographic groups, to avoid the commercialism that disaffects them.

In spite of this, everyone in the ad biz never ceases to drink the Kool-Aid of the next paradigm shift. Leaping on whatever is being hyped in the current issue of *Wired, Red Herring,* or the *Harvard Business Review* dashing off to suck at the teat of the latest business book from Peters or Gilder, spending big bucks to hire futurists such as Faith Popcorn. Hopefully *The Ubiquitous Persuaders* will join their exalted ranks.

But, as I never cease telling anyone with the stomach to listen, if I could read the future the way some of these charlatans claim to, I would sell the house today and put everything on Lovely Lolita running in the 2:30 at the "Big A" tomorrow. Damn, we don't even learn from the past, so how the hell can we forecast the future?

What far too many people in the advertising business, particularly those slaving in the salt mines of the BDAs, fail to realize is that all this breathless excitement is merely about the means of delivery, rather than the content of the message. What's even more disturbing is that in spite of all the data mining, metronomics, research, and all the other marketing babble that agencies love to lay on their clients, there is no actual accountability, because what they are selling to advertisers is all about process with very little substance.

Marshall McLuhan once said, "The medium is the message." Personally, when it comes to advertising, I think he was dead wrong. In my opinion, the message is the message. Really good advertising is all about content. As several of the younger, smarter people doing good things in the business today - probably because many of them work outside the smothering influence of BDAs - are putting it so well, "Good advertising is about telling stories." Many years ago, a long dead San Francisco ad man by the name of Howard Gossage, who strangely enough was a great friend of Marshal McLuhan, said, "People don't read advertising; they read what they are interested in. Sometimes that's advertising."

And that, if you happen to be sitting on top of an ad budget the size of the GDP of a small African nation, is something worth thinking about.

At the time Vance Packard was writing *The Hidden Persuaders*, we were at the beginning of what has since been called the Creative Revolution. Up until then, agencies believed in what was known as "the hard sell" (some dinosaur BDAs still do) in as much as they considered it necessary to hit the audience over the head with product benefits in excruciating detail, repeated over and over., In the case of TV, this meant visuals of flaming stomachs, hammers beating anvils inside your head, and white coated doctors telling you that Camel cigarettes not only soothed your throat, they also gave you a ten hour erection... Oh, sorry, wrong product.

Then in the late fifties and early sixties a few agency luminaries, including David Ogilvy, Bill Bernbach, and George Lois - there were others, not a lot, but a few, so please forgive me if I haven't mentioned your dad or grandmother - decided that it would make sense to stop treating consumers like idiots. Hence the Creative Revolution was born and Americans started to enjoy some of the ads they were being exposed to.

Many famous campaigns originated in that era. Breakthrough work for Avis, VW, Hathaway Shirts, Xerox, Eastern Airlines, Rolls Royce, Hasselblad Cameras, Schweppes, Wolfschmidt Vodka, and many others, broke completely with tradition by not taking themselves too seriously, but above all by being engaging and informative. The sad thing is if you look at the current advertising for those brands that still exist, it's crap. Why? Because, both advertisers and their respective BDAs have long forgotten David Ogilvy's excellent advice, "The consumer isn't stupid, she's your wife."

Back in those days, Bill Bernbach could convince the CEO of Avis to run a campaign that had researched badly through a number of focus groups. "When you're number two, you try harder." But because Bill believed in the work passionately and knew it was right, in spite of the research, and because the client trusted him, the client accepted it, saying... "Well, you know best!" And so the campaign ran.

This could never happen today. Here's why.

The problem with most major companies today is that they

have their advertising produced by large advertising agencies which are, with a single exception, part of four multinational conglomerates, Omnicom, Publicis, Interpublic, and WPP, all of which are publicly traded and run by MBA bean counters. Everything they do is driven by the numbers, particularly those they have to make at the end of each quarter to keep the razor-fanged, blood-sucking analysts of Wall Street at bay. Then each can look forward to going through the same debilitating process three months later. Strangely enough, when you consider the size of their respective operations (all are global in scope) at the end of the day, they don't seem to make a great deal of money in return for all the effort they claim to put into it.

At the time Vance Packard wrote *The Hidden Persuaders*, there were virtually no publicly traded ad agencies, let alone holding companies. The first out of the blocks was the Interpublic Group of Companies (IPG) created in 1960, with McCann-Erickson and McCann-Marschalk as its two major subsidiaries. Thanks to the efforts of Marion Harper, the wunderkind CEO of McCann-Erickson, within a couple of years, IPG had grown into a family of about forty ad agencies, PR companies, and direct marketing specialists. In the seventies, the reigns were taken over by Phil Geier, who became vice chairman of the holding company until he retired at the end of 2000. Under Phil, IPG grew to become the eight-hundred pound gorilla on the advertising scene. Unfortunately, since 2002, the group has suffered continuing losses precipitated by an accounting scandal that has seen them restate earnings for the last four years. Strangely enough, Michael Roth, the guy running IPG since 2004, and a member of the board since 2002, had never worked in advertising. His entire career was in financial services. Remind me never to ask the guy for any financial advice. At the time of writing, IPG's stock is worth less than it was at the end of 1992. Yet the Adverati never cease telling their clients how they create value for them and their brands. Unfortunately, many of them seem incapable of doing it for themselves.

Omnicom Group currently claims the mantle of being the world's largest advertising agency holding company. But, if Sir Martin Sorrel of WPP Group, referred to by me in my various blogs as "The Poisoned Dwarf," has anything to do with it, it won't remain that way for long. Amongst Omnicom's agency roster are BBD&O, TBWA, DDB, and what I consider to be the most consistently creative agency of the last twenty years or so, Goodby, Silverstein & Partners of San Francisco.

Formed in 1986 by the merger of two giant agency networks, BBD&O and DDB Needham, Omnicom was the super nova of ad agency mergers, as no one had ever put together two global networks of this size. With the acquisition of the TBWA network in 1993, Omnicom became by far the largest of the conglomerates.

Publicis is currently the smallest of the four. This must really piss off its president, Maurice Levy, to no end. Particularly as he hates WPP Chairman, Sir Martin Sorrell's guts (I'm saving him for last). Based in Paris, Publicis is obviously run by a bunch of Chablis-swilling, cheese-eating, surrender monkeys. Just kidding guys! I love the French, even though you didn't invent French fries, or even French toast. But then I'm English and we didn't invent English muffins. And let's not get started on what happened at Waterloo.

The best known agencies in the Publicis roster include Leo Burnett, D'Arcy Masius Benton & Bowles, Hal Riney, and Bartle Bogle Hegarty. They also have an ongoing strategic partnership with Japanese agency giant, Dentsu. Interestingly, Maurice Levy became CEO of Publicis in 1987; before that he was their IT director, which might explain why they're so much more profitable than IPG.

And finally we come to WPP. The title is meaningless, but it did originally stand for Wire and Plastic Products, plc.; a British company that originally manufactured supermarket shopping trolleys. Currently trailing Omnicom by a lousy few million dollars, there is no doubt it will eventually overtake them to become the world's biggest advertising holding company - even if Sir Martin has to kill everyone standing in his way to achieve his ambition.

Martin Sorrell was originally the CFO to Saatchi and Saatchi of London in the glory days when Maurice was collecting Rolls Royce's and buying castles as places to park them, while Charlie was indulging his Damien Hurst modern art fantasies by buying dead sharks and rotting sheep floating around in giant fish tanks for a few million pounds a pop. Martin Sorrell looked at these goings on, and thought, I'd like some of those perks for myself, and so decided to do his own thing. Maurice and Charlie begged him to stay on as CEO, but he wanted to build his own empire. And he's been doing it with a vengeance ever since.

In the first two years, WPP stock grew by 2,000 percent. Over at IPG, Michael Roth's eyes would bleed for a fraction of that financial performance. It helped that the Saatchi brothers had put over a million pounds of their money into the venture, but Martin was recognized as the driving force.

At first, WPP started buying up fringe companies in Britain that specialized in design, audiovisual production, and sales promotion. He soon started buying similar companies in the U.S., but seemed to intentionally steer clear of traditional ad agencies. This all changed with a vengeance in 1987 when he made a hostile bid to buy out J. Walter Thompson, one of the oldest ad agencies in the world. Not only was little known about Sorrell in the U.S. agency community, it flew in the face of conventional wisdom, which held that any takeover had to be with the agreement of the agencies existing management if it wasn't to jeopardize the relationship with its clients. But Sorrell prevailed, even though it meant he ended up paying twice the value of the company just a couple of months before.

The buying spree continued over the ensuing years with the acquisition of Grey, Young & Rubicam, and Ogilvy & Mather. The battle for O&M was particularly acrimonious with David Ogilvy reputedly calling Sir Martin, "That odious twit!" Although I have it on fairly good authority he actually said, "That nasty little shit." Either way, David fought the takeover tooth and nail, but as usual, Sorrell got his way.

As I write this, there is just one large, successful agency left that doesn't belong to one of the big four holding companies. Situated in Portland, home of some of the finest beers you can buy in America, sits long time Nike agency, Wieden & Kennedy, with an impressive array of clients, from Proctor & Gamble to Pizza Hut, for which it is doing an impressive array of work. Because they are not a public company, they aren't vulnerable to a hostile takeover, and the principals are adamant they have no interest in selling, but nothing lasts forever. We shall see.

Most agencies operate these days on a fee basis with their clients, whereas traditionally, an agency's income had been almost completely derived from commissions the media rebated to them when they placed their client's advertising in newspapers and magazines, or on TV and radio. This was an anachronism based on practices dating back to the nineteenth century when newspapers would refund 15 percent of the cost of the ad space to the ad agency and the agency would bill the client the full 100 percent cost of the space. In other words, an ad agency's income was based on kickbacks from the media they persuaded their clients to run ads in. I have a strong suspicion that in any other line of business, you would probably go to jail for that.

Now agencies work out a mutually agreed fee based on the amount of work they expect to do for the client over a contracted period of time. Although this is no longer as lucrative as the old 15 percent days when in a great many cases owning an ad agency was like having a license to print money, fees still provide a healthy income as long as the agency is primarily churning out TV, radio, and press advertising. And by the time man hours, expenses, and production costs (generously marked up) are loaded in on top of the fee, few agency principals would complain.

Obviously, their clients did. As I've previously mentioned, there has always been a nasty perception in the minds of corporate America's senior management that a healthy proportion of the money they were continually pissing away on grandiose branding campaigns, was in fact doing no more than footing the bill for their ad agency's CEO to go golfing on Bora Bora. Whilst at the same time attending yet another American Association of Advertising Agencies conference entitled "Delivering real value to clients in the twenty-first century." But basically things were going along swimmingly for the moguls of Madison Avenue until Al Gore had to go and invent the Internet!

Then, almost overnight, things changed with the advent of new media and other nontraditional ways of communicating with the consumer, many of which I'll talk about in detail in later chapters.

God knows, it was bad enough with the proliferation of cable and satellite channels, that a BDA media "heavy" could no longer wrap up a clients TV schedule over lunch at the Four Seasons, courtesy of NBC, CBS, and ABC, while making sure his Christmas list was taken care of.

Now the whole media scene, as well as the nature of the content you could deliver on it, was starting to transmogrify into a nightmare of choices. And the scariest thing for Big Dumb Agencies was that they didn't have a clue what to do about it. This was particularly true within the conglomerates. Never forget that most of the management running these multi-national agency holding companies have never actually worked in the creative or account management trenches of an ad agency. As I have repeated ad nauseum, the vast majority are bean counters, whose so-called expertise is purely in finance. These are the clowns who deal in numbers, balance sheets, forecasts, and head counts. They could just as easily be running a dry cleaning establishment. But they'd probably fuck that up too!

For years agencies were run on the silo principle, often with each department functioning as a separate profit center. All activities were divided between what is more logically known in Europe as "above the line" and "below the line." Above the line (ATL) was concerned with all forms of regular media: TV, radio, print, etc. Whilst below the line (BTL) was all about direct marketing, sales promotion, and all the other ancillary activities the guys on the upper "creative" floors usually felt were not worthy of their valuable time. Yet, funny enough, it was usually these nonglamorous below the line activities which generated the most income and profit for the agency. Not to mention it was often a hell of a lot more effective in driving sales for the client than the three million dollars a pop Super Bowl TV extravaganzas the agency creatives lusted to get on their personal show reels.

Another great attraction of many of these nonmainstream media activities to agency clients was that it was possible to precisely target their products or services to specific audiences in ways that mainstream media buys couldn't. ABC, or any of the other networks, might try to convince you that you could reach 40 percent of the hemorrhoid suffers in the U.S. by spending a few million dollars on TV spots that would run during the evening news, probably putting the poor souls watching off their microwaved macaroni and cheese in the process. Whereas, a good direct mail agency could pinpoint 90 percent of hemorrhoid sufferers who'd just received their tax refund from the IRS and were primed and ready to splurge out on the "for a limited time only, 20 percent off offer!" Which would get them three cases of doctor recommended "Super Bum Salve." And if they called the eight-hundred number right away, they'd also receive a free tub of "Super Naso Nose Hair Remover."

Best of all, these miracles of quantifiable commercial efficacy could be achieved at a fraction of the cost of buying all that network TV time.

So, you might ask, if this below the line stuff was so much more effective and cost efficient, why didn't all advertisers use it and simply forget about the wasteful mainstream media? Because the smarter companies realized that in many ways the heavy handed use of these direct marketing ploys, while showing immediate short term benefits, could quite easily cannibalize the brands they had invested so much in to build over the years.

Consider that in 1980, advertising comprised about two thirds of all marketing expenditures by U.S. manufacturers and providers of services. Ten years later, that share had fallen to less than a third. What was happening to these companies then is what is happening to advertising agencies and the conglomerates that own them today. The focus was (and is now for agencies) on short term, immediate returns. By putting money and resources into couponing, premiums, price promotions, buying in-store shelf space and displays, funding distributor conferences (golf fests), conventions, sponsorship, and so on, owners of recognized brands could immediately boost their sales and thus enhance the perceived value of their companies. And remember, all this was happening in the takeover frenzy of the eighties and early nineties, when every stock broker's newsletter and financial columnist was continually harping on about "increasing shareholder value." How many times have you heard that old chestnut?

The contradiction within this whole scenario is that the very reason that persuaded the takeover "barbarians" to make a run at a successful company in the first place was for them to profit from the undervaluation of many of these companies brand franchises as they were perceived on "The Street." Once it was taken over, the brand was then milked by launching numerous brand extensions, which very often had nothing to do with the core values of the brand, but merely relied on its well established and trusted name to generate healthy secondary revenues.

Meantime, the core products, which had created the brand in the first place, were starved of advertising support and used primarily as providers of cash flow to make the quarterly numbers look good. The result being that once the profitable marrow had been sucked out of the ossifying bones, all that was left was a pale reflection of what had once been a great company/enterprise/brand. This was of little consequence to the takeover "barbarians," who, by then, would already be moving on to their next target.

During those years, agencies begged, pleaded, and cajoled their clients not to give up on mainstream advertising, even while they endeavored to provide a Chinese menu of alternative options. They did this by buying direct marketers, PR outfits, sales promotion houses, and film and video production companies. It was in effect, the reverse of the early WPP days, as most of them came at it from the top down; whereas the "Poisoned Dwarf" worked his way up from shopping trolleys

Once they'd bolted on all these ancillary services to the hull of their leaking ship of state, they proceeded to bang the drum about offering truly "integrated services." This somewhat murky and usually unrewarding concept will be dealt with in more detail in the next chapter. Suffice it to say that at the time of writing, very few BDAs, let alone the conglomerates they belong to, have successfully cracked the code of this particular business model.

This brings us back to the "New Media" and how it is radically changing the playing field for everyone involved in the advertising business, particularly the Big Dumb Conglomerates. What many fail to understand is that it isn't about consumers now having so many more choices for entertainment and information retrieval.

It's about the fact that consumers have so many more ways of switching off, or choosing to screen out advertising messages. Yes, every paid-up member of the Adverati now pays lip service to their ability to "come in under the radar," which is why there is so much hype about the effectiveness of guerrilla advertising; something I will also talk about in greater detail in a later chapter. But I prefer to think of new media being primarily in the digital domain, which exploded in the early nineties with the ascendancy of the dot com companies, only to implode in the late nineties leaving many BDAs and their parent BDCs holding the bag for millions of dollars in unpaid fees and outstanding media debts. This was their own fault for being both insatiably greedy and dumb enough to believe their own bullshit.

Now, through their constituent agencies, the conglomerates are jumping on the new media bandwagon with a vengeance, buying up anything that smells like it might be the next big thing. Unfortunately, because of the glacier like speed most of these organizations move at, by the time they get around to buying these hot companies, they usually end up being cold companies. And as all too often happens, the entrepreneurial spirit that made them desirable in the first place is stifled within the bureaucracy and risk-averse culture of the parent company. The principals soon walk with their multimillion dollar payoffs, hack management from the parent company is put in to replace them, and eventually everything that made the company desirable turns to shit. It is then either rolled into another of the BDCs stone-cold collection of once hot companies, or is quietly taken out behind the woodshed and shot.

Then the Big Dumb Conglomerate goes off and buys the latest hot company that might provide them with the key to the next big thing.

What these organizations haven't faced up to is the fact that there's now a shift in the mindset of even the biggest clients, which is leading them to believe they no longer have to go to their traditional agency of record for their communication requirements. In fact, clients are increasingly recognizing that by perhaps dealing directly with outside specialists in the fields of new media, digital content, product placement, word-of-mouth, and so on, they will not only get better work, they will undoubtedly save themselves a shitload of money. Proof of this growing trend is the stated intention of Google, the eight-hundred-pound gorilla that will eventually take over the known universe, not to have their account handled by some clueless BDA, but to work with individual specialists and small hot shops with proven expertise in specific areas of advertising, marketing, and communications. Look for this trend to grow in the future.

Does this mean there is no future for the BDAs? Suffice it to say, that like many of the financial institutions we are currently told (late 2008) are too big to fail, many of them will fail if they continue to maintain a business model that is increasingly divorced from the markets and consumers they are supposedly addressing. It is a business model that discourages creativity and risk-taking. What it does encourage is marketing and advertising, which invariably consists of homogeneous, vanilla-flavored pabulum put together after extensive, expensive marketing and advertising research. All of which is supposedly designed to eliminate risk, but which merely results in lowest common denominator solutions that not only fail to produce meaningful results. They also guarantee the frustration and dissatisfaction of the people working in the BDA, the unfortunates who are shareholders in it, the sharks on Wall Street who are peddling its shares, and last, but not least, the poor client, who we should never forget is the one ultimately footing the bill for all this lunacy. Oh, and I almost forgot, the consumers, who are forced to put up with the ever increasing proliferation of soporific junk they are exposed to on a daily basis.

Every year millions of dollars are poured down the black hole of new product development, marketing, and advertising, of which a select few proceed to launch, whilst the great majority are strangled at birth. The most amusing aspect of all this is that these multimillion dollar decisions are often based on the words of a few dozen bored housewives, who for the princely sum of twenty or thirty dollars are more than happy to sit for a couple of hours in a sub-basement below a suburban mall. Here they are encouraged to talk and express their opinions about the merits of Schmucko's "New and Improved" garlic flavored ice cream and whether they would be happy feeding it to their unfortunate family. Pseudo-psychologists engage them in inane brand association tests to discover if the product makes them have wet dreams about Tom Cruise - Or nightmares about Jack the Ripper – Or perhaps the other way around.

Little wonder, after spending millions of dollars on ambitious advertising campaigns, 80 percent of new products fail within six months of their launch, even though most of them tested like gangbusters with a couple of dozen housewives in Boise. To repeat myself. As William Goldman once said when talking about Hollywood and the movie industry, "No one knows anything." Perhaps he should have spent some time on Madison Avenue!

chapter FOUR. *more gets you*

LESS

Agencies are being handed ever bigger budgets by their clients. Media costs are escalating, while effectiveness is diminishing. Yet, they continue to flog the concept of "total integration," which is a direct contradiction to the way most agencies are structured and financially managed. Everyone claims the days of the thirty-second TV spot are numbered, yet they keep making more and more at an ever increasing cost.

The most visible part of any well constructed marketing program has traditionally been the advertising component. After all, not only has a significant part of the overall budget always been allocated to this, it was for years one of the few ways a company could present itself to the consumer in a form were they could completely control the timing and content of their messaging while defining the target audience. Yet, even though the high cost of mainstream media options has traditionally dictated ad campaigns should command the largest share of most companies advertising dollars, many of these media are now being recognized as the least cost efficient and results effective way for a company to get their marketing messages out to its target audience.

So, shouldn't we find it strange that what has become known as the Super Bowl of advertising, which takes place as an integral part of the Super Bowl, seems incapable of delivering the ROI even the most deep-pocketed advertiser might have a reasonable right to expect after shelling out close to three million dollars for a single thirty-second TV spot? Particularly as we are continually told by such media hacks as *USA Today* that the game is watched by viewers as much for the TV commercials as for the actual football

Yes, in recall studies after the game, a great many people are able to conjure up every detail of a TV spot featuring a large breasted, scantily clad woman appearing before a house congressional committee, who in the middle of her testimony manages to make one of her spaghetti thin shoulder straps slip from her shoulders to reveal even more cleavage. The problem is most viewers are hard pressed to actually name the advertiser. During the same eight hour broadcast of a ninety minute game, they may have snorted streams of Bud Light out of their pizza inflamed nostrils as they watched the hilarious antics of a chimpanzee dancing on an upturned pail somewhere in the Ozarks. But ask them who coughed up the millions of bucks it cost to buy the airtime, let alone the outrageous cost of producing the spot, and they don't have a clue!

And who could blame them when after spending all those millions of dollars to capture the audiences attention, the commercial concentrated on the entertainment shtick of its brief thirty-second life, rather than its informational value, and dare I say "selling" content? That is why, in the ad biz, there have always been three guaranteed ways to rapidly turn a client's multimillion dollar ad budget into a smoldering ash pile: Stupidity, profligacy and television.

For years in the agency world, TV advertising was where it was at. Such mundane disciplines as sales promotion and direct marketing were regarded as the red-headed stepchild in the attic, recognized, but looked down on as a lesser skill by the Armani-clad, Gucci-loafer wearing, Adverati of Madison Avenue. Plus, in the happy days of 15 percent agency commission, TV advertising was equivalent to the conquistadors landing in the new world and finding the city of gold within ten feet of the beach. There simply weren't enough ships to carry the loot back to the treasury. Now, things are somewhat different. The conglomerates and their constituent agencies have recognized the value of the "lesser arts." Not just in terms of the additional income it can deliver, but because only the dumbest of their clients are not demanding a range of services that are quantifiable, accountable, and most of all, can be proven to deliver some kind of ROI. Interestingly enough, back in the pre-conglomerate days, many major agencies did offer direct marketing, sales promotion, PR, and other ancillary services as an overall package, which is why most of the big shops considered themselves to be a full service agency. They realized, rather smartly, that throwing in many of these services for no extra charge made sense, as long as the tsunami of revenue from the 15 percent commission teat they were hungrily feeding off made all this possible.

Today, everything has changed.

Since the eighties, the income agencies derived from big media campaigns, particularly TV has been shrinking. They can no longer afford to throw in all those extra services for free. Agencies have had to start charging clients for direct marketing, sales promotion, PR, and other activities. This had the obvious effect of causing many clients to consider hiring independent vendors of these services. It also caused clients to begin questioning the effectiveness of what they had been spending billions on over the years. The big package goods and grocery guys had always known the value of in-store promotion, couponing, sampling, discounting, and even downright payola to get their product the shelf space necessary for heavy consumer face time. But for years, big consumer goods advertisers had also been drinking the agency Kool-Aid of branding.

Now, don't get me wrong here, I'm not saying that creating, building, and then supporting a brand is wrong, or that it can't be done through advertising. Some very big, very successful brands have been built through highly effective and original brand advertising. Nike, Apple, Coke, and quite a few more, are perfect examples. On the other hand, some well recognized and humongously successful brands have been built with virtually no traditional forms of advertising. Starbucks, Red Bull, and the Body Shop are just three. Although, since the Body Shop was bought by L'Oreal in 2006 it has joined the ranks of the heavily advertised, heavily bastardized, me-too cosmetic products, which will inexorably destroy the "brand equity" L'Oreal shelled out nearly seven hundred million dollars for in the first place. It's also sadly worth noting that everything the Body Shop brand stood for was, within a year or so of the acquisition, jeopardized when L'Oreal was forced to withdraw mega millions of dollars worth of ads for one of its mascara cosmetic lines that supposedly made natural eyelashes look like Betty Davies' in *Mommy Dearest*, after it was revealed that Penelope Cruz, the uber-film star who was featured wearing the product in the TV campaign, was actually wearing gigantic false eyelashes. Apart from the fact that this was a massive contradiction of everything the Body Shop stood for, why on earth did they have to use a member of the Hollywood Glitterati to sell a product aimed at women who supposedly rejected such much-abused stereotypes? I am left to wonder if the recently deceased founder of the Body Shop, Anita Roddick, is, at this very moment, spinning in her multi-million dollar Carrara marble mausoleum.

Every big agency worth its salt will hammer away at existing and prospective clients about the value of branding. Each and every one of their Web sites will be full of the same old bullshit wrapped in meaningless MBA-generated chat about building brand share, maintaining brand Integrity, creating core brand values, and increasing brand equity. Some will even invent proprietary catch phrases such as "360 degree branding," or "pinpointing brand essence." And even though today all these agencies will profess they can now create, build, and maintain brands by exploiting the potential of the various, much hyped, new media, the emphasis will continue to be that clients should keep pouring dumpster loads of money down the rancid tubes of traditional media, particularly television.

Yet, at the end of the day, there is little evidence advertising is *the* unqualified brand builder. Obviously, there has to be some form of *communication* between a brand and the consumer it is aimed at; but there are many non-advertising influences that have always entered into the equation. Product uniqueness, name, packaging, pricing, perception of value, quality, service, PR, and many other diverse factors all contribute to the creation and maintenance of a brand. Some internationally successful brands are not even products in the accepted sense of the word, and rely on little or no advertising.

Think of Manchester United Football Club, with fan clubs and enormous merchandise sales from China to Chile, as an example. Its fans have not been influenced in their loyalty by thirty-second TV spots or full color magazine spreads. No, theirs is a devotion advertising dollars cannot buy, even when millions of these fans have never actually seen "The Reds" play a live game. Few brands of this iconic nature owe their recognized power and influence primarily to advertising, even though the Adverati of Madison Avenue would like their clients believe otherwise.

One of the most egregious mistakes agencies make when it comes to their "brand stewardship," as they love to call it, is that they look at brands as a static entity rather than something that is constantly changing and organic in nature. This is particularly true with most advertising aimed at younger target audiences. Whether it be clothes, music, beverages, autos, and many other categories ranging from condoms to condos, when attempting to influence the eighteen- to twenty-eight-year-old demographic, only companies and their agencies prepared to move at lightning speed will be able to make any kind of meaningful impact on them.

Existing brands have a repository of historical perceptions, images, and impressions, which were made against an audience that has now grown older, changed habits and shifted on the socioeconomic scale. Advertising that worked on them ten years ago, may not work now. Even worse, the advertising that worked ten years ago, will not work against the new generation of consumers who now occupy that demographic sector. This is the continual conundrum clients and their ad agencies face. Yet, as I've mentioned before, when they do, the temptation is to rely on what has worked previously. Whatever it was that made sales spike, got the dealers and bottlers excited, or gave the company the best kick-ass financial quarter in years, is unfailingly rolled out for one more trot round the track.

Compounding the problem is the fact that virtually all those charged with this "brand stewardship," on both the client and agency side, are completely divorced from the life their target audiences experience on a daily basis. Which is why, if the primary objective of your "bleeding edge" brand creation plan is to make it into a household name, you'd better be damned sure you understand exactly what kind of household it is you're talking about. Meaning if you live in a four thousand square foot Soho loft, work out of a twenty-fourth floor corner office with a view of the East River, and you're attempting to sell stuff to people who live in a trailer park in Louisiana, you might be well advised to jump in the old BMW once in a while and at least get your ass down there and do a few circuits of the neighborhood just to get a feel for the place.

Another aspect of branding few agencies seem to consider is that for a product, service, or company to achieve brand status, its recognition must extend beyond those considered to be its target group. Previously mentioned Manchester United is a good example of this. Millions of Americans know it exists and what it stands for, yet they are not football fans; in fact, they don't even call it football, reserving that title for a peculiarly American game played by men who rarely touch the ball with their feet. They also know by association, one of the team's most famous ex-players, David Beckham, and by further association, his pseudo-famous wife, Posh Spice. The cumulative effect of this "brand fame," is what sets them apart from identical products that are not perceived as having the same intrinsic value. When the Hummer was launched, no one in their right mind should have bought it. It was a converted military vehicle with limited interior space, outrageously inefficient gas mileage, and it was God-awful ugly. And yet, it became a marketing success, a lot of which can be attributed to "the Governator's" involvement in its launch during post-Iraq invasion fever. Having said all that, only a minute proportion of Americans would consider owning one, yet the vast majority knows and recognizes the vehicle and its various brand extensions. This is what, through the building of "brand fame," a real brand is all about.

Much has also been made by the legions of MBAs and consultants, who make obscene amounts of money advising grossly overpaid and incompetent captains of industry how brands do not actually belong to the companies that create them. These Svengalis of snake oil claim the most valuable attribute of a true brand, the one which separates them from mere products, is not in the possession of the company who created it. Instead, it is in the universe of consumers who buy it. This is an unnecessarily convoluted and confusing way of talking about loyalty. The drive that makes consumers go out of their way to find, and willingly pay more for a product they could buy a generic and equally functional version of for a great deal less. Finding ways to perpetuate this aberration of the human condition is what causes the CEOs of pharmaceutical companies to awake in a cold sweat at two in the morning. It's also one of the main reasons why drug companies have replaced cigarettes and booze as the number one Madison Avenue milch cow.

I recently had an experience that demonstrates how true brand loyalty comes about; not because of multimillion dollar advertising budgets, but from a company's commitment to creating better products and an overriding dedication to customer service - something all companies pay lip service to, but few execute well. I have long been a customer of Amazon, buying primarily books, videos, and music, although less and less of the latter because of the many choices now available to me to stream and download music tracks. I bought a Kindle, Amazon's version of the electronic book; I used and enjoyed it for three weeks, and in my opinion, it is without a doubt a unique product and far superior to anything else on the market. After three weeks, I dropped it and broke the screen. I called Amazon and explained what happened, expecting to be told what I had in the past when calling manufacturer's help lines after doing the same thing to several laptop computers: "Oh, sorry sir dropping the appliance is an event not covered by our guarantee and terms of service." Meaning, tough luck, you will have to buy a new one. Exactly the response Apple delivered to those unfortunates who'd bought the first versions of the iPod, and after discovering that their battery would no longer recharge after a years use, were told you couldn't replace the battery, you had to cough up a couple of hundred bucks for a new bloody iPod. So, imagine my surprise when Amazon said they would express deliver me a new Kindle that same day. No charge. No questions asked. Needless to say, I am now an Amazon fanatic. Interestingly, as I am writing this, the current issue of *AdAge* has an article titled "Consumers become Kindle ambassadors." It points out that Kindle users are so enthusiastic about the product, they are volunteering to demonstrate it to prospective purchasers as part of Amazon's "See a Kindle in your city" marketing program. These volunteers are setting up meetings in coffee shops and other social venues where they pass along their knowledge and enthusiasm for the product to prospective purchasers. And, they do this for free. Amazon doesn't pay them a penny. Not even expenses. This to me is a perfect example of what "brand fame" should be all about.

Back in the days of *The Hidden Persuaders*, booze and cigarettes were the perfect examples of how customer loyalty would help build brands, even though that loyalty could often guarantee an early death. If you are long enough in the tooth, you might remember such classics as, "I'd walk a mile for a Camel." Or, "I'd rather fight than switch." One of my all-time favorites is, "If you're out of Schlitz— You're out of beer." Advertising lore (Adverati code for bullshit) tells us that many years ago, the creative director working on the Schlitz account at a big agency in New York, Chicago, or some other big metropolitan city had to come up with a new campaign by the next day for a major client presentation. He'd been working on it for weeks, but had arrived at exactly, fuck all. So, he went down to the corner tavern for a glass or two of inspiration, or as my old friend Chris Jones, ex-chairman of JWT New York used to call it, "Writer fluid!" He sat at the bar having a Scotch or three, when a guy came in, sat down a few stools further up, and asked for a Schlitz. The bartender told him they were out of Schlitz, but not to worry, they had plenty of other beers. To which the customer replied, "If you're out of Schlitz, you're out of beer."

Obviously, the light bulb went off in the CDs Scotch-addled

brain and eureka, a star was born. This is inviolable proof that if you are in urgent need of inspiration, my advice is to hit the nearest bar. It's always worked for me. It's also an excellent demonstration of the inexorable link between loyalty and brands - even if the whole thing is one giant fairy tale. Having said that, the Joseph Schlitz Brewing Company went out of business in the nineties, not because it lost the loyalty of its customers, even though it was once the second largest selling beer in America, but because they screwed up the product by introducing something called high-temperature fermentation, more than likely because the bean counters said they could save two cents a keg in production costs. The end result? It made the beer taste like yesterday's horse pee, or even fucking worse, today's Bud Light.

This then begs the question, should a brand constantly reinvent itself, or should it leave well enough alone and not change a single thing over the years? Schlitz ruined a mammoth brand through the mealy-mouthed meddling of the financial people to extract the last vestige of profit from a successful product. It is a perfect demonstration of the dangers inherent in allowing those who operate on the fringes to meddle with and influence the values that have created and maintained what made the brand a success in the first place. Rarely is it the fault of the people actually making the stuff. They have a genuinely honest stake, not to mention pride, in what they are doing. So, is there any excuse for those charged with the marketing and advertising of a brand when they decide to screw things up? I would unhesitatingly say no. The launch of New Coke in 1985 is a perfect example of how quickly the aberration of some marketing genius can endanger a brand that has been built over generations. It was decided to reformulate Coke to taste more like its rival Pepsi. Personally, I think they both taste like ten year old battery acid, but perhaps their zero alcohol content has something to do with this. Taste tests and focus groups showed conclusively that consumers loved the taste of New Coke over old Coke and Pepsi which, when you consider 80 percent of all new products test like gangbusters in research yet die a horrible death within months of their launch, it should have immediately raised a giant red flag. But no, Coke thought they were onto a winner here. The agency was chomping at the bit to blow mega millions on a campaign based on the Shakespearean-esque line, "The Best Just Got Better!" This probably raised a red flag in the consumer's mind that if it was already the best, how could it possibly get better? You'll have to pardon me for asking patently dumb, yet obvious fucking questions here. Anyway, the rest is history, and is doubtlessly enshrined in thousands of business school case studies. All of which will no doubt be ignored by legions of freshly minted MBAs as they move on to the position of fast-food marketing fuehrer at the Acme Cola Company. Tasked with developing strategies capable of persuading John Q. Public to supersize their new improved Acme-Coke to the five gallon bucket size when purchasing their next ten-pound Acme "BlastaBurger."

I guess at the end of the day, when it comes to branding, the client, in reality, knows very little about what created their brand in the first place. No, I should correct that. They probably know a great deal about its creation, in terms of design, manufacture, pricing, distribution, sales, etc. What they know very little about is what turned it into a brand; what were the factors which enabled it to be seen as superior to its competition and made people willing to pay more for it? They certainly know nothing about how they can maintain it as a brand with its current degree of dominance. Yet having said all that, the agency tasked with representing the client's brand knows even less.

The erstwhile Dr. Dichter would have had a field day with present day agency management and their state of denial regarding the increasing precariousness of their situation. No doubt he would put it down to their potty training as a child or a bad case of penis envy. But whatever the reason, we may be reaching a turning point in the way the ad agency business will function in the future. The four giant holding companies are buying up ancillary businesses like crazy. These range from Web design shops to market research outfits. Sir Martin Sorrell, chairman and CEO of WPP Group, in a recent speech stated that within ten years, more than 80 percent of the group's revenues would be coming from non-advertising activities. Perhaps he's thinking of getting back into the supermarket shopping trolley business.

In the days of *The Hidden Persuaders* when the legendary Doyle, Dane & Bernbach agency was starting out, and before it revolutionized the business in the early sixties with its iconic advertising for VW, Avis, El Al, Chivas Regal and many other clients, Bill Bernbach said, "Advertising is fundamentally persuasion, it happens to be not a science, but an art." He was, still is, and always will be right. Because, in spite of many attempts over the years, it is still virtually impossible to know up front if a particular campaign is going to work. This is why so much of the advertising that consumers are subjected to is exactly the same as all the other advertising within that particular product category. In this way, advertising is remarkably similar to the movie and TV business where sequels and spin-offs abound, because the showbiz rationale is that if something has worked before, it should work again. However, the truth is that it rarely does, and no one has a clue why this is so. Yet, this is exactly how virtually all agencies approach their business, particularly today. As I will unashamedly continue to hammer away about it, advertising as practiced by the BDAs is strictly about making the numbers every quarter. As a result, agencies rarely take chances when they are part of a publicly traded company, and they certainly don't want to upset their present clients by doing anything that might be considered risky. Yet, eventually and inevitably, this leads to the loss of the account, because one day the client gets out of bed, looks in the mirror, then scratches his or her head and says, "Goddamit, all those agency people ever do is give me the same old crap. I think it's time I started looked around." Which then leaves the agency CEO scratching his or her head, saying, "Goddamit, we gave them everything they asked for, and now they're looking around" This is the single most common reason why most advertising agencies lose accounts; failing to understand that the most important thing an agency can do for a client is not to give them what they want, but to give them what they need.

Many clients are now not only pulling their non-media advertising activities out of their agencies, they are also going to specialist shops or groups that have arisen in the last thirty years to do nothing else but plan and buy media. This is ironic if you consider that when ad agencies first came about in the late nineteenth century, their only function was to place media for their clients. This move towards media specialists started in France. Yes, trust those cheese-eating, burgundy-swilling French to throw a wrench in the works. In the 1960s, un homme (for the benefit of Alaskans, that means "a dude" in French) by the name of Gilbert Gross started a company called Carat, which was based on a simple, obvious, but rather clever idea. He went to all the major media, newspapers, magazines, TV, and radio networks (although there was little commercial TV or radio in Europe in those days) and offered to buy large blocks of space and time well in advance of publication or broadcast dates. This way he could secure huge discounts from the normal card rate. Then he would resell it to clients and agencies, still at a discount, but a much smaller one than he had negotiated for Carat. The economies of scale and savings this method of buying media produced for all concerned convinced most advertisers it was the way to go in the future.

This was, however, taking place in "old" Europe, to the point where by 2000, close to two thirds of all media was being bought through media planning and buying specialist companies. Not until the late eighties and early nineties did America wake up to the benefits of centralized planning and buying. But of course, in the U.S., and to a lesser extent, the UK, it was done in a completely different fashion. WPP, Omnicom, and Interpublic simply spun off the media departments of their major agencies, tarted them up in new party frocks and re-presented them as entirely new entities. In the case of WPP, these so-called autonomous outfits go by the names of Mindshare and Mediacom. Interpublic has Universal McCann and Initiative. While Omnicom's media operations opt for the much simpler and less grandiose names of OMD and PHD. Publicis seems to be content with a single company, MediaVest Worldwide. But, irrespective of the cute names they have decided on, all are simply suppliers of the same old grist to the mill necessary to keep these behemoths churning out profits for the shareholders; which when you look at the actual operating profit of these trans-global titanics, you would have to ask yourself, wouldn't they have been better off investing in something as mundane as frozen pork bellies? Or, perhaps in the unfailingly enterprising way BDAs have managed to survive through their never ending ups and downs, rather than subjecting themselves to the risks of the Wall Street casino, they might be better served by jumping on the next big thing, because in the wonderful world of *The Ubiquitous Persuaders*, there is always another next big thing. One of which we shall deal with in the next chapter.

chapter FIVE.   *is there a*

GUERRILLA IN THE ROOM?

The advent of "new media," a great deal of which is actually, pretty old. Everything from viral, buzz, word-of-mouth, seeding, shill marketing, street teaming, to ambient. To be honest, most of it's been done before, but if you give it a funky new name, you can charge extra big bucks and your clients will eat it up.

It seems like only yesterday when visiting the men's room in one of my favorite Greenwich Village watering holes, I was greeted by a talking urinal. In actuality, it was seven years ago, and even though it made a lasting impression, particularly on my shoes, I must confess I have no recollection what the bloody hell the thing was trying to sell me. Today, talking urinals are somewhat old hat and we have moved on to such things as life-sized cars carved out of ice parked on London streets until they eventually melt away, steaming manhole covers in the middle of gritty, metropolitan streets that, upon closer inspection, appear to be the top of a coffee cup, or a woman apparently sleeping blissfully in a full-sized, canopied bed on a Tokyo subway platform, while the "salary-men" scoot off to their respective cubicles. These and many more increasingly bizarre events are fairly representative examples of what has now become known as guerilla marketing; a subject that dear old Rosser Reeves would be at a complete loss to understand.

As I've pointed out in earlier chapters, conventional forms of advertising are proliferating whilst for obvious reasons, they are becoming increasingly ineffective. At the same time, new media and digital choices are exploding whilst their costs are minimal compared to mainstream media. All of which presents today's advertisers with a dilemma; in a rapidly changing media landscape, how can they best reach their target audiences with messages that engender some kind of favorable response, and how can they do it cost effectively?

Could they perhaps take advantage of the much vaunted new media options and guerilla marketing methods we seem to hear about on a daily basis in both the general and business press? After all, these new ways of communicating with potential customers are claimed by their proponents to be capable of breaking through the barriers consumers are increasingly putting up to block traditional forms of advertising. Unlike most new media, which is primarily digital in nature, guerilla marketing, even though it can use elements of digital messaging, is much more physical, often relying on live interactions with the selected target groups.

This is why those who specialize in the black arts of guerrilla marketing would have you believe they achieve "indifference-breakthroughs" by involving the consumer in messaging they'll hopefully perceive as non-threatening, particularly when it occurs in noncommercial environments. Do these guerilla gurus have a point? I would have to say, they do, but only up to a point.

As someone who's been in advertising and marketing for well over thirty years, I can assure you that the basic principles and methods of communication, which have worked so well, for so long, to the enrichment of both agencies and their clients, no longer necessarily apply to a society that can instantly, and forever, tune you out because you haven't given them a good enough reason why they should keep you tuned in.

Overcoming that problem is what guerilla marketing claims to be about; it allows advertisers to engage, entertain, and interact with customers in ways traditional marketing does not. And, because it's an experience the consumer unknowingly becomes an integral part of, there's hopefully less inclination for them to disregard the message.

There's no question many companies have come to the realization the marketing and advertising model they've always relied on is rapidly becoming both ineffective and expensive. This means advertisers are increasingly willing to look at other ways to get their marketing message out. Obviously online, interactive, and other forms of new media are being used on an ever increasing basis, and this is dealt with in more detail in chapter nine. But guerilla marketing is increasingly becoming an important part of the communications mix.

The one thing everyone can agree on is that everything is changing, and it's doing it at a pace that is far more rapid than the Adverati of Madison Avenue would like to acknowledge. After all, it wasn't that many years ago when network TV, agency media buyers, and the couple of thousand TV viewers who'd agreed, for the sake of a few lousy bucks a month, to have a Nielson monitoring device sitting on top of their TV set, or even worse, to fill in a weekly diary listing what TV programs they watched, decided what the entire nation would be forced to watch for the next twelve months. This handful of people would also inadvertently, dictate how many millions of dollars the Johnson & Johnsons, P&Gs, General Foods and Colgate Palmolive's would have to cough up for the airtime necessary to reach the American consumer. Ah, the good old days! Today's Madison Avenue media buyers must cry themselves to sleep every night on their martini-soaked pillows thinking about how wonderful those halcyon days were.

So, exactly what are these revolutionary forms of non-traditional marketing? I'll briefly spell out most of the current forms, bearing in mind that by the time you read this there will undoubtedly be a great many new variations. Even more strikingly, you might perhaps think after going through the list that some of them are not quite as revolutionary as their practitioners would have you believe.

Guerilla: An overall catch phrase for non-traditional advertising coined by Jay Conrad Levinson more than twenty years ago when he wrote his seminal book *Guerilla Marketing*. In subsequent years it has exploded into a veritable cornucopia of amoeba-like, rapidly-reproducing, big–dollar-earning stuff that has embedded itself into the geek speak of corporate America. As Jay puts it so eloquently on his Web site, "Guerrilla Marketing started out a single volume and has since acted biblically by being fruitful and multiplying into a library of 35 books and counting, an Association, a lush Web site, an abundance of video and audio versions, an e-mail newsletter, a consulting organization, an internationally-syndicated column for newspapers, magazines, and the Internet, and presentations in enough countries for us to consider forming our own Guerrilla United Nations."

Damn, I'm jealous!

But Jay was on to a good thing. The primary premise of guerilla marketing was that you could use unconventional tactics to perform promotional activities that had been considered as too expensive for small companies to engage in. Examples of this in the early days were such relatively mundane things as sticking insta-print circulars under windshield wipers, leaving discount vouchers hanging on the door knobs of hotels and residences, giving out samples in shopping malls, using flags, banners, balloons, even giant purple blow-up dinosaurs or lumberjacks outside your premises. Yes, I know most of these would now be regarded as the kind of tacky merchandising props best left to used-car dealerships who still think the offer of a free hot dog will convince you to come in and sign up for a new seventy-five thousand dollar auto, but at the time these were introduced, many were considered by mainstream businesses as truly unconventional.

Buzz: Also known as word-of-mouth marketing (WOMM). This revolves around creating favorable personal recommendations to someone else by users of a product or service. Although in the past, this would have been the natural reaction of a happy customer who was so impressed by a company's product, he or she would spontaneously tell all her friends about it. Today, WOMM campaigns are designed to give consumers more than a little encouragement. A few years ago, Ford gave a new car to 125 influential young consumers in different parts of the U.S. to drive for six months in order to generate talk amongst their peers about this "hot" new model. As a result of this program, initial sales were 120 percent over the original estimate. Hebrew National organized 250 PTA presidents in twelve cities to drive around hosting hot dog barbecues and pass out coupons at local events. Each was given the use of an SUV for the summer. It goes without saying that each SUV was plastered with very big, very ugly, Hebrew National logos. Although the initial reaction was favorable, interest soon dropped off after the program ceased. That's why WOMM is increasingly moving away from the free product and couponing model, and more towards the seemingly innocent introduction of brands into apparently spontaneous conversations, which if you think about it, is going back to the kind of nefarious mind manipulation Vance Packard was getting his knickers in a twist about in *The Hidden Persuaders* fifty years ago. Which provides a nice segue to:

Stealth: A rather more devious form of buzz marketing in that the people who are being targeted don't realize it's actually taking place. Stealth marketing can involve hiring attractive couples to sit in bars and engage each other in conversation about this fantastic new drink they've discovered within earshot of total strangers. Then when they've drummed up enough interest and enthusiasm amongst the other customers, they'll offer to buy them a drink; perhaps using the excuse that it's some kind of special occasion like a birthday or anniversary to alleviate suspicion on the part of the listener. As most of these stealth marketers will very likely be unemployed actors, they should be able to play their roles in such a natural way that their audience will not realize they are being marketed to. This engenders a much better response within the target audience than a sponsored event, which is seen as obviously staged. I'm sure Dr. Dichter would have been a huge proponent of the method, no doubt seeing it as an extension of mans subliminal need to be sexually promiscuous with complete strangers.

Ambient: This is a form of participatory marketing aimed at a specific and well defined group or class of people, i.e. golfers, NASCAR fans, students, surfers, nose-hair groomers, or anyone with an overriding, even obsessive, interest in a specific activity. You then create events, promotions, and offers that are of particular interest to these groups. You reach them through parties, fan clubs, reunions, anniversaries, membership lists, club literature, sponsorship, and anything else that can be specifically tailored to them. The great thing about these groups is that the members are usually fanatics verging on the weird, so if it has anything to do with their particular sphere of interest, they want to know about it and be involved. Members of these networks are also incredibly loyal to the companies that support them. Red Bull has created a huge brand in the extreme sports community with this kind of below the radar marketing, and they've done it without spending the fortune it would have cost them if they'd used traditional mainstream marketing and advertising. However, one of the inherent problems with this kind of marketing is the more successful it is, the less cost effective it becomes. At the time of writing, Budweiser has just dropped out of NASCAR race sponsorship, no doubt because they came to the realization that the mega millions they've spent on it over the years can now be spent more effectively elsewhere. On the other hand, if you strike up a loyal relationship with a small, but fanatic niche market, such as the aforementioned nose-hair groomers, the odds are you can own that entire culture for the foreseeable future with a relatively meager outlay of bucks.

Experiential: In an earlier life, this would have been called sampling, as it is based on getting your product into a potential customers hands and letting them use it and enjoy the benefits. In the beginning, it was used mostly by cigarette, liquor, and specialty food companies when launching a new product. And if you get lucky on your exotic beach vacation in Cancun or Rio, you can still be offered free cigarettes by a bikini-clad babe anxious to get you hooked on the pleasures of the evil weed. Again dirty old Dr. Dichter must be excitedly spinning in his grave at the wonderful sexual/death wish connotations of this particular strategy. Today, this form of marketing has become much more sophisticated and is used by many mainstream companies. The key is to let the product speak for itself, as what the donor is looking to achieve is getting a favorable reaction from the recipient, who will then become an evangelist for their company, hopefully spreading the word to friends, family, and work colleagues. Experiential marketing can be looked at as being diametrically opposed to the hard sell that was so beloved of major marketers of consumer products and their advertising agencies in the fifties and sixties, as was spelled out in detail in *The Hidden Persuaders*.

Viral: This relies on using existing networks of people and societies to expand awareness of products and services through the ripple effect of viral communication. Think of it in the way a computer virus spreads - but in a much more benign sense. The effectiveness of the communication is enhanced through its transmission, because it's only passed on by the participants within the network if they are favorably impressed by it. This form of marketing is very much reliant on the explosion of digital communication in recent years via cell phones, text messaging, blogs, and Web sites, with particular emphasis on the rapid growth of the many social networking sites such as MySpace, LinkedIn, Facebook, and video sharing sites such as YouTube.

Swarm: Sometimes known as "smart-mobs," is a form of social networking that enables large groups of people to connect, usually by cell phone or computer, often for political purposes, but increasingly for commercial purposes. Smart-mobs have been known to congregate on the premises of particular retailers to negotiate group discounts. One of the interesting aspects of this form of participatory marketing is that it can be instigated by the very retailer the Smart-Mob shows up at.

Astroturfing: Although primarily applied to the marketing of politicians and political movements, such as getting amendments, propositions, and write-in candidates on state and national ballots, its primary purpose is to drum up support for some kind of initiative by making it look like there is a grassroots movement in its favor. This usually involves hiring paid-for "volunteers" to collect signatures, create "spontaneous" rallies, and man phone banks. This form is not recommended for anyone in a legitimate business who isn't entirely devoid of scruples, and is best left to the politicians and their hacks.

Undercover: Somewhat of a catch-all description for all forms of marketing that targeted consumers do not see as marketing. It should be realized that whereas stealth marketing is completely subversive, even elements of experiential marketing when consumers are given free product, can be perceived by the recipients not so much as obvious merchandising, but perhaps as acts of benevolence. This is certainly true of ambient marketing, as the target groups are such fanatics about their particular interests they are grateful and become extremely loyal to the companies they recognize as supporting them and their activities.

Product Placement: Although not usually considered as a guerrilla marketing tactic, there's no question this is a form of promotion that works in the same subliminal way by introducing brand name products to consumers as a supposedly natural part of another experience. This is different from product endorsement, such as took place in the early days of television that I talked about earlier, when even the Flintstones would smoke a particular cigarette because the brand was sponsoring the show. Product placement occurs in today's TV programs when characters such as Carrie in *Sex in The City* writes her columns and her nonstop whining about Mr. Big on an Apple PowerBook, always making sure the Apple logo is prominently displayed - or in the long running animated series *South Park* when the

P.F. Chang's restaurant franchise is sometimes featured in episodes. Many claim that product placement is a relatively new phenomenon, yet as I mentioned in an earlier chapter, it's been part of the movie business for a long time. When 007 fired up a smoke after killing a SPECTRE agent and knocking back a stirred, not shaken, vodka martini, it was always a Lark. He even shared them with whatever sultry babe was occupying his bed at the time. Now, product placement is in everything from TV and films, to video games, plays, and books, with the most notorious example of the latter being Fay Weldon's book, *The Bulgari Connection*, which was chock-full of the Italian companies' jewelry. No surprise when it came out that Bulgari had actually paid Ms. Weldon to write the book. Wonder how slim the chances are of a Big Dumb Agency paying me to write a book for them? Yeah. OK, pretty slim.

Virtual Worlds: There has been tremendous growth in the last couple of years of both MMORPGs (massively multiplayer online role playing games) and virtual world social sites, of which second life is the prime example. Both are outgrowths of earlier variations in both the gaming world and social networking sites. Increasingly addictive and commercialized, I shall also deal with them in more detail in chapter eight.

So, these are some of the choices companies are currently faced with when it comes to guerilla and non-traditional marketing. No doubt, by the time you read this there will even more, but most of them will simply be variations of the above, which are in turn, mostly up-to-date tactics of long used strategies to capture the consumers attention.

But even though the big package goods and other FMCG (fast moving consumer goods) companies are still primarily reliant on mainstream marketing and advertising programs Many are starting to reallocate substantial parts of their budgets into new media vehicles and guerilla marketing tactics. In fact, as far back as 2000, Proctor & Gamble formed their own in-house agency, Tremor - you just have to know that this name came out of a multiday, multimillion dollar brainstorming session replete with agonizingly trite

PowerPoint presentations and the kind of soporific corporate-speak that was invented within the marble canyons of P&G's headquarters in Cincinnati. This in-house organization is completely dedicated to guerilla marketing, with particular emphasis on word-of-mouth or "buzz campaigns. Interestingly, the agency has become so successful that a large part of Tremor's business now comes from outside P&G. This is a trend that will no doubt continue.

Because of its well publicized growth and the newsworthiness of some of its more outrageous executions, one of the key questions being asked about guerilla marketing is whether or not it can be used to the exclusion of other forms of traditional marketing and advertising. In my opinion, the answer is yes, but with this caveat: to do it well, it demands the investment of a great deal of time and effort by the people tasked to execute it. It also means companies engaging in it must commit to a radically different mindset than that with which they've approached their marketing in the past.

It means not treating guerilla marketing as a bolt-on to an existing mainstream media campaign. Which is why so many large Madison Avenue advertising agencies are often so pathetically bad at virtually all forms of non-traditional marketing and advertising. Only after the mainstream TV and print advertising has been produced to guarantee maximum income to the agency are the digital people brought in to create the Web sites and other Internet communications. Then, just before the office cleaner comes round to empty the trash baskets and put out the lights, some junior account executive pipes up with the suggestion that maybe they could do a few of those ambient or viral gimmicks. You know, like we should put on some "stunts" to prove to the client we're really up to speed on all that *"Long tail, Cluetrain, Tipping point"* stuff you read about in the *Harvard Business Review* and *Wired*. So, less than enthusiastically the BDA throws together some "way out" stuff, like perhaps employing a few dozen homeless people to stencil the client's logo in fluorescent paint on the sidewalks of Manhattan, even though the prime target audience they need to address live in Louisiana. Then just to show everyone how "hip & groovy" they are, they shoot a video of the early morning stencil battalion, stick it on YouTube, and enter it in the

"Best Viral Campaign Featuring Homeless People" category of the Cannes Film Festival.

One of the great opportunities guerilla marketing offers to companies with marketing budgets less than the GDP of a small African nation, is that it can level the playing field in respect to their competition, particularly if they have fallen into the habit of spending most of their marketing and advertising budget on traditional media to little effect. All they have to do is outsmart their competition, rather than try to outspend them, which is obviously easier said than done; but there's another benefit to this approach, which is rarely given the recognition it deserves. Namely that being perceived as the underdog can be appealing to customers who have had less than sterling experiences with the market leader in a given category and are looking to make a change to someone they hope will at least treat them with the respect they deserve. Remember the original Avis "When you're number two, you try harder" campaign? (Interesting enough, at the time, Avis was actually fourth or fifth in the car rental business). The key requirement for any company adopting this approach is that it has to live up to the expectations of their new customers. Unfortunately, many fail to do so.

However, *"The Ubiquitous Persuaders* is not intended to be a how-to book. Rather, it is intended to show how much of the executional mechanics of the advertising business have changed since the publication of Vance Packard's classic, whilst at the same time many of the fundamental principles have not. Over the years, I've seen great amounts of money wasted by both agencies and their clients because they jumped into the newest "tactic du jour" without thinking things through. This is particularly true with many of the new media and guerilla marketing activities. I feel driven to offer some thoughts on what I think companies should consider before implementing guerilla tactics as part of their advertising. Some of the most common mistakes companies make include not recognizing that whatever they do, it must be an integral part of their overall marketing program, and that although guerilla marketing tends to be less costly than traditional media, it still needs to be funded sufficiently for it to attain worthwhile results. By its very nature, guerilla marketing embodies change as a way of achieving impact, and an essential component of the program is momentum. Doing a series of one-offs or stunts will never deliver the cumulative benefits realizable by developing and executing a well architected and consistent program. And finally, to be successful, a guerilla marketing program must be based on the logical principles and outlining of attainable objectives you would expect to find in a traditional marketing plan.

These general principles of guerilla marketing are applicable to most companies, irrespective of whether they are business-to-consumer (B-2–C) or business to business (B-2–B) focused. Another appealing aspect of guerilla marketing is that it can be effective for companies of all sizes, irrespective of whether they are startups or have been in business for some time. Small companies can utilize many guerilla tactics without the use of outside agencies. And who knows, when they achieve the magnitude of a P&G or General Electric, they might very well decide to have the equivalent of their own Tremor working for them.

Guerrilla marketing has been around and talked about in its modern interpretation for about twenty-five years, yet in actuality it's been with us for centuries. When Nero provided bread and circuses (not to mention a large number of unfortunate Christians) for the pleasure of the mob in the Circus Maximus, he was ensuring his popularity through a lethal combination of PR and guerilla marketing. It's no different from a liquor company hosting a tasting of their hot, new rum - which within twelve months will be last year's "lukewarm" rum - in a trendy Soho bar to encourage New York's coolest to get plastered for free on this exotic foreign libation. Creating this kind of exposure properly is simply a matter of superior planning and execution. And, unlike Nero, it shouldn't be necessary to stage crucifixions on the dance floor.

It's important to realize that because of the ubiquity of advertising now, some forms of guerilla advertising are becoming the realization of Vance Packard's worse nightmares, or Dr Dichter's wet dreams. If you see the ice car melting on a London street, or the lady in the four poster bed sleeping in a Tokyo subway station, you know it's some kind of publicity stunt or marketing activity that a client is paying through the nose for. You may think its crazy, but there is obviously nothing ominous about it. On the other hand, the new form of stealth marketing that I talked about earlier with the couple in the bar encouraging complete strangers to try this great new drink they have discovered, takes guerilla marketing one step further by wherever possible disguising the fact that the people involved are actually actors engaging in a marketing activity. This is quite different from the launching of the new "hot" rum mentioned above; where the guerilla marketer makes no secret the tastings are being hosted by the company providing the booze. In fact, the person handling the event will make sure there are plenty of bottles of the product highlighted behind the bar, as well as display materials, coasters, and literature on view promoting the product. There will also probably be "resting actress" hostesses serving the drinks, dressed in suitably evocative and skimpy tropical attire in the colors of the brand being promoted. Everyone in the bar will be left with no doubt that a promotional marketing activity is taking place, and will raise their glasses of free booze accordingly. Then, they will all trot off to another bar where the next "hot" product is on offer for free.

With participatory marketing, the essential tactic is to make sure that those it hopefully makes the most impact on are part of the game and don't mind participating because they haven't realized it's a marketing activity. An example of this a couple of years ago was when a well-known camera company employed a bunch of actors to be pseudo-tourists who would ask genuine tourists to take their picture in front of the Statue of Liberty, or on the Staten Island ferry, all the while raving about the incredible features of their new camera.

Even though the Adverati of Madison Avenue would have you believe this is all part of some incredible new-fangled piece of marketing expertise they have recently invented, just like Nero's bread and circuses for the masses, most of it is not even close to being new. As I've mentioned, ever since the earliest days of the motion picture industry, cigarette companies have spent untold fortunes convincing us that smoking was sexy and glamorous. Not only would "Bogie" light two cigarettes at the same time and pass one over to Lauren Bacall while curling his upper lip in a way I have been practicing for years, but never managed to pull off, but Sean Connery's portrayal of James Bond unfailingly required him to smoke Lark cigarettes. Even though in Ian Fleming's original books, 007 wouldn't have left his Mayfair apartment without his hand rolled Morland, cork-tipped, Turkish/Virginian-blend cigarettes in his gun-metal-grey Dunhill cigarette case; the same one that saved his life on numerous occasions by fortuitously deflecting a SPECTRE agent's bullets. And yes, his vodka martinis always had to be made with Smirnoff, which went out of fashion for several years (probably because Smirnoff wouldn't cough up the money) but has now come full circle with the latest Bond caper *Casino Royale* prominently displaying Smirnoff as the twenty-first century spy's essential martini ingredient. Actually, all the Bond movies have been rife with product pitches form Omega watches to Aston Martin cars, and 007 wouldn't be caught dead in Monte Carlo Casino's "Salon Prive," drinking any champagne other than Bollinger. Today, this is just one very expensive tactic within the sphere of guerilla marketing and is known as product placement. Back in the days of *The Hidden Persuader* it was known by the far less glamorous name of payola.

There are many attractions to the stealth and participatory forms of guerilla marketing, because it is based on the principle that consumers will be more receptive to your messaging if they perceive it as coming from fellow consumers who have simply stumbled across this wonderful new product, rather than having been obviously influenced by paid-for advertising. This form of consumer promotion can be so much more effective, because it's delivered under the radar. This is particularly important when more and more advertising is perceived as a less and less credible source of consumer information.

One of the greatest appeals of guerilla marketing for a small- or medium-sized business is that not only is it less expensive to execute than traditional marketing and advertising, but the company can also do a great deal of it themselves without the help of a specialist marketing and advertising agency. Although, I would certainly be the first to recommend that when any enterprise gets to a particular size, they might benefit from hiring such a specialist. But that's certainly true of all forms of advertising; the client just has to be sure they manage the process effectively to guarantee a reasonable return on their investment.

Having waxed eloquently about some of the advantages of guerilla and other non-traditional forms of advertising, it has to be acknowledged there is a downside, one which is becoming increasingly obvious. The reason this book is called *The Ubiquitous Persuaders* is because traditional advertising is now almost everywhere, and where it isn't, these spaces soon become occupied by increasingly intrusive non-traditional forms. Supermarket eggs now carry logos and ads for TV programming. That's right. The ads are on the eggs, not the carton they come in. Pizza boxes and take-away Chinese food boxes carry ads for airlines, while airline sick bags carry ads for insurance companies. The conveyor belt at the supermarket checkout carries ads, which seems to me somewhat redundant as the reason you're at the checkout is because you've already completed your shopping.

There are an increasing number of companies who do nothing but offer free supplies and products covered in advertising to professional groups who can save on their operating expenses by using these branded items. Doctor's offices are increasingly looking like market stalls with logos and messages on everything from the pens you use to fill in the reams of paperwork necessary to get your two minutes with the physician, to the paper cover on top of the examination table you park your frigid bum on, so that when you stand up, your rear end will have an ad on it for hemorrhoid suppositories.

Even though the American public (and increasingly, the rest of the world) has been able to manage an ever-higher tolerance level towards most forms of advertising, there will eventually be a reaction. Yes, people will put up with advertising if they get something in return. This has always been the broadcaster/audience compact with commercial television and radio. If you wanted to avoid the ads, you subscribed to cable or satellite TV, or listened to PBS for commercial free radio (and hopefully made a donation to the station). By the same rationale, if newspapers and magazines didn't carry advertising, very few publications would exist, and only the very rich would be able to afford them. This accepted state of affairs is now starting to spill over into the areas of wireless telephone service, downloadable music, online video sites, and other current forms of communication and entertainment. If you are prepared to watch an ad on your one-and-a-half-inch cell phone screen while listening to the scratchy soundtrack on a pea-sized earpiece, then this will get you a few dollars deducted from your next cell phone bill. The youthful inhabitants of this increasingly wired world - actually, I should say unwired, but you get my drift - are conditioned to accept this arrangement as part of the deal. In some cases, they have no choice, as many school buses now have video screens featuring commercials for junk food and fashions, along with public service messages about not doing drugs, or engaging in premarital sex on the way to school. But even they will eventually rebel and say enough is enough.

So, how will the consumer of the future be reached and persuaded when they have become increasingly saturated and eventually turned off by a 24–7–365 barrage of hype? That, dear reader is a subject we'll save for the last chapter.

chapter SIX.

ESCAPE from REALITY

Why it is virtually impossible for Big Dumb Agencies, because of the archaic way they are staffed and structured to create advertising that can possibly have any meaningful impact on the consumers they are addressing. And, why this situation is becoming worse as BDAs increasingly divorce themselves from the audiences they claim to address.

Back in the late fifties when *The Hidden Persuaders* was published, the vast majority of people who worked in the advertising business could be considered as belonging to the middle class, in common with most of the population of America. It didn't matter if you earned your daily crust as a copywriter at Sullivan, Stauffer, Colwell and Bayles (a long since defunct agency of the fifties and sixties), on a production line assembling Fords, collecting tickets on the Long

Island railroad, or, God forbid, had the misfortune to be stuck in the hell of a middle management job for Proctor and Gamble or Colgate Palmolive. The fact is, most Americans lived in a comfortable two or three bedroom house in the suburbs. Their 2.3 children went to public schools. They owned two big, gas-guzzling cars, which cost less than five dollars a week to fill up. The majority of the wives stayed at home. The extended family could afford to go on vacation for two weeks every year, and they even managed to save a modest amount of money out of their fortnightly paycheck. Fifty years later, things are drastically different for the average working/middle-class American family, to the point where all of the above parameters no longer apply to the vast majority of U.S. citizens.

Without going through a litany of how drastically things have changed, suffice it to say that the archetypical American family described above is now only to be found on late-night television when watching reruns of the classic fifties "nuclear family," *Ozzie and Harriet*. This is particularly true when it comes to a day in the life of the lady of the house, who is increasingly the only adult in the house. This unfortunate woman, after a hard day at her place of employment, can barely manage five minutes to gulp down a stiff pick-me-up, before taking the kids off to soccer practice, returning to feed them their micro-zapped macaroni and cheese, while watching a rerun of another nuclear family in *Leave it to Beaver*. This is assuming she isn't disturbed in the middle of dinner by the ringing of the phone as some wanker calling on behalf of Jerry for the March of Dimes, implores her to help out "Jerry's Kids," even though she's registered at least a couple of dozen times on the national "do not call list."

The big disconnect here is that although, at the beginning of the twenty-first century, we all know America has changed drastically, this fact doesn't seem to have penetrated the minds of the people charged with convincing the unwashed masses they should go out and buy mountains of unwanted junk on their already maxed-out credit cards. That's because a great many of the people employed at BDAs live a life that is a total opposite to that of their intended audience. Consider that those who've backstabbed their way to the upper reaches of management are blessed to live in a huge loft in Soho, have a weekend place in the Hamptons for summers at the beach, a place in Vermont for skiing in the winter, travel to the office in a limo, work out with their personal trainer at Equinox, have another limo drop off and pick up their kids from their thirty-thousand-dollar-a-year private school, enjoy season tickets to the Met, and order bellons by the bucketful at Balthazar. Which leads you to ask the twenty million dollar question? How the hell can they relate to, let alone empathize with those unfortunates who troll the aisles of Wal-Mart looking for affordable polyester bed sheets or Chicago Bears sweat shirts, after they've been forced to take out a "pay-day" loan three or four days ahead of their actual pay day? This is a mystery I've spent a great many years trying to solve, all to little avail, even when aided with many fine bottles of the cognac distiller's art. Nevertheless, I shall push on with my quest, again with the aid of the cognac.

Compounding this weirdness is the fact that the advertising business is based on a series of unfounded myths its practitioners would have the public accept as sacrosanct. You should never forget that these are the people who expect you to believe there is absolutely no truth to that hoary old chestnut, "If you invent a better mousetrap, the world will beat a path to your door." Threatening that unless you wish to spend the rest of your days in penury, you must utilize their services to let the world know you have invented this super new mousetrap. In these days of advertising ubiquity, that means they will advise you to blow massive amounts of cash creating brand-building TV campaigns that can only achieve their full impact if they are aired on the Super Bowl, the Oscars, the hot and cold varieties of the Olympics, and numerous golf tournaments.

Yes, they will pay lip service to the wonderful opportunities now available through the use of new media and other much hyped ways to interact with prospective customers. What they will invariably fail to recognize (and certainly omit to tell their clients) is that they are by far, the least best equipped organizations to maximize these new opportunities. By their nature, BDAs are slow, hide-bound, unadventurous, and because of their financial structure and necessary obeisance to their various holding companies, little more than a collection of scum sucking, bean counting wankers, and if that's not strong enough language for you, they are also outrageously expensive.

Consider that advertising is definitely not a science; it certainly isn't an art, even an applied art. It's more like a trade. It requires certain skill levels that can only truly be acquired, as with a trade, through an apprenticeship. Yes, there are now schools of advertising where gullible people who are deluded enough to think they are some kind of nascent creative genius are conned into handing over thousands of dollars by signing on for a portfolio building program. All in the hope that after a short period of time they can walk out with a diploma, a book of sample ads, and assorted digital odds and ends that will be the key to a high-paying job with a thirty-fourth floor corner office enjoying a view of the Hudson River. This rarely happens, and all these graduates have done is enriched the con men who run the schools. At the other end of the scale you have MBA business school mills at just about every university on the face of the earth, all churning out pod-like, brain-dead people whose only skill is that they can now do mind-numbing PowerPoint presentations in three colors, while talking a variety of nonstop, verbal diarrhea discernible only to their fellow brain-dead MBAs.

The reality is that advertising is like showbiz - you can only learn it by being in it. And if you ask me how you get in it, that's the old catch twenty-two, to which there is obviously no answer. All the best people I've ever known in advertising just fell into it, and after a few years, the vast majority of those blessed with a sufficient amount of brains, couldn't wait to fall out of it.

However, I digress. Agencies would have you believe they have some kind of exact scientific methodology that they employ on behalf of their clients to come up with "killer solutions" all guaranteed to increase the client's market share and send their competitors sliding down a feces-slimed slope to oblivion. Any agency worth its salt will dress this methodology up in various grandiose titles such as "360 degree branding," "return on ideas," or "the Klingon Empire USP." However, whatever they call it, it is invariably complete bullshit. Simply realize that no agency has come up with anything original in terms of a business model since our scaly ancestors dragged themselves out of the swamps and discovered the use of hand tools.

Perhaps the best example of the lengths to which BDAs will go to present themselves as having discovered the Holy Grail for building brands was when at a recent advertising conference in Cannes (where else would you hold an advertising conference?) Lord Maurice Saatchi - He of the original Saatchi & Saatchi fame - declared that by a process combining intuition and astrology he had come up with an entirely new way to create unassailable brand superiority. This miracle was to be known as "one word equity." The noble Lord claimed that because the consumer is increasingly bombarded by thousands of fragmentary messages via traditional and non-traditional media, the agency must now finesse and whittle away at any brand proposition until it is boiled down to one word. That's right, a single word; whether it is "power," "truth," "clean," "refresh," or perhaps "bullshit!" His thesis was that once the agency and its client had jointly found this single word, they should then use it relentlessly as the core of their messaging. In fact, they should commit to beating the crap out of it in all of their advertising, and they should do it forever! Half the stunned audience obviously realized he was a genius, as this "one word equity" would allow them in effect to continue doing what they'd always done for their clients; inventing new terms and descriptions for doing the same old stuff. The other half thought he was insane, pointing out that it required Lord Saatchi to give a two-thousand-word speech to explain his minimalism breakthrough of "one word equity." Besides which, shouldn't the title of his brilliant concept have been executed in one word instead of three?

The thing almost everyone in the advertising business quickly realizes is that whatever name, description, or acronym you choose to give to your "killer solution" this week, the basic objectives, strategies, and methodologies have changed little over the years. Before you start blowing lots and lots of money on an ad program, you have to decide what it is you wish to achieve as the end result. Oh yes, you might say, that's bloody obvious, and maybe it is to someone as perspicacious as you, but you might be amazed to be told that I've worked with numerous clients over the course of my career that had absolutely no idea why they were spending millions of dollars every year on their advertising. Obviously, this didn't stop me from helping them spend their money. After all, if I didn't do it, someone else would have.

Consider that before any advertising campaign is produced and run, whether it requires an outlay of hundreds, thousands, or millions of dollars, its objectives should be defined in such a way that they are crystal clear during both its creation and execution. The strategies to achieve these objectives and the messaging that best reflect the brands character, are essentially in the purview of the agency. This is not to say the client shouldn't have any input at this stage, but they should recognize this is the added value the agency brings to the table; otherwise the client may as well do all their advertising in-house and save themselves a ton of money.

After the advertising has run its course, both parties should evaluate if the objectives have been achieved. This is only possible if all elements of the program have been mutually agreed at every stage. It is a situation that rarely happens, even with the most competent of the BDAs. Compounding the problem is the fact that the agency creative team responsible for this particular account must be capable of translating the unfathomable ramblings of the MBA "suits" (the agency account executives) into something that hopefully will not lull the target audience into a total state of narcolepsy. Hard to do when the average "creative brief" contains such nuggets as, "Client wishes to be the category leader in the global market." Well, yes, and I would like to be the emperor of the known universe, but it would help if I had some kind of clue as to what it is that makes the client and his/her products capable of achieving this worthy ambition. This is why so much advertising is smoke, mirrors, and large helpings of bullshit built on a never-ending series of generalities. It's also why there is so much of what I call "your logo goes here" advertising, which is overwhelmingly generic in nature, with the only differentiator between your advertising and your competitors being the logo in the bottom right-hand corner of the page. Is this all too frequent state of affairs because of ignorance, apathy, or laziness? I have a long held suspicion it's probably a combination of all three.

We can look back at most of the advertising produced all

those years ago during the era of *The Hidden Persuaders* and snicker at its general amateurishness, not to mention its homogeneity. Yet when we look at the efforts of most of today's BDAs, we may be impressed by the quality of its production (as we should be when considering what it probably cost), but the content has barely improved. In fact, I would suggest that in many ways it has regressed. Why? Because now with the advent of new media, "consumer generated content," and "social networking" it seems there is a conscious effort to dumb down the message to the point you would expect it to be painted in day-glo colors on the walls of your local Toys "R" Us. At the time of writing, there are a number of agencies who seem to be striving for a never-ending diet of frat house humor in the work they produce. OK, a lot of it is for burgers, pizza, and tasteless, colored water, otherwise known as light beer, which appeals to a younger audience who would-n't be caught dead reading a paper or considering what might be happening in the world outside of MySpace. But eventually, most of these people must move on and join the ranks of those working for a living, raising a family, or God forbid, voting. In which case, I would hope they may have advanced to the stage of becoming receptive to advertising that's a tad more sophisticated than the "crushing a beer can on your head" variety. Or, maybe not! I don't claim to be a social scientist.

Irrespective of whether the advertising is sophisticated, naive, or simply moronic, I can assure you that if it is produced by your average BDA, it will have gone through the mill of numerable client/agency meetings, followed by untold numbers of focus groups and various other methods of testing to the point were any spark of originality will have had the crap beaten out of it. This unfortunate sequence of events will be covered in nauseating detail in a later chapter.

The major problem most BDAs seem to have is their failure to distinguish between strategy and execution. This is particularly true with their late acknowledgement and current infatuation with all things new media. Their eagerness to jump on this bandwagon usually blinds them to the fact that they not only don't understand it, they probably don't have anyone on staff capable of executing it, and will invariably end up losing money trying to execute it. Yet, because they have been lectured to at numerous advertising and marketing conferences they have paid thousands to attend, this is the future, it is unquestionable the path they must now proceed down.

To paraphrase Sir Winston Churchill, "Advertising is a riddle wrapped in a mystery inside an enigma." That's why nobody can give you a definitive reason why, or how advertising works, if indeed it does! OK, as I've already mentioned, you can prove that the direct marketing branch of the advertising industry works because the ads are coded in such a way that when people visit a Web site or call an eight-hundred number, the resulting sales are attributable to the effectiveness of the advertising, which makes you wonder why more clients don't do it? However, trying to credit some kind of effectiveness to generic and brand advertising is almost always impossible. Even though occasionally we get an ad (usually a TV spot) that generates great Monday morning "water cooler" chat. An ad that through the wonders of recall studies might do pleasant things for the clients brand recognition, and will undoubtedly be used by the agency to justify even more millions being thrown onto the burning pyre of brand building, there is usually no way you can quantify if it *actually* translated into increased sales.

As I said earlier, we are dealing with something very inexact here. When you consider some of the classic campaigns since the publication of *The Hidden Persuaders,* we have such gems as the Hathaway shirt campaign from David Ogilvy. The only reason he put Baron von Wrangel in an eye patch was because as he was on the way to the photo shoot, he realized he was going to have a stultifyingly boring series of ads, so, on a hunch, he stopped off at a drug store and bought an eye patch. The rest is ad biz history. Although, I've often wondered how pissed the Ogilvy art director on the account must have been when the agency CEO showed up with a ten-cent eye patch and made the model wear it. Not to mention wondering why the agency CEO found it necessary to show up at the photo shoot in the first place, for what I assume was a relatively minor account. Oh well, David always was a law unto himself.

We also have from the same period the Avis "Number Two -

Try Harder" campaign, the VW "Think Small" campaign, and the Alka Seltzer "Whatever shape your stomach's in" campaign, all flying in the face of advertising convention fifty or so years ago. In fact, if you look at most of the advertising we are currently subjected to, those classic campaigns would probably be flying in the face of advertising convention today! But they were immensely successful, both in terms of brand building and generating sales. However, ask any advertising guru to explain why these ads worked and they would find it almost impossible to give solid, quantifiable reasons. Just as they would be hard pressed to explain why campaigns that tested like gangbusters in Dubuque, and in spite of having tens of millions dollars shoveled behind them, died like mangy curs in the aisles of the nation's supermarkets. But, as I have said, advertising is not an art, and it's definitely not a science. Anyone who tells you otherwise is either an idiot or a charlatan.

If we go back to the days of *The Hidden Persuaders,* probably the single most advertised product in the U.S. was cigarettes, yet there is a great deal of evidence that both the content of the advertising, and the amount of money budgeted to run the advertising, had very little, if any, effect on the sales of one particular brand over the other. The same can also be said about the anti-smoking ads that now run fifty years after the publication of Vance Packard's classic. They, along with increasingly dire warnings on cigarette packaging, have had virtually no impact on the desire of people to smoke. The banning of smoking in public places and increasingly high taxes on the sale of tobacco has perhaps had an effect... However, in spite of the claims of the Adverati, the millions of dollars spent on advertising campaigns for both smoking and anti-smoking have had virtually no effect on the rate of smoking, or indeed on any other kind of addiction. Which is a chilling reflection on just how effective advertising actually is.

Perhaps the least understood thing about what makes an ad successful or not is the manner of its execution. In a traditional sense, this would mean the copy, layout, photography, and even the choice of typeface. To the people creating the ads, the copywriter and art director, these are no mere details and are often things they consider worth falling on their swords for in the interest of artistic integrity. Once again we can rely on David Ogilvy to encapsulate the absurdity to which this fanaticism is sometimes taken. In his book, *Confessions of an Advertising Man,* he describes the hypothetical conversation of two housewives riding on the top deck of a London bus. During the course of their chat, one of them points out to the other that she was put off from buying Persil detergent because the headline in the newspaper ad had been set in Bodoni Bold, and she had always been a big fan of Times Roman. Yes, agreed, it does sound a bit far fetched, but no more so than the irrational fanaticism I've witnessed on the part of art directors I've been partnered with at various stages of my career. There was a time back in the seventies when I was working in a major London agency with an art director who invariably insisted on having complete fonts of metal typefaces flown over from the U.S. for whatever particular masterpiece he was crafting at that moment. With a completely straight face he would claim that even though these typefaces were readily available in the UK as photo-type fonts, they lacked the crispness and "bite" of real metal type. Apart from the fact that this difference was only discernable with the aid of an electron microscope, and the ads were destined to run in a tabloid newspaper that most people bought for the naked girl on page three and would probably be used for wrapping tomorrow's fish and chips in, if you factored in the shipping costs of several tons of lead type, there was no way the agency would make money on this venture. Unless of course, they could find a way to pass these costs on to the client. Which they invariably did.

This is further proof of my thesis that the vast majority of people in advertising have absolutely no understanding of, or relationship to, the people they are advertising to. And, what's more, they couldn't care less about it.

Hastily backtracking here, this is not to say that creativity plays no part in solving the conundrum that is essential to the creation of great advertising - far from it. As someone who has made a nice living peddling my so-called creativity over the years, I would claim it is the absolute core of the process. Everything else, strategy, positioning, research, media, production, and the other disciplines their practitioners would claim to be fundamental to the process, are actually secondary to the message content. That is something which relies on great creative work. This explains why so much of today's advertising is mundane and pedestrian. Because, it may be based on perfectly sound strategy, positioning, etc. However, it's invariably executed badly. Perhaps the housewife on top of the London bus would have bought the Persil detergent in spite of the headline being set in Bodoni Bold if the ad had actually said something that grabbed her by the throat and made her jump off the bus and run into the nearest supermarket. This has always been, and always will be, the great challenge for people who create advertising. No matter how much research has been done to provide them with "unique" consumer insights, even though these are usually nothing more than common sense facts a twelve year old could tell you for a lot less money, in spite of the mountains of market research and competitive information dumped on your desk, and even if you've been in the business of creating ads for more years than Madonna has spent reinventing herself, at the end of the day, no one knows what makes a great ad.

It's like the movie business, where 99 percent of the movies made for millions and millions of dollars are sheer unadulterated crap. Yet the studios invest many, many more millions in increasingly stultifying formulaic films, all based on previous films that have been box office successes. Unfortunately, what is so predictable is that there is absolutely no guarantee the numerous copy cats, spin-offs, or remakes will become the next blockbuster. The same is true in advertising. This is why most car ads look like other car ads. The same is true of much bank and financial services advertising, or pharmaceutical advertising, and indeed a great many other categories. As I've written earlier, this is often because there is less risk to middle management at both the agency and client if you dumb everything down to a general standard of mediocrity. But mostly, it's because no one knows if a particular advertising campaign is great or not until it actually runs and you can measure the results. And as I've also said earlier, if the campaign is that pabulum lovingly described by BDAs as brand advertising, you'll be hard pressed to find out conclusively if it worked or not.

I guess in my forty-year career, I've been involved in thousands of campaigns. Several have won awards for creativity, which have been decided on by juries of other creatives who couldn't give a toss how the ads actually performed in the market place. No, it was all down to whether the copy was clever, or the art direction and photography was "hot." When it came to being judged on TV and film work, the fact that you used the "director du jour" everyone wanted to work with, would more often than not guarantee you a spot on the winner's rostrum. And it certainly helped if the other judges on the panel knew that in a couple of weeks you would be judging their own particular "breakthrough" work at the next big awards show in Cannes, Rio, or wherever was a rather nice place to escape the misery of New York, Minneapolis, London, or Moscow in winter. Not to mention, there's a certain attraction to being able to spend a couple of weeks getting deeply tanned and shitfaced at someone else's expense in the sunshine of some exotic location. I can even claim that some (not the majority, I'm afraid to say) of the campaigns I have been responsible for did work and actually sold product. This was particularly true when I worked on Dell's advertising for Chiat Day in San Francisco and when it became Goldberg, Moser, O'Neil in the late eighties. Because, as Dell only sold computers direct, if the ads didn't make the phone ring, then the ads weren't working, and the agency would have been shit-canned. But to be honest, for the vast majority of the work I have produced over all those years, I have no idea if it worked or not. And in fairness, I also must own up to knowing I've produced my share of ads that have definitely not worked. But in common with most people in advertising, I choose to ignore this disturbing fact.

Will BDAs change? I doubt it, and not just because they are entrenched in their ways and methods of working, but primarily because, as I have said previously, their business model is too rigid and structured, and the fact that they are beholden to their conglomerate masters will not allow it.

Will advertising change? Definitely, but it will be the new agencies and startups that will be responsible for it. These are individuals and companies intent on breaking the mold, not just in terms of what they do, but in how they do it and how they get paid for doing it. Many specialize in particular aspects of new media, viral, gorilla, stealth, and a dozen other names, some of which will have changed by the time you read this, for what is in reality an escape from the traditional, expensive, and wasteful methods that have persisted since the days of *The Hidden Persuaders*.

However, having said that, it's a fact of life that as these new kinds of advertising agencies grow and become successful, they will be courted by the BDAs and their conglomerate masters. Eventually the owners will cash out, sell their shop, and go off to buy that house in the Hamptons they always lusted after. Meantime their company will be sucked into the black hole of the BDA that has just bought them. The originality and new ways of working, which made them attractive to the BDA in the first place, will have their life force sucked out of them by the sheer mediocrity of the BDAs management and methods of working. Within months, everything will be back the way it always was, and the BDA will be out shopping for the next "hot shop" that currently enjoys the kind of reputation that makes it a desirable target for the BDA.

This is the way it has always been in the canyons of Madison Avenue. I would put money on my belief that this is the way it will always be.

chapter SEVEN. *will the*
DIGERATI
eventually KILL the
ADVERATI?

As we move towards a totally digital, totally connected world, the functions of the ad agency become increasingly decentralized and irrelevant. Specialist companies and in-house departments will supersede traditional functions of agencies. Is the Madison Avenue model broken? Can it be repaired? Will new media kill old everything?

A note of caution here: At the time of writing - mid to late 2008 - what I am describing as new media, by the time you read it, will, probably be "old media," and will, without question, have been replaced by "new, new media," or "uber new media." In fact, I shall go beyond that and talk about social media, which is in reality, a subset of new media. The great attraction of many of the social media initiatives is that they are often aimed at the youth market.

A demographic advertisers perennially lust after in their unfailing belief that these kids sit atop mountains of disposable income. Hence social media has become the flavor du jour for the Adverati in their never ending chase of the next big thing. Something you should definitely climb aboard before the express train leaves the station and you end up in penury for the rest of your miserable life. Personally, over the years I've realized that sometimes it's better to grab a cup of coffee (or a beer, in my case) relax, and wait for the next train. Most of the time, you'll be far better off having missed out on the sheer exuberance and froth of whatever was on offer.

As I mentioned in chapter one, when *The Hidden Persuaders* was written, in the halcyon days of low stress, two-parent families, pre-equal rights legislation, and let's just smoke and drink ourselves into happy oblivion, it was possible to reach 80 percent of the American population via three TV networks and three national magazines. In the fifty years since, this situation has radically changed. Not just because of the explosion in TV choices via cable and satellite, the hundreds, if not thousands of magazines that now pander to virtually every niche interest, and the deluge of guerilla marketing tactics described in chapter five. Hell no. The overwhelming change in the way companies are now attempting to reach their potential customers has been with the explosive growth of the Internet. Although the Internet had been around since the early eighties as a development of the earlier military driven ARPANET, it wasn't until the nineties, thanks to the wondrous creation of the World Wide Web and the development of easy-to-use, intuitive graphic interfaces, that the so-called dot com boom really took off, fuelling a frenzy of activity. The "Digerati" would have had you believe it was going to change the way we gathered information, communicated with each other, and most importantly for advertisers, shopped. Hopefully, doing so 'til we dropped!

Initially, though, it didn't quite work out as planned. Many of the dot com startups failed, not just because they were merely electronic versions of traditional brick-and-mortar stores, or because their business model was incapable of being transferred to an online presence in spite of the hundreds of millions of dollars venture capitalists were throwing at them. Buying dog food or groceries over the Internet made absolutely no sense, which made the ultimate demise of such companies as Pets.com and WebVan inevitable. However, perhaps one of the largest problems affecting most of these startups, which they and their investors deliberately chose to ignore, was that the customers they were addressing lacked the bandwidth necessary to properly communicate with their sites. Meaning that if you were trying to shop from a vendors Web site over a dial-up telephone line, which in the late nineties was what the vast majority of Internet users were stuck with, you would have been quicker jumping on your bicycle and riding down to "Main Street, USA," for whatever it was you absolutely had to have.

Perhaps the most famous example of how naïve many of these startups were, was the infamous Boo.com, a company formed in Britain to sell high-end, branded fashion wear. The Swedish founders, Ernst Malmsten, a former professor of Norse literature, and Kajsa Leander, a retired fashion model, didn't have a clue about commerce, let alone the Internet, yet this didn't stop investors from pumping hundreds of millions of dollars, pounds, and Euros into the venture. The basic principle of the site was that you would log on and then proceed to wander through multiple pages of semi-3D views of all the merchandise available, accompanied by your very own personal avatar-shopping assistant, "Miss Boo." Unfortunately, because of the limitations of the technology, and the over ambitious design of the site, you could grow old and grey waiting for pages to load via your slow dial-up connection. As a result, even though the Boo.com brand received tons of favorable PR and press coverage, potential customers quickly became frustrated and refused to stick around for the hours it would take to choose the latest gear from Gucci, Versace, or Louis Vuiton.

Boo.com rapidly burned through hundreds of millions of venture capital dollars as they opened plush offices in London, New York, Paris, Stockholm, and whatever other exotic locations the founders took a fancy to. No surprise that Boo.com became known in the dot com business as the enterprise that ran on "the three Cs": champagne, caviar, and Concorde - there were also many rumors of a fourth "C," namely cocaine! After a few short, exotic months and several hundred million dollars worth of funding, Boo.com was out of business. The company name and the Miss Boo character (two of their few remaining assets) were sold for a mere two hundred and fifty thousand dollars.

Even though Boo.com was one of the most visible failures of that heady period, there were hundreds, if not thousands of others that rapidly collapsed as they ploughed through mountains of VC cash while trying to peddle everything that had always been conveniently available at your local supermarket or corner drug store for as long as anyone could remember. What most of these startups failed to realize was that unless you're counted amongst the Trumps of this world, why would you bother to order dog food and diapers online, particularly when the delivery charges often doubled the cost of the product? Few of these "new models in retailing" brought anything different to the consumer's table, merely being online variations of the brick-and-mortar retailers who'd been around for the last hundred years or so. However, in fairness, I should point out there are a couple of great survivors from that era who have toughed it out for over a dozen years to ultimately achieve success and profitability: eBay and Amazon.

To date, eBay is by far the only e-commerce, new media, Internet-based company that has uniquely demonstrated the much hyped and long promised paradigm shift we were told to look forward to in the way business would be done in the future. I hate the word paradigm, with or without the addition of shift. However, I think in this case, eBay deserves it. I will promise though never to use the word again. EBay is truly different, because it has fundamentally changed the way millions of companies, small businesses, and customers are now doing business with each other. Based on the principle of an online auction, flea market, thrift store, and general repository for all the crap you've accumulated over the years and thought you would eventually have to rent a U-Haul to get rid of. It is without a doubt a unique business model. Without the Internet, it couldn't exist. Amazon, on the other hand, could, although it would not be as successful or efficient as it has now become, in spite of soaking up massive amounts of cash for nine years before showing its first profit. When Amazon opened its "virtual" doors in 1995 it was little more than an online bookstore. Today, it is the world's largest online store, where you can buy virtually anything. Yet as a business model, it is still really only a twenty-first century electronic version of a nineteenth century Sears's catalogue; albeit, one with incredibly effective data tracking systems and highly sophisticated customer relationship programs, including making superlative service virtually a religion.

But even though both these companies are often described as eMarketeers and are regularly written about in the advertising trade press, they are not really representative of how new media is changing the way increasing numbers of people find, pay attention too, and react to advertising when it is presented in a digital form. The overriding consideration of what new media will eventually mean in virtually all modern societies is summed up in the title of this book - it will make advertising truly *ubiquitous*. And yet, because it will therefore be everywhere, there's no question, its effectiveness will inexorably diminish over time. Successful practitioners of the advertising arts will be those who can create effective communications without obvious intrusiveness.

Consider the word "media." It's merely a catch-all method of transportation for words, pictures, ideas, and increasingly, experiences. In its early stages, media consisted of graffiti covered walls in cities such as Pompeii, which eventually transmogrified into the billboards that clutter our highways today; with the exception of Sao Paulo, Brazil, which at the time of writing has just banned the use of billboards throughout the city. Then the invention of moveable type by Caxton gave us editions of books, rather than hand-written originals. This eventually gave us newspapers and magazines. After a few hundred years, wireless and television followed. But until Tim Berners-Lee invented his unique filing system, which we know today as the Internet, very little had changed in the preceding fifty years. Those fifty years of an exploding economy when the dramatic increase in the average American's disposable income allowed them to indulge in the odd luxury, rather than strictly necessities, made it an advertiser's paradise. And this is the primary reason why traditional advertising agencies, which I shall continue to lovingly call BDAs, gradually became complacent, fat, and lazy.

Scrambling to jump aboard the moving train before it leaves the station, they are now all paying lip service to new media, emphasizing how they "get it!" But what they don't get is that although there is now no shortage of new media choices that enable them to bombard audiences with a tsunami of messages. There is also an increasing shortage of the consumer's time and attention. *Wired* magazine has described it as "the Attention Economy" and rightly so. Because people, particularly in the U.S. are working longer hours with less and less leisure time, so the chances of you catching and holding their attention for a specific message or piece of communication are diminishing. Overlay this with the acknowledged fact that more than half of all consumers already go out of their way to actively avoid most forms of advertising and you have a situation where from the advertiser's point of view, things can only get worse.

The true Internet media choices for advertisers are known as neutral trading platforms, because unlike Amazon and other merchandise vending sites, they are providing services, rather than selling products. They are in effect, merely the "tubes," to paraphrase the geriatric senator from Alaska - who by the time you read this, may no longer be the geriatric senator from Alaska - through which the visitor avails him or herself of the particular service the site offers. The successful ones enjoy high volumes of traffic, and are smart enough to control the advertising they carry so as not to make it offensive or obtrusive to the users of the site. Also, unlike brand sites that are dedicated to a single company and its products, these sites make great efforts to appear as neutral, trustworthy, and nonpartisan to their users.

The single most used category of these sites is the search engine, and the eight-hundred-pound gorilla of them all is Google. In less than ten years, this company has gone from a Silicon Valley startup to an international giant with revenues of more than twelve billion dollars. In the late nineties, there were many search engine companies, the vast majority of which have either fallen by the wayside, become vertically, or niche, specialized, or have been absorbed by one of the remaining big three: Yahoo, MSN Search (now known as Live Search), and Google, with Google having close to a 60 percent share of the entire global search market. Available in more than 120 languages, including even Klingon and Elmer Fudd, the swift success of Google was driven not just by its superior Web search capabilities, but primarily by its lean, exclusively, all-text design, which was maintained when the company started selling advertising in its third year. In the early days of Web advertising, and even today on far too many sites, the pages were a nightmare of spinning banners, star bursts, flashing neon type, and whatever else the ganja-influenced designer could think of inflicting on the site visitor. In other words, far too many Web sites looked like your average used-car dealership newspaper advertising.

The principle of advertising on these sites was simplicity itself. The advertiser could negotiate to purchase keywords associated with the subject the viewer was searching. The purchaser was able to do this through a system of bidding, starting at five cents a click, and in the case of Google, because of the volume of traffic the site was generating, these nickel clicks quickly grew into millions of dollars. This initial program was known as Google AdWords. Every single day, vast numbers of people perform millions of searches on Google. With AdWords every single search acts as a niche specific marketing vehicle, the ads associated with that search mean that the advertiser has the opportunity to connect with a potential customer who is probably in the market right now for their product or service. Very few marketing channels deliver such targeted specificity. The company then introduced Google AdSense, a program whereby Web site owners agree to host Google ads on their site, earning money for every click through to the advertiser. Google now has dozens of products from e-mail, to maps, to news. All are linked into Google advertising, most of which no longer rely on counting clicks, but now measure the income generated by each lead, which is a far more satisfactory and fair arrangement for the advertiser.

Google is also now moving into some forms of traditional advertising, including radio and newspaper. In fact, in a speech in Paris (July 2007) Eric Schmidt, CEO of Google, announced the company's commitment to expand into many of the traditional areas of advertising agencies had always considered their natural purview. Naturally, this is causing the BDAs to wet their knickers as they wonder just what the hell is going on. But based on their past track record of reacting to change, by the time they wake up, I'm sure it will be too late. Even Sir Martin Sorrel, chairman of WPP has expressed concerns that Google is bypassing his agencies and going directly to clients. He thinks Google is attempting to become the world's largest advertising agency. In common with the senior management of all the conglomerates and their constituent BDAs, Sir Martin is dead wrong. Google does not want to be an advertising agency; it wants to replace advertising agencies.

Even more interesting, at the time of writing, Google is eyeing the TV market in an effort to provide advertisers with yet another option to reach consumers by harnessing the power of the Web and its interactive direct channels of communication to specifically target offline ads, delivered via TV to consumers who are predisposed to buy certain products. This new method of delivery to cable homes in California takes the data from Google user's search activity, then pumps out specifically tailored content relative to their searches in the form of TV ads they will be exposed to during their viewing sessions. Meaning that if you've been searching online for information about health insurance you will now find yourself being targeted by TV spots for health insurance next time you're in the middle of your favorite soap or game show. This method of data mining people's online activities obviously raises worrisome questions about privacy. Is Google in danger of becoming George Orwell's long ago forecast Big Brother? An all seeing, all knowing presence that monitors our actions and thoughts 24–7. Could this become the digital version of Vance Packard's mind controlling army of shrinks in *The Hidden Persuaders?* One that doesn't have to rely on the pseudo-psychiatry and crackpot theories of the Dr. Dichter's of this world, because now, thanks to "datametrics" and "psychometrics," and all the other metrics, we can look forward to hearing about in the future, much of the guesswork will be taken out of marketing and we can expect to be relentlessly targeted, based on our interests and activities.

Obviously, this is an issue Google is very much aware of. It recently announced it would be erasing giant chunks of personal information on user's searches in an attempt to reassure the masses that their privacy is a major consideration for them. They will, however, still cache data from billions of searches for a period of two years, something they are legally required to do, as the data can be requested by law enforcement agencies when pursuing an investigation. The trick now is for Google to find a way to churn this information for financial gain, without pissing off its tens of millions of users. If they can manage to do this, they would completely transform the way most advertising in the future might be targeted and programmed. It would also make Google even more obscenely rich than it already is.

This brings us to Facebook and MySpace, two of the leading, and by far, most-hyped examples of the current "digital craze du Jour," social networking. Even though they originally started out in life as little more than small networks of people with common interests, they have rapidly developed into an incandescent nucleus of the Web 2.0 phenomenon. Ah, yes, Web 2.0; that much talked about phenomena that will transform humanity from here going forward. If I may, I would love to take the opportunity to cut through the layers of bullshit the media has been shoving down our throats for the last couple of years about how Web 2.0 is going to change the way people connect, eat, drink, and even have orgasmic sex. I prefer to defer to the wonderfully simple explanation of British actor/author, Stephen Fry:… *"Web 2.0 is an idea in people's heads rather than a reality. It's actually an idea that the reciprocity between the user and the provider is what's emphasized. In other words, genuine interactivity if you like, simply because people can upload as well as download."* My God, Stephen, I couldn't have put it better myself, so I shan't bother to make the effort. But, back to social networking. Although, at the time of writing, social networking is constantly being declaimed as the next big thing, and therefore, humungous amounts of money are being forcibly poured down the goosenecks of its various versions. I find it somewhat amusing that Eric Schmidt, the CEO of Google, and therefore one of the richest people on the face of the planet, reckons that social networking is little more than the twenty-first century digitization of address books and the content of corporate America's Rolodexes.

Yet, in spite of Mr. Schmidt's statements to this effect, Google itself is already investing boatloads of money in the next big thing. The proof is that they currently own Orkut, one of the largest social networks in Brazil and Asia. Thereby proving that Mr. Schmidt obviously speaks with a forked tongue, or that both he and I, in common with all the other pundits out there, have no idea what the hell we are talking about. But then again, who does in this perpetually changing and paranoid business?

MySpace was the first of the gargantuan social networks and now boasts more than a gazillion million members, all of whom seem determined to create the most ugly, busy, and totally incomprehensible to read home pages. Yet in a strange, but understandable way, all of this will eventually become counter productive. For as Silicon Valley uber-pundit Paul Saffo has stated from the heights of his soapbox, "The value of a social network is defined not only by who's on it, but by who's excluded." This is simply another way of expressing the old truism - familiarity breeds contempt. An observation that might eventually come back to bite Rupert Murdoch in his Ausie arse, in spite of the fact he paid what was considered at the time to be the bargain basement price of a mere six hundred and fifty million dollars for MySpace in 2006. Why do I feel the "Dirty Digger's" backside is in danger? Because, though that paltry sum might have been considered a steal at the height of the exploding Web 2.0 frenzy, by the time the "Wizened of Oz" has finished larding MySpace with lots and lots of up your nose ads and blatant promos for Fox movies and News Corporation's insanely bad TV shows, he may actually have succeeded in driving away a large percentage of the target audience he shelled out all those millions of bucks to capture in the first place. This seems to be an increasingly common scenario in the way many media companies go about acquiring desirable properties these days.

My favorite MySpace quote is from the original founder and CEO, Brad Greenspan, who after the launch, as the Jolt Cola sucking, ganja smoking, stale pizza eating guys were trying to figure out some kind of comprehensive business plan that would hopefully convince the VC sharks residing on Palo Alto's Sand Hill Road to cough up a few million dollars in startup money, team member Chris DeWolfe suggested that perhaps they should start charging a fee for the basic MySpace service. Greenspan quickly poured shit over the whole idea, because as he put it so eloquently, "It was totally not necessary, as many mindless youths and adults will donate money to us anyway" A true summation of the attitudes of current and future generations of MySpace users.

The biggest problem non-fee based social networking sites face is the creation of a realistic, long lasting business model based on the generation of sustainable advertising revenues. MySpace can more than justify its existence as a platform for promoting its parent company's programming, because as part of the News Corp. Empire it is able to relentlessly push Fox movie and TV networks products. Any ancillary advertising then becomes the gravy on the News Corp. meat and potatoes, and if you go to the MySpace home page, you'll find there's no shortage of this kind of advertising. The difficulties facing MySpace competitors - and there are many - is the risk of trying to take on the monster at its own game by creating sites that simply pile feature on feature. This will inevitably lead to failure, as not only is MySpace already bursting at the seams with features, and continually adding new ones, their key advantage is that they rapidly acquired a formidable critical mass of hundreds of millions of users. It's like trying to take on Microsoft in the operating system arena; there is no way a competitor can beat their head bloody on the brick wall of Microsoft's huge installed user base and ever imagine they can catch up. Instead, smart people operating in the social networking space have opted to use MySpace as the "mother of all hosts" in which they can embed their own add-on services. Startups such as Photo Bucket, Image Shack, Rock You, and Slide, are doing well on MySpace by providing Web widgets that allow users to post photos, videos, and slideshows on their individual pages. One of the biggest winners to have associated itself with MySpace is YouTube, but I shall deal with them in detail later in this chapter.

Pretenders to the MySpace throne seem to pop up on a weekly basis, many of which disappear just as quickly, yet some seem to be surviving and building an audience based on having some kind of perceived difference from the competition, whether it be content, features, the uniqueness of the interface, or simply a harder, often "in your face" attitude the members find appealing. A good example of this is the Web site "I'm in Like with You!" Which has been described as a flirting/dating social network. Boasting the usual features, it adds a different twist by allowing users to make friends by bidding points through a series of games, that purport to offer better, more compatible matches than most social networking sites offer via the simple process of signing on to someone's list of friends. Users can also place comments on stories directly into both the text and visual elements. As is usual with most of these sites, the news section seems to consist solely of the latest gossip about showbiz and celebrities. As there is no advertising on the site, and no membership fee, I am at a loss to figure out how they intend to make money. But having said that, in true next-big-thing style, investors have already dumped buckets of cash into the startup.

Perhaps the greatest current challenge to MySpace is relative newbie, Facebook, which in a short period of time has made great strides in the social networking arena. Only three years old at the time of writing, its current valuation, based on the 240 million dollars injected into the company by Microsoft to purchase a mere 1.6 percent stake, is already more than fifteen billion dollars. Which is somewhat amazing for a company whose revenues are probably still only in the tens of millions. Founded by Mark Zuckerberg, as a college student listing service aimed initially at fellow Harvard classmates, it then spread to other Ivy League colleges, such as Yale, Columbia, and Stanford, before bursting out beyond the bounds of academia. It should also be pointed out that at the time of writing, Mr. Zuckerberg is being sued by three fellow Harvard alumni who accuse him of ripping off their original idea for a Web site, "ConnectU." As of now, the matter remains unresolved.

Perhaps the biggest problem facing social networking sites is that their business model is based on the same shifting sands and bottomless bogs so prevalent during the dot com explosion of the late nineties. Everything is always about building vast armies of users, or a customer base, as the MBAs refer to it. Think of the movie *Field of Dreams.* If you build it, they will come. The problem is that they may come, but once you give them the impression they are being taken advantage of, they won't stick around. Sad to say, but for builders of social networks, life isn't like the movies. This was best demonstrated when Facebook introduced a new technology by the name of Beacon in late 2007. This particularly insidious gizmo automatically alerted Facebook users to what books, clothes, music, videos, or virtually anything else their friends were buying or merely browsing in anticipation of possibly buying online. Unfortunately, Facebook didn't ask its millions of member's for their permission to make this information available to other users and legions of potential advertisers. Unsurprisingly, a great many people were pretty pissed about this, actually having the nerve to consider it as a gross invasion of their privacy. Within days, Facebook backed off and stated that Beacon would be an opt-in system only, while issuing assurances that community member's purchasing information and preferences would be completely private from that point on. The problem for Facebook with this is not just the massive amounts of egg the whole debacle places fair and square on their face; it's a further reinforcement of the questions that keep me awake at night: How the hell do these non-subscriptions based social networking sites make money? Exactly what is their business model? Will the Segway replace Hummers? Does a bear shit in the woods? Does the Pope wear little red shoes? All important stuff, right?

As the title of this book suggests, advertising is now ubiquitous. If I am a regular user of a social network that bombards me with obtrusive advertising or that seems to be increasingly inhabited by people I have no desire to meet or communicate with, I will simply move to a network with more exclusivity and less intrusive advertising. After all, there's no shortage of choices out there. That's the beauty of the Internet. Creators of social networking sites should never forget wise old sage Yogi Berra's observation that, "no one goes there any more, it's too crowded!"

On the other hand, social networks that charge users a monthly or annual fee are usually organized on an entirely different business model and give the perception they are more exclusive.

Because they actually sell themselves on a subscription basis, they do not have to rely on advertising revenues to cover their costs and throw a profit. And even though some carry advertising, if they stick to their guns, they can be selective about it, thereby avoiding falling into the trap of carrying the kind of advertising they initially claimed they would avoid. By charging members a small annual or monthly fee, whilst delivering content perceived by members as something they are prepared to pay for, community centric social networking sites actually have a viable and sustainable business model. The success of which will obviously be dependent on membership numbers. There are many of these sites out there, but currently, one of the best examples of a community based social networking site, which not only has it's organizing principles sorted out from a smart business perspective, but also enjoys a huge and extremely loyal community of members, is Suicide Girls. Started in 2001, long before the Digerati had coined the catchphrase Web 2.0 for what they envisioned as the next stage in the development of the World Wide Web, Suicide Girls offered a forum for women who wanted to express a nontraditional view of themselves, their fashions, and their particular lifestyle. Sometimes described as "soft porn," the site is actually much more meaningful than that. As "Missy," who founded the company in 1991 in Portland, Oregon, relates it, the site can best be equated with *Playboy* in the sixties, when people would describe themselves as buying the magazine "for the articles," rather than the massively retouched art. And, thanks to the legendary Hef's editorial policies, there was in fact a great deal of truth to this claim. Suicide Girls online content ranges from images of community members' posing in various degrees of dress or undress, which undoubtedly has an appeal to those trolling the Web in search of titillation. But if that was all Suicide Girls offered, there are far more satisfying sites available to the legions of voyeurs seeking it, and SuicideGirls would not have gone from strength to strength over its seven year history, to the point were at the time of writing, the site is now pulling in more than one million visitors per week. No, the beauty of Suicide Girls is that it offers a far richer experience to those who commit to becoming part of its family than is offered by the vast majority of existing social networking and collaborative sites.

This is why Suicide Girls is also probably one of the better examples of that much abused and misunderstood term, "stickiness." A word those involved in Web 2.0 and new media love to throw around when meeting with investors they are trying to persuade to cough up millions of dollars, in order to be in on the ground floor of the next big thing. Yet, in essence, "sticky" simply means developing a site so unique, experiential, and mind blowing that visitors are not only prepared to dwell on it for hours, they can't stop themselves from having recurring wet dreams about the site, hopefully suffering severe anxiety when deprived of the experience. To appreciate the ultimate demonstration of this twenty-first century aberration, simply think of Dustin Hoffman's character in *Rain Man*, when he couldn't get his daily dose of Judge Wappner. Translate that insatiable need for a daily fix to the average social networking junkie. Then you will understand why the promise of "stickiness" is indeed the Holy Grail of the blogosphere. Even though, unfortunately, far too many of current Web 2.0 sites demonstrate that they have little or no understanding of the concept.

Which is a nice segue into the subject of YouTube, the video sharing site "par excellence," now in a league of its own. Founded in 2005 by three ex-PayPal employees, within eighteen short months, this startup was acquired by Google for what at the time was considered as the outrageously exorbitant sum of 1.65 billion dollars. Admittedly, the buy-in was in Google shares, which are not really hard cash, or even real money, but, looking at the current market valuation of those shares, if the ex-PayPal guys should happen to cash their equity in before the next dot com implosion, I can guarantee you, they won't be signing on for food stamps for the rest of their lives, or their children's, or even their grandchildren's.

OK, enough bullshit. There's no question there are dozens of video sharing sites in existence, and there has been for years However, YouTube is by now far and away the biggest. Why? Because it was one of the first to launch, and it was smart enough to realize users wanted a no-brainer interface that allowed them to quickly upload their "Fellini-esque" video efforts to share with other cine-auteur's, while partaking of their equally ambitious efforts. This leads me to believe, there are an awfully large number of people out there, who like them, seemingly had nothing better to do with their time. Moreover, what made YouTube even more appealing was that there was no software to download and no need to sign legal bullshit disclaimers, you didn't have to register on the site, and there seemed to be no structure or plan to the whole thing - something the dinosaur "mega media monopoly" buyers of these sites unfailingly forget within days of making their multi-billon dollar acquisition. If you think about it, this was the perfect, click the remote and scratch my ass, vehicle for all those unwashed masses lying around on their purple, Naugahyde, covered Barco-Loungers with a case of Bud Light duct taped to their chest while they trolled the Internet for XXX rated freaky videos. Because here was a veritable cornucopia of self-made amateur videos of dogs riding skateboards, weird guys burying themselves on the beach, acne encrusted teenage blimp-freaks miming to Eastern European pop songs, or in the vast majority of cases, simply sitting around doing nothing. In fact, if this kind of thing turns you on, you can still access "WebLog.com," as there seems to be an unlimited number of people out there with nothing else to do but produce vast numbers of very boring videos. However, while the mainstream media firms were trying to capture the video market, YouTube has been consistently getting on with it, and after a mere twelve months in business, by 2006, YouTube was getting a gazillion video downloads a day. However, as they seem to be rather reticent about disclosing their viewership numbers, at the time of writing, I would think it's a great deal more than that. But, what the hell do I know; that's just guesswork on my part. Or, as we say in the ad biz. It's a synergistic supposition.

In the early days, the TV networks and movie studios viewed the screening of film clips and program segments as an infringement of copyright, but as traffic to the site ballooned, they eventually came to regard it as positive exposure for their product. This in turn, has reinforced the positioning of YouTube as a neutral platform. The actual business model for YouTube has changed since its beginnings. Originally the founders stated that it was advertising based, and indeed it still carries advertising. But unlike so many others, it does-n't rely on banners. Pop ups and Flash segments. The prominent video, with screen clip, that's featured in the top right hand corner of YouTube's home page is always an ad promoting an upcoming film or TV show (seemingly, very often, a pay-per—view sports event). There are also a dozen or so featured videos" listed, many of which are com-mercially sponsored and are barely disguised pitches for particular advertiser's products and services.

YouTube, along with many other Web 2.0 and social net-working sites, is gradually changing the media landscape. Advertisers are no longer locked into mainstream media (MSM) with its accom-panying baggage of overly structured and dated demographics, high costs, and suspect ratings. Much of new media is collaborative, mean-ing it no longer merely pushes content to consumers after having arbitrarily decided what they should be grateful to receive. Now, it's all about engaging in a dialogue with the audience, responding to their demands and most importantly, understanding that the con-sumer is no longer locked in to your media channel. If they don't like what's on offer, they will go somewhere else, and even worse, they'll tell everyone else that you're stuff is absolute crap.

One of the single biggest influences new media has had on advertising and the agency business in the last few years has been the surge in what is now known as viral marketing. Although this is bandied about as yet another next big thing, and even though I lay myself out for criticism as an old fart who thinks there is nothing new under the sun, I would describe viral marketing, as simply the digital extension of something that's been around for a very long time: word-of-mouth - a guerrilla marketing tactic covered in chapter five, which is simply based on the hope that the audience you are addressing will pass along your marketing message to others voluntarily and enthu-siastically. However, it's worth bearing in mind that if the people you are hoping to influence should think your message is sheer, unmiti-gated rubbish or a load of old bollocks, they will pour shit all over it, and not hesitate to impart their opinions about it to others. So, never forget, word-of-mouth and other viral marketing techniques can work for you, or against you, if your messaging or product is inferior.

As the computer geeks say, "Garbage in, garbage out."

At the time of writing, it's no secret that increasing numbers of companies are rethinking why they should continue blowing hundreds of millions of dollars of their hard-earned profits on massive and often totally useless brand building TV campaigns. Instead, they are exploring other less expensive, and often more effective ways of getting their message out. Remember the Diet Coke and Mentos video that appeared on YouTube a couple of years ago, and within days it was getting millions of hits? There are now hundreds of spin-offs on YouTube; many, not with Coke, but with Diet Pepsi, or various brands of beer. The value of this publicity for both Coke and Pepsi, even though most of their product ends up foaming away in a geyser-like eruption, is immeasurable. And none of these companies have paid a penny for it. I was recently at a marketing symposium in New York where speakers from various companies talked about their current marketing programs. General Electric went through a twenty-minute presentation in tandem with their global agency, BBDO, showing the elements of their "Innovation" branding campaign. This involved spending three hundred million dollars on extremely beautiful and evocative TV commercials. For example, one showed how if GE had been at Kitty Hawk in 1907 when the Wright Brothers first achieved the miracle of powered flight, GE could have strapped one of their turbo jet engines onto the balsa wood wings of that frail, rudimentary biplane, and then merrily proceeded to circumnavigate the globe. And, thanks to the power of obscene amounts of production money and tons of computer generated graphics, every TV spot in the campaign was a thing of beauty; extremely well executed, but, somewhat expected. As a direct contrast, next up was a presentation by George Wright, the marketing manager of Blendtec, a Utah manufacturer of industrial strength blenders. I'm talking about the ones that sit behind the bar of your local Polynesian restaurant or Tiki bar, so that when you demand a mariner's grog, a pirates punch, or any other lethal cocktail which requires the blending of twelve kinds of rum with vast quantities of fruit, coconuts, and conch shells, this sucker doesn't even blink! The Blendtec guy proceeded to blend an eight foot garden rake, a dozen golf balls, and a BlackBerry some idiot in the audience had offered up. The crowd went nuts, not just because it's always fun to blend a BlackBerry, but because everyone in the place knew that "Will it Blend?" is one of the most successful viral campaigns ever.

Comprising a series of thirty-second to two-minute videos, which *never* run on paid media, relying solely on video hosting sites such as YouTube, the "Will it Blend?" series features company founder Tom Dickinson blending almost any object you can possibly imagine. Not only has the phrase itself become an Internet meme, the campaign has produced significant results for Blendtec, with millions of views, significantly increased sales and new lines of distribution. The videos are shot in-house at Blendtec's factory in Orem, Utah, literally for pennies. The company is now also selling "Will it Blend?" merchandise such as tee shirts and hats from their Web site. And interestingly, the videos are earning an annual payout of about fifteen thousand dollars from the video hosting service, Revver, which splits revenues fifty-fifty with people who upload their content onto their site. This means that not only is Blendtec getting mass exposure and increased sales for their products, they're actually making money off their advertising. Eat your heart out GE!

This is merely a single example of how new media is changing the traditional advertising landscape. Smart advertisers are beginning to realize that as advertising becomes ubiquitous, they have to find new, better, and more cost effective ways of addressing consumers. This is why a new breed of advertising agencies is springing up, while the Big Dumb Agencies are desperately trying to reinvent themselves. I'll talk more about this state of affairs in the final chapter.

chapter EIGHT. *get 'em* WHILE THEY'RE
YOUNG

Why the Adverati are hell bent on persuading children they should eat crap and play with things that might just kill them. The vast majority of advertising aimed at children is for junk food; lead painted plastic toys and electronic gizmos that break before the batteries run out. Teens must have everything "cool" and Madison Avenue will make sure they do.

Make no mistake here; advertising aimed at children has been around for a long time. As I mention in chapter one, Packard talked of how in the early fifties, a major Chicago agency was using psychiatric probing techniques on little girls. (The self same little girls who are now, fifty years later, buying Feng Shuie positioned and decorator furnished retirement lodges in the Adirondacks, in spite of the effects those deep probes may have had on their young psyche.) He goes on to describe how the inimitable Dr. Dichter and his staff of Igor, "shall I pull the switch now, Master?" assistants at the Institute of Motivational Research were engaged in studying such esoteric subjects as the effect of TV cartoons on the toilet habits of children at different times of the day. Strange and scary stuff, but eaten up by the news media of that time, as it delivered even more proof that the Adverati were hell bent on corrupting the minds of clean-living Americans from the cradle to the grave. Perhaps a more rational approach to the subject was taken by Dr. David Riesman in his seminal study of American character, *The Lonely Crowd*, which was published in 1950, seven years before Packard's blockbuster. In it, he describes how modern society is less and less defined by preceding generations, and is even more driven to acquire and consume material goods, obviously, aided and abetted by the advertising industry. He goes on to imply that this process begins at an increasingly early age, or as he puts it: "Today, the future occupation of all moppets is to be skilled consumers." Looking around in this day and age, I would suggest this goal has definitely been achieved.

Even though as far back as 1874, the British Parliament had passed legislation intended to protect children from the efforts of merchants to induce them to buy products and assume debt. It's a fact that before World War II, most advertising for children's products was aimed at their parents. Yet social scientist John B. Watson, of Johns Hopkins University, wrote in 1924 that advertisers should direct their messages directly at children because their minds were a "blank slate" and their characters yet unformed. As he put it, at this stage of their lives, the prejudices they picked up from their parents would not yet be fully developed. A year later, another psychologist working with ad agencies, Alfred Poffenberger, recommended appealing directly to kids when facing "the great difficulty that one meets in breaking habits" among parents. He went on to stress "the importance of introducing innovations by way of the young." I have to confess the thing that strikes me as most insidious about what these characters were suggesting is that it wasn't about selling toys and fast food to kids; it was about instilling in their blank-state minds brand preferences they would hopefully carry throughout their life.

This is something that thirty years later would be described in the McCarthy hysteria of the fifties as brainwashing. However, these extremes were rare, and most advertising to children would probably be best represented by what appeared in such publications as *Parents Magazine,* introduced in 1926, featuring ads for food, clothes, educational materials, and yes, even toys. But unlike today's advertising, the content was written to parents, using grown up language that stressed the beneficial or educational aspects of whatever they were selling. And even though it is still published today, *Parents Magazine* is just one of a great many publications that are aimed at this lucrative and ever growing market.

Perhaps what is most different and certainly more pernicious today is not only the sheer volume of advertising aimed at children, but also the outright manipulative techniques used to persuade them. The latest figures I could find at the time of writing showed that children under twelve spend more than ten billion dollars a year, while teenagers spend close to eighty billion dollars. Even more amazing is the fact that children also influence more than 225 billion dollars spent annually by their parents. This is a startling amount of money when you consider the little buggers are still light years away from their first paycheck. No wonder a whole subcategory of advertising agencies, marketing companies, and research organizations have sprung up aimed at cherry picking the ripening fruit of the children's market, with many sporting such whimsical names as Kid2Kid, Kid Connection, Just Kids, Small Talk, and my all-time favorite, The Gepetto Group. I have to imagine everyone working there sports a twelve-inch wooden nose that grows by the hour every time they convince some snot-nosed five year old to persuade their long suffering parents to spend lots of hard earned dollars on the next piece of worthless plastic shit the little monster has to have to have, right this fucking minute. There are also numerous conferences, studies, and publications such as: *Selling to Kids, Marketing to Kids Report,* and *Youth Market Alert* - all aimed at promoting to eager advertisers with deep pockets, an array of strategies cooked up by child psychologists, which are little more than recommended methodologies for ways to get children to bug the crap out of their parents until they either shell out for whatever junk is being advertised, or, the parents decide they've had enough of this, kill their whingeing kids, and ride off into the sunset to enjoy the money they had previously been blowing on the obnoxious little wankers!

One of the more disturbing aspects of this involvement of child psychologists with ad agencies and marketers is that we are increasingly finding out just how much advertising affects children. Some experts even believe that brand loyalty begins as early as *age two*. Additionally, we now know that successful advertising to children not only begins to cultivate their brand loyalty, it can also affect their entire outlook on life. As Douglas Rushkoff writes in his book *Coercion*, "The fresh neurons of young brains are valuable mental real estate to admen. By seeding their products and images early, the marketers can do more than just develop brand recognition; they can literally cultivate demographic sensibilities as they are formed. A nine-year-old child who can recognize the Budweiser frogs and recite their slogan (Bud-weis-er) is more likely to start drinking beer than one who can remember only Tony the Tiger yelling, 'They're great!" Well, all I can say is that personally, I'd rather eat the croaking frogs than drink anything brewed by Budweiser, as I've made it a rule never to drink anything that claims to be beer when it actually tastes like watered down horse pee.

The one overriding fact to be considered when talking about the business of advertising to kids is that whenever young children are exposed to commercial messages, particularly via television, until they've developed a certain level of sophistication and awareness; they are unable to distinguish between the commercials and the programming. Today, with the massive amounts of cross-promotional activities occurring between game and toy manufacturers, in league with movie production companies and TV content providers; this tenuous line is becoming increasingly blurred. However, efforts to institute some kind of regulation limiting the amounts of advertising directly targeted to children are more often than not, unsurprisingly, doomed to failure. As far back as the midseventies, the then Chairman of the Federal Trade Commission, Michael Pertschuk, tried to introduce restrictions on TV advertising aimed at children under the age of thirteen. His efforts were met with a ferocious lobbying campaign from food, soft drink, toy, and game manufacturers. Needless to say, the regulation was killed. As indeed, have virtually all other attempts since.

Interestingly, the French government has just introduced legislation prohibiting the creation of any TV programming (and its constituent advertising content) aimed specifically at children under the age of three. You have to do a Paris Hilton "Oh My God!" And wonder how any company (French, American, or even Bulgarian) might think they could influence a two and a half year old to jump in the family limo and pop down to Saks to stick a few Ks on their Black Kindergarten-Kard. But then again, why would the French ban the practice if they didn't have evidence it was a problem?

Without a doubt, by far the most amount of money spent year after year on advertising to children has been by the food, candy, and soft drink industries. Yet, in the last few years we've been bombarded with nonstop news stories about the emerging crisis of childhood obesity. We've also heard about the new "healthy" menus available at your local "Fat-Burger" joint. So, is this self-imposed restraint on the part of the food industry working? Well, according to a 2007 research report from the University of Arkansas, a year after major food companies announced new advertising policies to combat childhood obesity and crossed their hearts and swore to die if they didn't shape up, there have been virtually no changes in the television food ads the food companies are continually beaming at children. The research showed that not only were unhealthy foods the most frequently advertised, but the TV spots continue to employ the production techniques and appeals that make it difficult for children to critically evaluate the ads they are watching. What this means is that unlike, supposedly smart adults, young children are more receptive to information presented to them in the form of colorful visuals and sound effects. Before they get to be eight or nine years old, children have difficulty processing information presented to them in the form of on-camera dialogue or voice-overs. This means that smart, or, as I prefer to think of them, devious advertisers, rely on animation, puppets, people in stupid costumes, (think Ronald MacDonald,

Jack In The Box with his ping-pong-ball head, Subservient Chicken, or the Burger King "King") visual effects, sound effects, and musical jingles. These not only appeal to children, they are proven to be effective in their ability to generate an easily understood sales message to the general population. Messaging that invariably promotes the idea that if you indulge in the lard enriched, uber-cholesterol loaded, artery-exploding product, you will be guaranteed lots of fun and happiness to enrich the experience. And if that isn't enough, what about a miniature plastic Darth Vader, complete with a hissing, emphysema-like voice chip, to go along with that super-gooey, ninety-nine cent "Choke Burger?" Never, ever forget that after your local car dealer, promotions are really, really big in the fast food biz. It all comes down to giving parents a guilt free excuse to shut the rapidly ballooning, never satisfied child up for a few more hours until the next episode of The Mighty Morphins is on the telly, or Hannah Montana is in town for a three hundred dollar a seat concert. Better yet if the long suffering parent can be persuaded to convince themselves, thanks to the messaging buried in the advertising, they are buying junior reasonably healthy food, and not driving them into an early grave with clogged arteries and bleeding ulcers. Then, what the hell, give the kid another Busta-Burger, as long as he/she shuts-the-fuck-up!

Even though TV advertising still has the most effect on children, the food and drinks industry is certainly exploiting the ubiquity of kid's entertainment channels by creating Web sites where they can play games, win prizes, or send messages and e-cards to their friends. Supermarket in-store displays and product packaging are designed not only to attract children to the product, but then to hold their loyalty by driving them to interact with the manufacturers Web sites. At the time of writing, the Federal Trade Commission has released a report showing that the food and beverage industry spent close to two billion dollars marketing their products to children in 2006. Twenty percent of that went into integrated programs guaranteed to create repeated product exposure over many varieties of media. This included movies, TV shows, and games via the Internet. Interestingly enough, viral marketing of the kind described above, is more common on sites specifically aimed at children and teens (74 percent) than those aimed at adults (34 percent).

One of the more disturbing aspects of the study, covering children between the ages of two and seventeen, was the amount of money spent on promoting what can only be categorized as junk food. 492 million dollars went on soda - what Steve Jobs once described as sugared, fizzy water when trying to persuade John Sculley to move from Pepsi to become CEO of Apple. 294 million dollars was spent by the fast food giants, and 237 million dollars on cereals, with the lion's share of that aimed at children under the age of twelve. Cereal makers seem to be particularly in kid's faces when it comes to promoting their brand. My favorite was on frootloops.com: "You can find new yummy smelling Rub n' Sniff Froot Loops cereal boxes in stores for a limited time." Apparently, when dealing with five and six year olds, you need to employ lots of that hard nosed marketing jargon.

In common with most marketing to children, great use is made of promotional tie-ins with high-profile movies such as *Spider Man, Pirates of the Caribbean,* and whatever the latest *Batman, Ironman,* or "superhero du jour" happens to be. But, we shouldn't gloss over the fact that the primary purpose of all these various "special edition" packaging iterations for food, drink, and candy products is to encourage kids to go online and enter the ever proliferating, prize eligible competitions. All of which are created to incentivise multiple purchases in order to encourage participants to get lucky, and find the requisite codes hidden inside bottle caps, or candy wrappers. Codes that will hopefully guarantee the young participants the opportunity to win one or more of the super prizes on offer.

Speaking of super prizes, as I write this, Tootsie Roll Tootsie Pops is offering a prize of fifty thousand dollars if you can answer Mr. Owl's forty-year-old question, "How many licks does it take to get to the center of a Tootsie Pop?" As Mr. Owl has been answering this question in TV spots aimed at kids since 1970, it should be a nobrainer, although anyone familiar with the commercial will know this is a trick question. Apart from the fifty thousand dollar grand prize (and what the hell is a five year old going to do with fifty thousand dollars?) there are also monthly drawings with five winners, who will each receive twenty-seven pounds of assorted Tootsie Roll candies! That's about three times the weight of the average five year old's head. Although, after eating twenty-seven pounds of sugar laden candy, most of their teeth will have rotted and fallen out, which should bring the average down a little.

For years, the single most effective way to influence kids in their buying habits was through massive amounts of television buying. Although this is still where a great deal of their marketing money goes, the food and drink industry is now increasingly starting to make big investments in new media, including both computer- and cell-phone-driven campaigns. Not only are these much cheaper to create and run than traditional TV advertising, they also enjoy far less scrutiny from the regulators. Parents who were able to exercise at least a modicum of control over what their kids were watching on TV now have little, or no, knowledge of what their kids are exposed to on the Internet via their computers, or increasingly, on their cell phones.

Another area beyond parents' control is the creeping influence of junk food manufacturers in the schools. We know, and are forced to accept, that the corridors of most schools are lined with vending machines pushing sodas and snack foods, but even more disturbing was the recent disclosure in the national press that in Seminole County, Florida, McDonald's had been sponsoring Happy Meals as rewards for children with good grades and attendance records in elementary schools. This only came to light when a parent, was upset enough to raise questions about the promotion printed on the jacket of her daughter's report card. A jacket which showed Ronald McDonald, the company's golden arches logo, a Happy Meal menu featuring items such as chicken McNuggets, and the advice to the five year old that they should "check your grades, then reward yourself with a Happy Meal from McDonald's." Apparently, the local McDonald's restaurants had replaced Pizza Hut as a sponsor of the incentive program, which Pizza Hut had been running for ten years, as part of a national campaign to encourage children to read. The bottom line for this whole enterprise was that apart from porking up the kids, the school board had saved themselves a few hundred lousy dollars by not having to pay for the printing of the report cards. Mmmm... Go stand in the corner, school board.

For a long time, brands have been presented as an integral and fundamental core component of a young person's life, from infancy to adolescence, from teen years to young adulthood. We continuously hear how clothes, make up, fashion accessories, music, electronics (particularly cell phones and even BlackBerry's and other PDAs) are now "must-have" components of increasingly younger girls' lives. As expected, boys are heavily into electronics, with an emphasis on gaming, yet are now seemingly just as fashion conscious as the girls. All of this activity is not simply aimed at the acquisition of "stuff;" it's also about having the right brands. Because then you'll have the cool stuff that will impress all your friends, even if all your friends have exactly the same cool stuff. However, we should never forget the kids themselves, via whatever social media is currently the flavor of the month, continually propagated this culture of coolness. Yes, the brands and their marketers drive it by seeding YouTube, MySpace, Facebook, and other social sites with content, some of it less obvious, but a lot of it very much in your face. And, as any avid follower of the new media landscape should be well aware, the key word here is, content. Because as kids are increasingly becoming less influenced by straightforward advertising, marketers are continually striving to come up with new ways to influence them. Yet, having said that, there's really nothing new about this form of marketing. When I was a snot nose working at Benton & Bowles, back in the Dark Ages of the nineteen sixties, they created a youth division designed to cut through the cliché ridden, expected advertising that was then the norm. It was supposed to achieve this by coming in under the radar and subliminally influence the purchasing decisions of the rapidly growing and increasingly affluent market of high school and college students. Unfortunately, it was, as is usually par for the course with these Madison Avenue breakthroughs, total bullshit. In order to be effective, the youth division would have necessitated being run and staffed with young, like-minded people, rather than the three martini lunch, thirty something hacks who would, through an alcoholically induced fog, crash out embarrassingly stupid ads to run in high school and college newspapers with absolutely no effect on the target audience.

Throughout their existence, agencies have never really understood the youth market, in spite of the billions of dollars they've persuaded clients to flush down Madison Avenue's rancid tubes in pursuit of this Holy Grail. That's why, you never stop seeing so many vapid "me-too" print ads, full of kids staring blankly into the camera while wearing a baseball cap backwards and sporting baggy pants, which due to some anti-gravity device, allows them to stay up, even when the crotch is below their knees. Having said that, the TV advertising aimed at young people has always been far worse. Remember the Sprite ad with the young African American kid glaring into the camera while proclaiming he doesn't want to be in a beer commercial? Apparently, making a few thousand by being in a Sprite commercial didn't offend his delicate sensibilities. But it did make the teenage viewers it was aimed at guffaw in disbelief. Numerous other examples of this advertising genre seem to announce nothing more than every kid's God-given right to the latest toys, fashions, electronics, and tchotchkes. Unfortunately, the parents of this devil spawn inevitably cough up enough money to bribe them to shut the fuck up, go and buy something and for God's sake, leave me in peace! Relative to that is a 2004 study by the American Psychological Association, which is one of the few dealing not just with the effect on kids caused by the consumption of products that may be inimical to their health and well being, it also discusses the increase in child-parent conflicts that occur when the parents refuse to shell out their hard earned dollars for the stuff kids demand after having been exposed to ad campaigns. One rather sinister aspect of the report is that it points out the increasing number of applied psychologists now working as market researchers or consultants to advertising agencies and their clients in order to enhance the persuasive effect of child-oriented advertising. Seemingly, the descendants of Dr. Dichter are alive and thriving in the new millennium.

Hence the current infatuation with what is called branded content; the latest smoke and mirrors solution to every marketers dreams. But in actuality, it's little more than an extension of product placement, something that has been going on for years in both tele-vision and the movies. This is why you always see Sarah Jessica Parker and Tom Cruise working out their various plots and schemes in either Sex and the City, or Mission Impossible, on a Mac laptop. It's also why James Bond wouldn't be caught dead driving anything less than an Aston Martin, and how TV panel hosts always seem to drink out of soda glasses with a Coke logo on them, while morning news show hosts often drink their coffee from a mug emblazoned with a Starbucks logo. What supposedly makes branded content different now from the old, in-your-face days of Desi and Lucy relaxing while puffing on their favorite brand of cigarette is that there is no longer any pretence these fictitious people use these products in their real lives. Everything has become theatre, because life has become theatre. Now Internet available, mini-movie, vignette's featuring fast cars driven by pseudo-secret agents (Guy Ritchie's wonderful series for BMW), or Rube Goldbergesque, white-coated scientists, blending garden rakes, bricks, and ball bearings in a Utah laboratory ("Will it Blend?" for Blendtec blenders) have little relationship to traditional advertising. Yet, in their own way, they seem to be having far more impact on their chosen audiences than the mega-million dollar extravaganzas we are relentlessly exposed to during the Super Bowl or on Oscar night. So, you have to ask yourself why these ultra-expen-sive, yet increasingly ineffective TV epics continue to be made. Is it because of the persuasive powers of advertising agency account exec-utives whispering in the ears of marketing directors over expensive lunches at the Four Seasons, or the malleability of clients when being treated to eighteen holes at Pebble Beach? To be honest with you, I don't know the answer. On the one hand, I continually read in the advertising and marketing trade press that clients are switching their marketing dollars from traditional media efforts into digital and other forms of new media, yet am still waiting for the first time a network TV show runs without commercial breaks because no one bought the time slots.

However, things are looking up. Some agencies are coming at this problem from a refreshingly new direction. A good example of this is collaboration between the Droga5 ad agency in New York, the Production Company, Smuggler, and the French-based conglomerate Publicis Groupe, to create something bearing the unfortunate name of "Honeyshed." A Web site that performs as a dedicated channel aimed at teens and young adults by making online shopping an entertaining and social experience. It does this by promoting brands, not through the expected, and increasingly ineffectual use of banner ads and pop-ups, but via a theatrical presentation of on-camera sketches, acted out by youthful presenters in the style of the never ending, increasingly boring, and well past its shelf life Saturday Night Live TV show. The sketches feature and promote products and services aimed at the youth market. They are paid for by the brands presented and talked about in each episode. Visitors digitally window-shop for these products on various sub channels, which cover a range of interests from girl fashion and tech and toys, to denim and sneakers. Visitors can place their selections on an "Amazon-esque" wish list of online purchases, which Honeyshed has dignified with the too-cute label "my stash." At the time of writing, Honeyshed is about to make the leap from beta (where it's been for almost a year) to the mainstream. The success of Honeyshed's business model will depend on how well it walks the tightrope requiring the balancing of enough selling communication to make the sponsors happy, with enough entertainment content to keep the increasingly suspicious, youthful visitors prowling the Internet from being turned off. Why don't we come back in a year to judge the ongoing results? But for now, kudos to Droga5 for a bold and interesting experiment.

Unfortunately, the reverse side of this coin is the many agencies now claiming to have tapped into the exploding children/youth market; all stating their core competency is now about "connecting brands with youth." This is nothing more than the rearranging of the deckchairs on the Titanic tactic all agencies engage in when the previous milch cow, such as hard liquor or big tobacco accounts begin to dry up.

Perhaps what we should be most aware of when it comes to advertising and marketing to kids, tweens, youth, and young adults is that even though as Marshall McLuhan once said, "The medium is the message," and the choice of media available to young people is constantly proliferating, the quality of the content delivered by these media will always be the essential ingredient necessary to influence them. Advertisers and their agencies continually fall into the trap of using technology for its own sake simply because it's cool, yet they rarely have anything of relevance to say via this cool technology. Then, when they do have something worthwhile to say, they often choose to say it in a tone of voice, or character, which is at odds with the content. More often than not, this is because it's being created and produced by people who are at least a generation removed from the target audience.

With the increasing use of handheld devices for voice and text messaging, music, video, GPS, and even shopping by the young, the desktop will eventually be relegated to a backup and storage box. In the U.S., the iPhone is just the beginning of what will eventually become the ubiquitous all-in-one device. In Japan, where 3G networks have been in place for years, all-in-one phones are consistently used by young people as an indispensable tool to facilitate their everyday lives. While the vast majority of Japanese teens have a Smartphone, in the U.S. that number is currently just under 20 percent. Without a doubt, this will rapidly change.

What we fail to appreciate fully is that a whole generation is growing up with the expectation of "ubiquitous connectivity." With platform agnosticism and total mobility, advertisers will be able to target young people via geographic, socioeconomic, ethnic, and environmental data with pinpoint precision. If the target audience has opted-in by giving marketers permission to advertise to them, they can be reached on their favorite social network, whether it be MySpace, Facebook, or whatever the next cool one is. And they can be reached via their Mac, PC, mobile, or God forbid, "Crackberry." Even though older generations would probably have been pissed off to be the subject of this nonstop attention, today's young people consider this to be the normal and expected way they go about their lives.

Perhaps the single biggest unanswered question that clients and their agencies choose to ignore is what effect years and years of advertising to the young has had on their receptiveness and reaction to even more advertising as they grow older and eventually become adult consumers. We shouldn't be surprised that teens and young adults are cautious, skeptical consumers inclined to disbelieve things that they do not hear from friends or peer groups. These kids have been bombarded with advertising since before they could walk. As I've mentioned earlier, the various tactics now being employed to pierce the shell of indifference, if not downright cynicism, displayed by today's youth may work initially, but as soon as they are recognized as yet another dumbass marketing tactic, their effectiveness quickly fades. Traditional advertising aimed at an older market has always worked on the principle that the advertiser's brand represents a unique selling proposition or attribute they would like the target audience to believe and accept as unique to their brand. Think "Volvo safety" or "Wal-Mart value." Once the older consumer does accept this message, providing the brand lives up to its promise, they are inclined to stay with it for a long time. This is not true of the young, whose thinking is much more ephemeral and influenced by peer groups rather than commercial communications. Not only are they turned off by blatant selling, they are much more cynical of product quality, longevity, service, and value. Their attention is focused on such attributes as functionality, style, and coolness. All of which can change more rapidly than companies have ever been used to when addressing product design, manufacturing, and marketing cycles.

Therefore, advertising to the young has become a never-ending, constant battle that yields ever diminishing returns as Madison Avenue jumps on the next big thing, whether it be social networking, patently obvious product placement, or uber-expensive celebrity endorsements.

In this contest, my money's on the kids.

chapter NINE. *is the*

PURPLE
PILL
MAKING YOU SEE RED?

Having persuaded us to smoke, drink, and eat our brains out for years, the Adverati have now discovered medicine, and are committed to having us all lead a healthier life. As long as Big Pharma, hospitals, and insurance companies are ready to foot the bill!

When *The Hidden Persuaders* was published, the three biggest cash cow accounts for Madison Avenue agencies were cars, cigarettes, and booze. Now, fifty years on, the auto accounts are still around and continue to be major spenders, although, the vast majority of them are no longer American. Even so, auto accounts never stepped away from being a giant pain in the ass to work on, particularly when the agencies are forced to deal with the Neanderthal-like mindset of the regional and statewide dealer networks. You know who I'm talking about, all those wonderful folks in the polyester suits who've never seen a Columbus-Thanksgiving-President's-Ground-Hog-Day sale they couldn't get behind with all the persuasive power of inedible free hot dogs, warm soda, and donkey rides for the kids.

On the other hand, almost all promotional activities associated with the demon nicotine weed have long since disappeared, even after its massive sponsorship of the good ole boys favorite pastimes, NASCAR and rodeo. OK, you still see cigarettes featured in TV advertising, but only as part of the pathetic and totally ineffective anti-smoking efforts "Big Tobacco" is obliged to pay for as part settlement of various law suits while, at the same time, large amounts of tax payer dollars continue to be expended in the form of massive subsidies for the K Street represented tobacco growers.

Meantime, alcohol, with the exception of beer, departed the mainstream media landscape many years ago, but is now starting to make a comeback; even on television, from which hard liquor had been banned since the fifties. Now, with the advent of flavored vodkas, patria tequilas, artisan grappas, and Dolce & Gabana designer anti-freeze, big time, ten dollars a shot booze is back with a vengeance. Although, it must be said that wine advertising never really went away because you could always find sophisticated, understated ads for Bacchus's favorite tipple in high-end magazines like *The New Yorker* and *Wine Aficionado*, as well as major metropolitan newspapers. Now, as we move into the early part of the twenty-first century, with many of Napa Valley's finest vineyards being snapped up for obscene amounts of money by Silicon Valley's nouveau riche at an alarming rate, we can look forward to digital wine tastings and Second Life cocktail lounge experiences in the company of the large breasted avatar of your dreams. Personally, I'd rather sit down in front of the "telly" with a couple of bottles of cheap plonk and a giant bag of deep-fried pork rinds. Although, if you promised to throw in a well endowed real, rather than virtual, female companion as a bonus, you'd certainly get my attention.

Then in 1998, everything changed. The FDA decided to allow drug companies to indulge in something called direct-to-consumer (DTC) pharmaceutical advertising, a practice that today is only allowed in two countries, the U.S. and New Zealand. And at the time of writing, New Zealand is seriously considering banning it, having come to the conclusion that it's little more than an obvious license to print money on the part of the drug companies and their bought and paid for mouthpieces in Parliament, or in the case of the U.S., the Congress and Senate.

For the last ten years, DTC advertising has been a cornucopia of unregulated, largesse for advertising agencies and the media. Which is not surprising when you consider that, in spite of the protestations by pharmaceutical companies that the reason their drugs are so expensive is because they have to invest so much money in their research and development programs, a recent study in *Medical News Today* points out that U.S. drug companies spent 57.5 billion dollars on advertising and promotional activities in 2004, the last year for which figures are available. By comparison, those same pharmaceutical companies spent a grand total of 31.5 billion dollars on research and development in that same year. In addition to the money spent on advertising and marketing, the pharmaceutical industry spends many millions of dollars lobbying Congress for more favorable legislation. In 2007 alone, they spent more than twenty-two million dollars lobbying the federal government, which was a 25 percent boost from the year before, but it did pay off on several key issues. Proposals aimed at lowering drug prices and restricting industry advertising fell by the wayside in Congress. The Pharmaceutical Research and Manufacturers of America, whose members include Pfizer, Amgen Inc., and Eli Lilly& Co. spent about twelve million dollars in the second half of 2007 to lobby on how prices are set for seniors' medications, and the toughening of rules governing drug imports and other issues. But lobbying experts say the road ahead for the industry is beginning to look increasingly bumpy, particularly if they face a Democratic president and Congress in 2009.

And yet, wouldn't it be less hypocritical on their part if they simply owned up to the fact that the purpose of spending these vast amounts is to get consumers to bug the crap out of their doctors in an effort to convince them to prescribe drugs they probably didn't need in the first place.

But who can deny this pressure works. I mean, come on, you know deep down inside that you really need Viagra if you are approaching senility, yet want to continue banging your brains out like an eighteen year old. Even better, you might be ambitious enough to be convinced you need Cialis after watching the TV ads warning you about seeing your doctor if, after taking the miracle pill you are blessed with a forty-eight-hour erection and a giant woodie that just won't go away! And what about that chronic "restless leg syndrome" you never realized you were suffering from? Or the "acid reflux problem," which might just be keeping you from rising to the top of the corporate ladder! As for sorting out the difference between good cholesterol and bad cholesterol, talk to your doctor, because he/she just got back from a week-long seminar in the Caribbean on that very subject. And please ignore the fact that the seminar was paid for by Pfizer, makers of Lipitor, one of the largest selling "Statin" drugs on the market, the ones that claim to dramatically reduce cholesterol levels in blood. Something obviously far better achieved (and way less expensively) by moderate exercise and a healthy diet. But, that wouldn't do Pfizer, its ad agency, the media, and your doctor who deserves the odd working/golfing holiday every couple of months much good, would it?

Yet, it's not as if all this healthcare advertising activity is new, it's actually been around for a long time. Hospitals, clinics, insurance companies, doctors, and the lunatic fringe of chiropractors, acupuncturists, crystal healers, aroma therapists, and feng shui practitioners have been advertising since the Aztecs promised better living through heart surgery. But, until the FDA opened the DTC floodgates, most of it was concentrated in business, trade, and professional media aimed at the health care industry. Local media was occasionally used to target messages at consumers who might actually be in the market for the particular services local hospitals, clinics, and other medical specialists were pedaling that week. The pharmaceutical company's promotion of prescription drugs was aimed specifically at doctors and would never appear in the mainstream media. Instead, they were concentrated in the medical literature, massive amounts of expensive direct mail programs, and armies of medical reps who would do the rounds of doctor's offices handing out free drug samples, and lots of office supplies, golf tees, golf balls, golf clubs, golf bags, subscriptions to golf magazines, and yes, invitations to medical seminars that for some reason or other, always seemed to take place at a Caribbean resort with multiple golf courses. This is why I came to the conclusion many years ago that the only people more enamored with golf than the medical profession are politicians and the hundreds of healthcare lobbyists tasked with the job of sucking up to them.

Until the floodgates opened in 1998, virtually all medical advertising and promotional activities were handled by specialist ad agencies. A perfect example of these would be Sudler & Hennessey, founded in 1941, bought by Young & Rubicam in 1973 and ultimately swallowed up by the WPP conglomerate when it acquired Y&R in 2000. In common with all these specialist agencies, the only advertising S&H produced aimed at consumers was for over-the-counter (OTC) drugs, such as cough and cold medications or headache and upset stomach cures. Because, prior to the FDA's landmark 1998 decision, anything requiring a prescription could not be advertised directly to the general public. Today, even though there are still many hundreds of these specialist agencies in existence (S&H alone has sixty-three offices worldwide) and they do hundreds of millions of dollars worth of advertising, marketing, and PR aimed at the many people, companies, and organizations within the health care industry, since the DTC ruling, the hundreds of billions of dollars spent on creating consumer demand for prescription drugs is now primarily spent through mainstream consumer agencies, most of which, unlike the specialist healthcare shops, have no one with any medical training, background, or expertise on staff. In fact, most of the people tasked with working on the newly acquired drug account, probably worked on beer, booze, or burgers the week before.

What has to be realized is that healthcare advertising has in less than ten years developed into a massive, self perpetuating, juggernaut involving ad agencies, the media, drug companies, hospitals, medical journals, and yes, even the MDs and other professionals working within the medical industry. Overlay this with the pernicious practices of the health insurance industry, and you begin to realize why the United States spends far more on healthcare, for far inferior results, than any other Western nation.

The evening newscasts of all the major networks, not only carry more healthcare advertising than any other kind, but a substantial amount of their broadcast content is devoted to healthcare matters. I recently watched an NBC Nightly News program that carried a segment pointing out that women could no longer rely on mammograms as a preventative screening for breast cancer. NBC's medical correspondent pointed out that doctors were recommending women should now have an MRI scan every twelve months. The correspondent failed to mention that most medical insurance does not cover MRI scans, which can be prohibitively expensive, and you can easily run up a bill for thousands of dollars. She also rather conveniently failed to mention that the largest manufacturer of MRI equipment in the U.S. is General Electric, who just happens to be the parent company of NBC.

Most of the pharmaceutical advertising the public has been subjected to since the DTC explosion has been television focused. This is because the majority of it is aimed at an older demographic. The popular perception among the Adverati being that people of my advanced age are pill freaks, although I hasten to add that in my case, I prefer to get my medication out of a bottle, which hopefully ends up in a martini glass with an olive in it. But media geeks will tell you that older people are bigger watchers of network TV, and so can be more easily targeted by commercials which show old geezers suffering from esoteric infirmities they never realized they had in the first place. These ailments can be everything from high cholesterol to restless leg syndrome to dry rot in their wooden leg. But then, after talking to their doctor – their medical advisor suggests they should take the purple/yellow/blue pill, and presto, before the sixty second span of the commercial is over, they are bronzed, fit, muscular, and climbing the Salathe Route on Yosemite's El Capitan in the company of their equally bronzed and fit significant other. And, best of all, because they took the purple/yellow/blue pill, they'll more than likely drink champagne and get laid on the summit! God bless America's drug companies!

Of course, one of the things you soon realize after you've watched a great many of these TV spots is that they fall into two distinct categories. The first kind tells you absolutely nothing about what the medication might be for. The second tells you far too much. Perhaps the best example of the former was the massive advertising campaign launched by AstraZeneca for Nexium. This is supposedly the panacea for acid reflux disease - or as it used to be known pre-DTC, heartburn. Something bicarbonate of soda, or a couple of Alka Seltzer would normally cure. Although, watching any of the numerous TV spots for the drug would not have made you aware of exactly what is was for, let alone what it was supposed to do for you. Instead, disgustingly healthy people of an advanced age perched on mountain tops, or whitewater rafting through raging torrents of water, would suggest that you talk to your doctor about the "purple pill." Amazingly, tens of thousands of people did. The doctors, in a desperate attempt to get these people out of their offices, gladly wrote up prescriptions for the purple pill, which they were fully up-to-speed on, having learned all about it during a five day AstraZeneca hosted conference at a hotel in Barbados surrounded by, you guessed it, golf courses.

The reason for these very ambiguous commercials that tell you nothing about the product, or even what it is intended to cure, is that although the FDA bequeathed a veritable cornucopia of riches on the drug companies by its actions in 1998, it did at least have the decency to recognize that once an advertized drug made claims about its efficacy, it also had to list its possible side effects and dangers. This is why print ads, direct mail pieces, and Web sites will often contain reams and reams of information the drug company would rather you didn't know about, but legally, are forced to explain. In the case of the purple pill, these are listed on their Web site as "Side effects with Nexium include headache, diarrhea, and abdominal pain. Symptom relief does not rule out other serious stomach conditions." Mmmm, that's funny, I thought Nexium was supposed to cure abdominal pain.

Another example of this approach was when Schering-Plough launched their allergy medication, Claritin, with a huge TV campaign. As it has always seemed to me that the entire population of the United States suffers from multiple allergies, many of which probably only exist in the sufferers head, this product turned out to be a gold mine for Schering-Plough, and the result was a nonstop stream of patients barging into their doctor's offices demanding drugs they knew absolutely nothing about, and which they very probably didn't need. Initially, many doctors regarded the Claritin campaign with suspicion, seeing it as a demonstration of the effectiveness of advertising programs that drive patients to demand medication for ailments they do not have. Since then, however, numerous medical conferences in exotic locations, coupled with lots of opportunities for golf, have calmed their fears while soothing their ethical dilemma.

The second form of marketing and advertising employed by the drug companies is one in which they are allowed to make beneficial claims for a drug, but they are also obliged to tell you absolutely everything about the product, both pro and con, and do it in excruciating detail. This means the TV commercials seem to last forever, with the bulk of the time being taken up by disclaimers about possible harmful, sometimes even lethal, side effects, which can run the gamut from extreme cramps and diarrhea, acne and boils, baldness and infertility, to blindness and brain tumors. But hey, if a well crafted and expensively produced spot for the new miracle "pink placebo" can convince you it will cure that "itchy elbow syndrome," which you didn't know you had until you saw it on TV five minutes ago, then it's worth bugging the crap out of your doctor for a prescription. That way you'll be cured of something you very probably didn't have, and your doctor gets to enjoy lots of "you know what," in Bali. Isn't capitalism great?

Having said that, to be fair, and yes, I occasionally do make the effort, I should point out that a recent study by a couple of Denver's leading hospitals found most physicians tended to view DTC advertisements negatively, saying such ads rarely provide enough information on cost (98 percent), alternative treatment options (95 percent), or adverse effects (55 percent). Most also believed that DTC advertisements affected interactions with patients by lengthening clinical encounters (56 percent), leading to patient requests for specific medications (81 percent), and changing the patient's expectations of a physician's prescribing practices (67 percent). Only 29 percent of patients thought that DTC advertising is a positive trend in healthcare and just 28 percent thought ads make them better informed about medical problems. Certainly, you would expect the drug companies to play down costs, alternative treatments, and possible side effects, but what is interesting is that the drug companies are actually making doctor's lives harder because their patients are taking up more of their time, not only demanding prescriptions for specific drugs, but also changing their expectations of what they want the doctor to do for them.

Perhaps one of the most disturbing aspects concerning the FDA's decision to allow DTC advertising is that after making it possible, it then chose to play very little part in its control or supervision. An AARP study three years after drug ads started to appear in the press and on broadcast media, found the following: "The FDA does not have authority to 'pre-approve' proposed advertisements unless requested to do so by a drug company. If the FDA finds a violation or violations in a particular ad, the agency usually issues a warning to the sponsoring company, which typically withdraws the ad; the company may later issue a modified version. The FDA does not impose penalties or other sanctions against manufacturers who broadcast or publish false or misleading information." When you compare this to the controls associated with food and cosmetics advertising, I find this to be extraordinary. It means that drug companies can say almost anything they want. If they get called on any of their claims, they simply pull the ad, suffer no financial consequences, and get the chance to come back at a later time with another variation on the same sales pitch.

At the time of writing, this has been perfectly demonstrated by the campaign Pfizer has been running to promote its cholesterol reducing drug, Lipitor. The TV commercials feature Dr. Robert Jarvik, the inventor of the artificial heart, who is shown running trails, sculling across a mountain lake, and generally looking like a perfect physical specimen while saying "I'm glad I take Lipitor." The problem is that he didn't start taking Lipitor until after he'd signed a big-bucks contract with Pfizer to promote the stuff. It also turns out that he isn't even licensed to practice medicine and it wasn't him in the boat, but a suitably athletic looking double. Even worse, ex-colleagues are disputing his claim that he invented the artificial heart, saying he merely refined other scientist's inventions. The Congressional House Energy and Commerce Committee decided this was all a bit misleading and asked the FDA to look into it. In early 2008, Pfizer saw the writing on the wall and decided to pull the ads, while issuing the following press release: "The way in which we presented Dr. Jarvik in these ads has, unfortunately, led to misimpressions and distractions from our primary goal of encouraging patient and physician dialogue on the leading cause of death in the world - cardiovascular disease. We regret this. Going forward, we commit to ensuring there is greater clarity in our advertising regarding the presentation of spokespeople in the statement." No punitive measures or fines were levied on the company, and you can be sure, that after having spent more than 258 million dollars advertising Lipitor in the last year alone to generate sales of nearly thirteen billion dollars. In the words of *The Terminator*, "They'll be back!"

In late 2002 only five of the FDA's, DDMAC (Division of Drug Marketing, Advertising and Communications) staff were dedicated to reviewing DTC ads. All the TV ads were reviewed. Many of the thousands of print ads were not. Legislation passed in late 2007 includes provisions for hiring another twenty-five DDMAC staff. At the time of writing, it was impossible to find out how many of these had actually been hired. This same legislation had originally included tough restrictions on DTC advertising. But it never made it to the final bill because of intense lobbying by advertising agencies, media, particularly broadcasters, and obviously, the drug companies. The toughest restrictions in early drafts of the bill gave the FDA authority to block pharmaceutical companies from advertising a product that carried serious safety concerns, but these were omitted from the final version. Instead, the FDA will get new powers requiring drug makers to submit TV ads for review before they run, but it can only recommend changes, not require them. The bill also proposes that the agency should levy fines for false and misleading ads. These will amount to two hundred and fifty thousand dollars for the first violation in any three-year period, and won't go above five hundred thousand dollars for any subsequent violation in a three-year period.

Now consider that in today's increasingly digital era, no one, whether it is the FDA or the DDMAC, is carrying out any kind of oversight on the tens of thousands of Web sites, newsletters and blogs that are disseminating pharmaceutical information and promoting specific drugs. And with the growth of Web 2.0 sites, it is now possible for drug companies to actually alter the content of some blogs and Web sites that are not even their own. In late 2007, it was revealed that employees of Abbott Laboratories had been altering entries on Wikipedia, the online encyclopedia, eliminating information that questioned the safety of its top selling drugs. Apparently, a computer at Abbott's Chicago office was used to delete a reference to a Mayo Clinic study revealing that patients taking the arthritis drug Humira faced triple the risk of developing certain kinds of cancers and twice the risk of developing serious infections. The study was published in the *Journal of the American Medical Association* in 2006. Then, the same computer was used to remove articles describing a public interest group's attempt to have Abbott's weight-loss drug Meridia banned after the drug was found to increase the risk of heart attack and stroke in some patients. WikiScanner, an independent site that allows users to look up anonymous changes to Wikipedia articles, showed that the changes were part of over one thousand edits made from computers at Abbott's offices.

The continuing increase in negative publicity may eventually have some effect on DTC advertising, but you can be sure that the immense strength and financial clout, of the pharmaceutical lobby in Washington will be brought to bear on Congress to put this day off for as long as possible, even with continuing negative news reports such as a recent one showing Merck & Co. and Schering-Plough, kept secret for more than a year, findings that their cholesterol drug, Vytorin, did not deliver the results promised in its advertising. Yet over the course of that same year, they spent more than one hundred million dollars advertising it to consumers. This PR disaster followed on the heels of a *New York Times* story spelling out that Pfizer's two billion dollar drug Lyrica was being consistently advertised as treating a condition, fibromyalgia, that a great many doctors don't even think exists.

Perhaps the current state of pharmaceutical advertising is best summed up by Dr. Sidney Wolfe, director of the Health Research Group for Washington-based advocate Public Citizen, when he said that he isn't surprised the ads continue to run. "There's a twenty billion dollar market for cholesterol-lowering drugs, and companies will do whatever it takes to get as much of that market as they can, even if it means letting people continue to take prescription drugs that they know are not beneficial and that even may be harmful," he said. "What's much more likely is that the companies put their stockholders above their responsibility to public health." Amen to that!

Another result of this unfavorable publicity is that Congress is at the time of writing considering legislation that may direct the FDA to scrutinize advertising for Over the Counter (OTC) drugs. This is a multibillion dollar business for both the media and ad agencies that has received very little oversight in the past. While the FDA can supposedly quash unapproved ad claims for DTC drugs, the ads for OTC drugs and remedies have typically been reviewed by the Federal Trade Commission, which handles this advertising in the same way it would for lawnmowers, home electronics, and footwear. It also doesn't engage in prescreening advertising content and only investigates complaints after the offending advertising has run. With possible new legislation, FDA supervision could force marketers to get prior approval before running ads and subject companies and their agencies to fines, not only if the ads are untruthful, but also if any potential side effects aren't displayed prominently enough.

If the 1998 enactment of legislation allowing DTC advertising opened the floodgates for pharmaceutical companies and proved to be a bonanza for the media and ad agencies, never forget, this was in addition to the enormous volume of healthcare advertising Americans have always been subjected to. Ever since the days of *The Hidden Persuaders,* hospitals have spent significant amounts of money on advertising and promotion. This is something uniquely American, in as much as the expenditure of millions of dollars in consumer media to promote the advantages of one hospital's lobotomy procedures over another's, is not only unheard of in any other civilized society, it would probably get you barred from ever practicing medicine ever again!

However, in America, this does not seem to be a problem. Here, hospitals come in two varieties, not for profit and for profit. Many of the not-for-profit hospitals originated in association with a religious order or denomination. Which is why so many of them still have a saint, or some other spiritual association as part of their name, although, it has to be admitted that today the connections with their saintly founders are tenuous at best. Along with large city public hospitals and those affiliated with medical schools, not-for-profit establishments comprise by far the majority of hospitals delivering a full range of health services in the U.S. Then the late sixties saw the creation of the first for-profit hospital groups, Columbia/HCA, and NME, which later became Tenet. These are investor owned groups whose admitted purpose is to generate profits for shareholders. Unfortunately, in many instances, these profits occur at the expense of their patients. Not just in terms of dollars, but even at the cost of their patient's health and life. Columbia/HCA has paid the U.S. government billions in settlements for fraud, the payments of kickbacks to physicians, and the overbilling of Medicare. Tenet paid more than half a billion dollars to settle charges of giving kickbacks for referrals and inappropriately detaining psychiatric patients to fill beds during the 1980s, when the firm was known as NME. In 2004, Tenet agreed to pay the government 22.5 million dollars to settle one of several cases; other allegations include performing cardiac procedures on healthy patients and exploiting Medicare loopholes to claim hundreds of millions in unjustified payments.

Perhaps the most notorious example of the way these for-profit organizations have conducted their business was Birmingham, Alabama based HealthSouth. Founded in 1984 by Richard M. Scrushy, this organization enjoyed explosive growth and after going public in 1988, Scrushy became the darling of Wall Street's investment banker and analyst community, while engaging in an aggressive expansion program. Unfortunately, all was not well in the accounting practices of HealthSouth and when Scrushy sold seventy-five million dollars in personal stock a couple of days before it tanked big time, the SEC stepped in and began an investigation. In 2003, he was charged with falsely inflating earnings by 1.4 billion dollars. No doubt he considered this largesse necessary, not only to pay for the company's fleet of eleven corporate jets, but also to cover the extensive and very expensive ad programs he'd committed HealthSouth to over the years.

After a well-publicized trial during which Scrushy apparently discovered religion, showing up in court every day hefting a portmanteau-sized bible and quoting scripture at every conceivable opportunity, he was acquitted by a carefully selected jury of religious zealots. But, the Feds eventually nailed him on bribery charges in 2007, and he's now serving an eighty-two-month sentence in a federal prison. Hallelujah!

Critics claim that for-profit hospitals specialize in such highly lucrative fields as medical rehabilitation, elective/plastic surgery, (meaning small noses, big boobs and a face that reminds you of a late eighteenth century alabaster death mask) and platinum credit card priced cardiology. All of which, fortunately for the investors, avoids providing those messy loss-making services such as emergency medicine, which would mean being forced to deal with the indigent. Always remember, "Indigent" is American code for people who either have zero health insurance, or are stony broke and currently living on the street. Either way, these are not the people who are going to enable the Scrushy's of this world to live like Eastern potentates, even if the hospital, puts a lien on their wages, takes their house away, shoots their dog and sells their children into slavery. And, believe me; if they think that's the only way they're going to get paid for their services, they will cheerfully undertake all of the above.

However, virtually all hospitals, including the not-for-profit institutions, engage in continuous marketing and advertising programs. In a recent study of 122 hospital ads from seventeen leading institutions aimed at attracting patients, 62 percent employed emotional appeal and 61 percent highlighted the institution's prestige. More than half mentioned a specific service or symptom and a third of them focused on technology, cultivating false hopes based on the perception that high-tech medicine is better. One advertisement for somnoplasty stated, "25 percent of all adults are habitual snorers. Fortunately, we have a solution." Well, as it happens, somnoplasty is "a procedure that has been shown to have no objective improvement and can in fact mask other problems like sleep apnea," one of the doctors conducting the study said. But when an influential medical center promotes somnoplasty, or a full-body CT scan, or a Venusian mind-meld procedure without a clear benefit, even though you will probably spend the rest of your life paying for it, "it kind of legitimizes it in the mind of the consumer," the same doctor said. One of my favorites was the ad from the University of Washington Medical Center. In 128-point type, "We Do Botox!" was the headline, which is kind of like "We Do Oil Changes." The ad continues, "You've probably heard that Botox injections can reduce wrinkles," and then goes on to say that the process is FDA-approved and available at the medical center. No mention that this simple procedure is probably going to cost you a fortune, won't be covered by any kind of medical insurance program, and in six months, when you look in the mirror and realize you're starting to look like a prune again, you'll have to come back, cough up a load of dough and do it all over! Yeah, and don't even think about trying to get it done for free in the emergency room.

Yet, at the end of the day, most hospital advertising is mind-numbingly similar, with each campaign pounding away at the same themes using virtually the same language. Which is invariably high-touch and feely-feely, often expressed in words like caring, close, sympathy, you, and, without question, experience is a particular favorite, as if the fact that they've been ripping off the local community for years should be considered as something they should boast about. They also love to hammer away about how they have enough high-tech and state-of-the-art technology to make Dr. Frankenstein swoon and stop beating Igor over the head. The ads often feature glistening chrome and white laboratory-like treatment rooms complete with giant scanning machines that have patients being fed into them on what looks like some kind of conveyor belt. The hospitals are so inordinately proud of all this stuff they can't resist telling you how many millions they've invested in it. Which, it seems to me, would raise a question in the readers mind as to whom the hell ends up paying for it all.

By emphasizing experience and the breadth of skills, hospitals put the spotlight on their well-trained staffs, their doctors, their nurses, and their investments in things like emergency Life-Flight helicopters, which if you should ever be unfortunate enough to need one will end up costing you several thousand dollars and necessitate you liquidating everything you and your children own. Not that they ever mention this in their advertising. Hospital branding campaigns invariably use taglines with such gems as: "Experience Better Care," "Exceptional Medicine. Extraordinary Care," "St. Blahs... Because we care!" And, if they've been around long enough, "Celebrating one hundred years of caring." Advertising for specific services or specialties are more focused, zeroing in on cancer treatments, heart surgery, orthopedic services, renal and respiratory expertise, services for the aged, and many others. But the mother of all services for a hospital which truly wants to make big bucks is providing for mothers. This can mean the provision of services that cover everything from maternity to infant care. I have been unfortunate enough in my long and checkered career to have worked on a couple of hospital accounts. This has entailed sitting in on numerous client meetings where the main topic has been how quickly the hospital can get the expectant mother admitted, have her drop her little bundle and then be speedily shipped out to make room for the next occupant of the birthing suite? Which in many hospitals are now themed and decorated in all kinds of exotic styles. The mother-to-be can have little "Cody" in the "Wild West Saloon." Or, her reincarnation of Edith Piaf in the "Bridget Bardot, St Tropez Suite." That's providing she doesn't hang around for more than the thirty six hours she or her insurance company have paid for up front. Most of the ads for these specialized services usually feature a doctor or nurse with a happy, smiling patient in an "after-birth" mode when the ordeal is over and all is well. It might be a little off-putting to show the patient undergoing the stresses of the "before-birth" mode.

Strangely enough, the not-for-profit hospitals significantly outspend the for-profit ones when it comes to marketing and advertising programs. I would have thought that if the for-profit operations truly believed in the free-market system, they would be ready to invest some of their staggering profits in such programs. But perhaps they are concerned this would have a detrimental effect on their CEO's gargantuan pay, bonus, and stock option packages.

Another well known and widespread part of the for-profit healthcare business are the HMOs, which are now the predominant means of delivering medical services in the United States. Such organizations claim they are able to provide superior care at lower cost due to higher efficiency. Others argue, however, this is pure bullshit, because the relative success of for-profit medical providers arises from their patently obvious and well-documented history of offering highly profitable care services for the affluent or well-insured customer, whilst avoiding unprofitable care options. High administrative costs and lower quality of service and care have also characterized for-profit HMOs. Many of these plans take 19 percent or more for overhead, versus an average of 13 percent in non-profit plans, just 3 percent in the U.S. Medicare program and a mere 1 percent in the Canadian version. It's also a little realized fact that contracting with private HMOs has substantially increased U.S. Medicare costs when Medicare has paid HMO premiums for seniors choosing to enroll in private plans. Compounding the problem, the HMOs have recruited healthy seniors who, if they hadn't switched to an HMO, would have cost Medicare very little. HMOs that were unable to recruit healthy people dropped out of their Medicare contracts, causing millions of seniors to lack coverage. In true Washington style, the government including forty-six billion dollars in additional HMO payments as part of the Medicare prescription drug bill.

At the end of the day all the claims of efficiency put forward by for-profit health organizations disguises the true facts. Investor-owned hospitals, clinics and HMO's have created a new value system. One that destroys the community roots and Samaritan basis of these establishments, while it makes doctors and nurses the employees of the investors, and views patients as nothing more than potential profit vehicles. In my opinion, investor ownership goes against the basic principles of responsible health care.

Having said that, I have to admit that I'm a fully paid up member of a profession that's unashamedly aided and abetted the American health care system to consistently provide the most expensive and least effective results in the Western world. Can this state of affairs change? Undoubtedly, in time it must. But as to how long it will take, I have no idea. While the pharmaceutical companies, hospital groups, HMOs, and yes, the AMA, continue to spend billions on marketing and advertising programs, not to mention the millions these interest groups spend on lobbying congress and supporting politicians through consistent donations to their campaign funds, I doubt it will happen in my lifetime. Never forget that the last time healthcare reform was attempted in the early years of the Clinton administration, the full force of a massive advertising program was unleashed by those in the industry who realized this could kill their golden goose. Remember the TV campaign featuring "Harry and Louise?" These were the professional, fortyish looking couple who spent every evening examining the Clinton healthcare bill in a campaign that ran in 1993 and 1994. They sat in their cozy middle class living room and spoke worriedly about hidden costs and the loss of provider choice and access to their "favorite doctor," that the Clinton health plan would allegedly force on America through the introduction of "socialized medicine." Never forget, that because of years of relentless brain washing, the term "socialized medicine" has acquired the stigma of being perceived as something between bestiality and necrophilia in the American psyche. The steady flow of these attack advertisements, principally funded by the Health Insurance Association of America and costing over fifteen million dollars, proved to be one of the most successful public relations campaigns in recent history. Within months, the Clinton healthcare plan was toast. It's interesting that when President Clinton presented his Health Security Act to a joint session of Congress and a primetime television audience in September of 1993, a *USA Today*/CNN/Gallup poll conducted shortly after the speech found that 57 percent of Americans approved of the plan. Six months later, the Harry and Louise campaign had caused a twenty-point drop in approval ratings, prompting Senator Jay Rockefeller (D-WV) to declare it "the single most destructive campaign I've seen in thirty years."

This, I suppose, goes to prove that advertising actually works! So much so that Harry and Louise were resurrected in 2000 on behalf of the Health Insurance Association of America in an attempt to lobby for insurance coverage for America's forty-four million uninsured. No doubt members of the association were only interested in those members of the uninsured who had a perfect health record and unlikely to make a claim against their policies. And just to prove that you can indeed flog a dead horse, Harry and Louise made another appearance in 2002, but this time they were shilling on behalf of an organization by the name of CuresNow. A pro-stem cell cloning organization opposing the recently passed Brownback-Landrieu legislation banning all forms of federally funded stem cell research. Amusing to think that Harry and Louise had switched sides and were appearing on behalf of the liberal, dare I say, "socialized medicine" fringe of society. In a series of TV commercials, they waxed eloquent about how scientists searching for a cure for cancer, Alzheimer's, heart disease and other serious afflictions could now go to jail because of their heroic actions. Unfortunately, third time around wasn't lucky, and Harry and Louise failed to carry the day.

The wonderfully ironic thing though, is that as a result of this TV battle over stem cell research, the Health Insurance Association of America sued CuresNow for allegedly misappropriating its Harry and Louise television icons. Perhaps that's the last we'll ever see of Harry and Louise on our TV screens.

One thing you can be sure of though is that you will be seeing lots of drug, hospital, insurance and healthcare advertising for many, many years to come.

chapter TEN.

the
FUTURE
was/is/will be TECHNOLOGY

In The Graduate, Dustin Hoffman was advised the future would be plastics. Close, but no cigar. What the guy at the cocktail party should have said was, information technology. 'Cos billions of dollars have been flushed away persuading captains of industry to buy technology systems they don't need, and which invariably become obsolete long before they've even begun to pay for them. No wonder BDAs love technology clients.

If you throw in the halcyon days of the dot com boom during the nineties, information technology has been very good to the advertising profession. It more than helped fill the yawning gap between the booze and cigarette bonanza of the sixties and the tsunami of "purple pill" pharmaceutical advertising we are now beaten over the head with on a daily basis. Yet, even though the IBMs, Dells, Ciscos, and Apples of this world now plow billions of dollars into the well churned loam of business targeted cable TV, The Wall Street Journal, Barons, Forbes, The Economist, the Summer and Winter Olympics and untold golf sponsorships, there was a time when a major technology account could be measured in tens of thousands of dollars, rather than the hundreds of millions many of them are now blowing on a regular basis.

For that state of affairs we would have to go back to the pre-Apple MAC and IBM PC days of the seventies; even though computers have been around since the midforties. Or, if you want to be really pissy about it, barnacle-encrusted artifacts have been dredged off the floor of the Mediterranean showing that the Phoenicians had various mechanical computing devices that enabled their seafarers to calculate, via the stars, what time the McDonalds on Crete would be open for a Minator burger with a supersized side of crispy virgin. I would even guess it's possible the Egyptian pyramid builders relied on very sophisticated computing devices to erect their alien directed structures. And, if you don't agree with me, I have an Erik von Daniken book to prove it.

Anyway, it doesn't matter, because I want to fast forward to the middle of the twentieth century. I'll even jump over World War II, ENIAC, and anything else that relied on vacuum tubes and relay switches to crunch numbers. Yeah, the self-same relay switches that malfunctioned when flying insects got trapped in them, which is where the phrase "computer bug" came from. But this isn't a book about bloody computers, it's a book about bloody advertising; let's cut to the chase.

As long as computers consisted of behemoth mainframe structures kept in cooled, glass-walled chambers, ministered over by white coated high priest programmers, data managers, IT professionals, and those weird people who spoke a different language, sported plastic pocket protectors, and wore spectacles held together with Band-Aids, there was no point in advertising. Because when the purchasing decision for something that's going to cost millions, rests on the expertise of a handful of geeks, you talk directly to the geeks. The function of corporate management is simply to suck it up and sign the check for whatever particular mainframe the geeks have decided they need.

All of this started to change with the introduction of computers that didn't need to be housed within their own specific environment, or require specialists to feed data in and interpret the results coming out. The first to break the stranglehold of the mainframe were much smaller machines known, unsurprisingly as minicomputers. These didn't take up tons of space, and people could work directly with them via desktop terminals. The most famous provider of these was Digital Equipment Corporation (DEC), which was eventually swallowed up by Compaq in 1998, which was in turn swallowed up by HP in 2002. Interestingly, when DEC was founded in 1957, it went looking for venture capital with little success, as in those days, the VC community regarded the computer business as being somewhat dodgy and having very poor prospects. The company eventually managed to raise seventy thousand dollars from Boston venture capitalist, Georges Doriot, who later sold his interest for 450 million dollars, which for those pre-Google days, was the single largest return on a VC investment.

By the seventies, computer designers were starting to develop what would come to be known as personal computers. Before the IBM PC, there was a whole range of machines starting with the Altair 8080 and including Commodore, TRS, Atari, Kaypro, Eagle, and others culminating in the introduction of the Apple II in 1977 (there was an Apple I, but only 200 of these were handmade by Steve Wozniak in the living room of Steve Job's parent's home). The basic premise of the personal computer is that it is a self-contained machine with its own processor, memory, and input and output devices. Unlike everything that had preceded it, it didn't operate merely as a dumb terminal attached to some unseen humming monster hidden away in the basement.

All these machines were regarded as the playthings of hobbyist guys (there were very few girls involved in the early days of the PC) who attended meetings of loose-knit organizations like The Homebrew Computer Club in the San Francisco Bay area. At these meetings they would share ideas and information, while getting excited over stuff that would make the average person's eyes glaze over after five minutes. But, everything changed with the introduction of the IBM PC in 1981, not because the IBM product was superior to all the other machines out there. No, it was simply because it was from IBM, which gave the idea of people actually having their very own personal computer tremendous legitimacy in the business world. Another major factor which opened the doors of corporate America to the PC was the introduction of software specifically written for individual users which increased their productivity tremendously. The first of these was the VisiCalc spreadsheet, quickly followed by the Lotus 1-2-3 program combing a spreadsheet with a database and graphics capability in a single integrated application. Lotus 1-2-3 soon became what the Technorati lovingly call a "killer application." - in non-geek speak, this means that the heavens open up and a great big hand descends and bestows upon you a license to print money. The rest is history. It would be hard to imagine any business being able to function today without having a PC on virtually every employee's desk. It's also worth considering that the PC has killed off the need for about 90 percent of the world's secretaries, except in Japan, where they are still employed serving tea and emptying the ashtrays.

In the pre- and early-PC days, computers were almost exclusively advertised in the computer trade press, the first of which was PC specific *Byte* magazine, founded in 1975 with an initial circulation of just four hundred. By the mideighties there were literally hundreds of titles covering everything from computers, networking, data management, hardware, software, systems, information management and just about every conceivable aspect of information technology. In those early days very little money was spent in the general business press and virtually nothing in general consumer media. This quickly changed after the introduction of the IBM PC.

In these early days, most IT advertising accounts were handled by specialist agencies versed in the esoteric culture and language of what was somewhat disparagingly called by its practitioners "bits and bytes," or when dealing with computer printer accounts, "speeds and feeds." If you were unfortunate enough to work in an agency handling these fledgling accounts in the early eighties, you quickly realized that when producing ads for IT companies, creativity usually came in a distant second to getting as much mind-numbing technical information on the page as possible. The result was that most early computer ads were little more than data sheets with postage stamp sized, impossible to read, visuals of monitor screen shots and motherboards. Yet, as many of these early computer companies originated and then grew to maturity in northern California's Silicon Valley, it provided a unique opportunity for a surprisingly large number of specialist agencies to grow alongside them. This was also true to a lesser extent on Route 128 in Massachusetts.

In the bay area, a few of these agencies were located in San Francisco, with the majority occupying the heart of Silicon Valley, stretching from San Jose to Palo Alto. Many of these helped such companies as Hewlett-Packard, Apple, Intel, Oracle, Cisco, Electronic Arts, and a great many others that no longer exist to communicate to their early audiences. But as is usual in the agency business, once the account reached a certain size, the client management would begin acquiring delusions of grandeur. They would start to think it was time to spread their wings and go after a more diverse audience. Then the high-tech agency that had put in all the heavy lifting creating the brand, usually for minuscule fees, would be unceremoniously dumped in favor of a BDA that offered the client more prestige, albeit with less expertise, and always for much higher fees. You also got a bunch of people working on your fiber-optic, mission critical, RAID, SQL Server, doohickey account, who just a week before had been working on suppositories and soap.

Having worked on IT accounts of all shapes and sizes, from Apple and IBM, to Intel and many others over the years, there is one thing you have to understand if you are to have any chance of surviving in the Silicon Jungle. If you work on the account of a company which is still run by the original founder, it means you must to be prepared to deal with a raging egomaniac who thinks he knows everything about everything, who has surrounded himself with boot licking sycophants, considers himself infallible and who will have the final decision on every single aspect of his advertising, from the size of the logo to how often they should be featured "reluctantly" in the ads.

If you are lucky, you will get Steve Jobs, who even though he will obsess over every detail, is a guy with great taste and the courage of his own convictions. After all, this is the CEO of a multibillion-dollar company who once demanded of his ad agency, "I want insanely great advertising!" On the other hand, if you have lived a very bad life and are destined to burn for eternity in the fires of hell, before you get there you will have to go through the purgatory of attempting to create advertising for Larry Ellison.

Let me explain. Steve Jobs, as I am sure you well know was co-founder, along with Steve "Woz" Wozniak, of Apple Computer back in 1976. Apart from being forced out of the company from 1985 to 1997, Jobs has done more than anyone in terms of innovation and esthetically driven design for both the computer and entertainment industries (he's on the board of Disney and is the company's largest shareholder since they bought his company, Pixar, for several gazillion dollars a few years ago). He has always recognized the value of creating advertising that "punches over its weight." Because if you can't outspend your competition, then you must outsmart them. Yes, I know this is glaringly obvious, but the vast majority of clients are prepared to continually spend dumpster loads of money running ad campaigns that are exactly like the ad campaigns their competition runs. This is what I call "your logo goes here" advertising. This state of affairs has always been so. It will always be so. This is particularly true of technology advertising.

Even in the days of the Apple II, long before the MAC and the IBM PC, Apple ran an ad headlined, "Will someone please tell me exactly what a personal computer can do," which spelled out one hundred different things, and hinted at even more, that anyone could do with the Apple II. They also ran ads that explained how you could use an Apple II to take care of your accounting, track inventory, and manage stocks and do many other things that until then had been laborious chores. But, the great thing about Apple's advertising, which is still true today, was that it humanized technology It talked about computing as an experience rather than a task, or even worse, as a chore. Which might not be considered a big deal now, but nearly thirty years ago, when computers were not as commonplace or accepted as they are now, this was revolutionary.

Apple was also responsible for what must be acknowledged as possibly the world's most famous ad. This was the TV commercial that launched the MAC computer during the 1984 Super Bowl. I wish I had a dollar for every client I've dealt with over the years who's asked me for "a 1984 commercial." When they do, I reply that I'm more than happy to oblige, but first they should realize there are a few things they need to understand. When the commercial was produced in 1983, it cost over six hundred thousand dollars (over two million dollars in today's money) making it the most expensive TV spot ever produced up to that time. When the finished commercial was shown to Apple's board of directors a couple of weeks before the game, they hated it and wanted to cancel the media buy. So, Apple's agency, Chiat Day, paid for four focus groups out of their own pocket to prove to the client it was a great spot. Unsurprisingly, everyone in all four of the groups hated it, which is further proof of my long-held belief that focus groups are a complete waste of time. Fortunately, the agency couldn't sell the time, as this was before Super Bowl mania had grabbed the ad industry by the throat, driving the cost of a single thirty second TV spot through the roof. Consequently, Apple was forced to run the spot.

The rest is history!

The publicity it generated was phenomenal. For days it appeared on every TV news program and was written about in virtually every newspaper. And, the single most important thing to consider about this whole situation is to realize that it only ran once (actually, it also ran one other time, very late at night on December 29, 1983, on a single station in Twin Falls, Idaho - not far from where I am writing this - for a cost of about ten dollars). Why? Because this way it would be eligible for the advertising award shows the following year, as entries for these ego-polishing competitions are required to have appeared in the preceding year. So, my answer to all those clients anxious to have the next "1984," is if you are prepared to spend more money than has ever been spent on a TV commercial, disregard any negative feelings you, your wife, your wife's dog, or God forbid, your board of directors, may have about it, and you promise to only run it once. Let's get cracking! Needless to say, no one ever took me up on the offer.

Then, on the other hand, there's Larry Ellison, founder and chairman of Oracle Corporation, one of the largest software companies in the world. He's also one of the richest people in the universe, with more money than Croesus, yet for all that, a guy who wouldn't know a good ad if you wrapped it around a brick and let it fall on him from ten miles up. This is a guy who during his continuing tenure as chief honcho at Oracle has subjected the unwashed masses of the business universe to some of the most horrendous technology advertising ever produced. Which is surprising, when you consider he's a close friend of Steve Jobs, served on the board of Apple for five years, and even enjoyed having Steve as his official wedding photographer during his fourth marriage a few years ago; a soirée which took place at his two hundred million dollar, reproduction, feudal Japanese Shogunate Palace, in Woodside, California! So why, I have to ask myself, why hasn't a scintilla of Steve's impeccable taste and insatiable desire to produce esthetically pleasing products and supporting advertising rubbed off on Larry?

Oracle's advertising has changed little over the years, even though the account has been through numerous agencies; the end result invariably being print advertising using simple black and red type against a white background, while rarely featuring any visual elements, apart from comparison charts showing the difference in performance and functionality between Oracle's products and the competition. As is de rigueur in this Neolithic form of IT advertising, the Oracle column in these charts is full of large, grease pencil, check marks, while the competition's column is empty, which makes you wonder how these companies, which include IBM, have managed to stay in business against the perfection of the mighty Oracle juggernaut all these years. And while many of the ads unfailingly make outrageous claims for the efficacy of Oracle's products, they are rarely backed up by facts. Personally, having had the misfortune to freelance on his account for one of his many ex-agencies, I believe the ads are merely an extension of the autocratic way Ellison runs his company.

Admittedly, he did have one foray into Super Bowl advertising during the dot com boom, producing a one minute extravaganza shot in Cambodia with lots of fast-paced action and explosions, ending with a rather strange reference to the "Red Chair of Knowledge!" The whole thing was acknowledged by many to have been a complete waste of time and money. Particularly money, as the production costs were rumored to have been more than Pol Pot's entire war budget during the Cambodian conflict. Larry has obviously since decided to keep his loot securely invested in pseudo-Japanese mansions, destroyer-sized yachts and the "cold-war vintage" fighter aircraft he collects, as Oracle has rigidly stuck to its simple print advertising format ever since.

Unlike Ellison, Jobs has used the same agency since he founded the company, although, to be strictly correct, Apple's very first advertising was produced by legendary Silicon Valley marketing and PR guru, Regis McKenna, who sold the advertising part of his business to Chiat Day in the early eighties so he could concentrate on plundering the mother lode of consulting that northern California technology companies love to blow their money on. And, even though, when John Sculley was running Apple in the late eighties, he moved the companies advertising to his old Pepsi agency, BBDO, as soon as Steve was back in the driver's seat, the advertising chores were swiftly given back to Chiat Day, which has consistently produced great advertising for Apple ever since.

Although not as glamorous and highly publicized as the Apple 1984 TV launch commercial, there is one other IT campaign that should serve as the perfect case study of how to build a brand from almost zero recognition to one of the best known names in the world. This is the "Intel Inside" campaign, which ran from 1990 to the end of 2005. The brainchild of Intel Marketing Director, Dennis Carter, it was not an advertising campaign in the traditional way. Just as I've had many clients asking for a "1984" campaign, I have also had many ask for an "Intel Inside." Forcing me to explain a couple of salient facts about why this was so successful. Firstly, if you wish to create a brand name for something 99 percent of users will never see (it's a microprocessor that sits inside a box that sits under your desk, for crying out loud) then you must be prepared to be in it for the long haul - in Intel's case, nearly sixteen years. You must also be prepared to spend a ton of money. Never forget that the most important thing about the "Intel Inside" campaign is that it is a cooperative program. That means Intel was prepared to pay for half the advertising costs for any other companies ad which featured the "Intel Inside" logo. If the ad didn't meet Intel's specific requirements, Intel wouldn't pay them a penny and the advertiser was prohibited from using the "Intel Inside" logo. Also, anyone taking the coop money for film and TV advertisements had to use the distinctive "Intel Inside" five note musical jingle whenever the logo appeared. I have no idea how much money Intel spent on this program over the sixteen years it ran, but, I'll bet it was well over a couple of billion dollars.

I can't leave the subject of egomaniac CEO's without mentioning one of my all time favorites. The larger than life, in so many respects, Philippe Kahn. This is a guy who arrived from France as a twenty-nine year old tourist in 1982 and because of his Masters degree in Mathematics, managed to talk his way into a job at Hewlett-Packard for a few months until they found out he didn't have a green card. Realizing the opportunities opening up with the desktop computing revolution taking place at the time, he decided his future lay in America, particularly in Silicon Valley, rather than his Gallic homeland. Managing to pull together a few consulting gigs he could bounce between before being asked to provide any kind of legal documentation to prove his immigrant status, he started to build a reputation for himself. To the point where within a few months he was able to start his own one-man company with the unashamedly grandiose title, Borland International, out of his apartment in Scotts Valley. In spite of the fact that it would be another four years before he actually acquired a green card, he was able to develop Borland into one of the leading software companies in the U.S. In 1986 the company filed an IPO in London (probably because Philippe was still not a legal resident of the U.S.) and before long Borland was in the top tier of PC software companies worldwide.

When Philippe started off, he would place small ads in the "geek" books, as his first product to market was the programming language, Turbo Pascal. But, because he had little money, Philippe would write and design the ads himself. This is hardly surprising when you consider that throughout his career he has always considered himself as some kind of modern Leonardo DaVinci. Truly a master of all things technical, artistic and entrepreneurial. As is usual with these kinds of people, they invariably surround themselves with ass kissing sycophants who never miss a chance to reassure their leader he is more than capable of walking on water. I have actually been in meetings with Philippe and his merry band of upper management churls, when they've dissolved into paroxysms of delight, jumping up and down and "high fiveing" each other whenever Philippe has suggested changing the typeface on a package from sixteen point Times Roman bold to eighteen point Bodoni extra bold. Through all this, Philippe sits at the head of the conference table with a Jaba the Hut smile of satisfaction on his face.

This is also a guy whose palatial office was replete with the toys necessary to demonstrate his expertise in all things esthetic. Not just computers, but also musical instruments of all kinds, tape recorders, still and movie cameras, art books, art materials, sketchbooks, notepads, I was surprised there wasn't a potters wheel tucked away in the corner. Unfortunately, the logical culmination of this explosion of creativity was that Philippe decided that as he had built a multimillion dollar company based on the ads he used to write from the laundry room of the apartment complex he once lived in. Well damn it, he obviously knew more about it than some high-priced advertising agency. So, he created his own in-house ad agency.

Now, as I explained in my previous book, *MadScam*, there are good and bad points about deciding to do your advertising in-house. On the good side, you can avoid having all those bastards on Madison Avenue, or down in San Jose, in Philippe's case, ripping you off. So, there are certain undoubted economies to be gained. But, on the bad side, there are a few things that can quickly outweigh these peck sniffing gains. For a start, few talented people in the ad biz want to work in an in-house agency. You only work on one account; there is no variety, no creative rub-off that comes from having to switch between different products and different markets. And you certainly

don't earn as much money as in a BDA. But the single most important reason why it is a bad idea is because the guy you have to present your ideas to, is the same guy who signs your paycheck, so the last
thing you want to do is piss him off. This means you will always ere
on the side of caution, never attempting to argue with the idiot.
Unless you've decided you can't stand sucking up to this bloated egomaniac any more. But, because of that warm, cozy and regular
monthly paycheck, this rarely happens. Consequently, Borland's
advertising was simply dreadful. Jargon filled data sheets, accompanied by cliché visuals of speeding stock cars denoting neck snapping
speed, or gigantic bank vault doors signifying impregnable security.
And, if you've ever browsed through an Information Technology
trade magazine (and who in their right mind would want to?) you will
still be bombarded by these kinds of ads.

Philippe was finally forced to resign as president, CEO, and
chairman of Borland after twelve years. Rumor has it that the board
decided he was spending more time, and money, outside the office
recording innumerable jazz CDs with extremely expensive sidemen,
than he was attending to the rapidly declining fortunes of the company he had founded. But, as is common with so many of the
Technorati, he has rapidly bounded back, founding, and selling for
obscene amounts of money a couple of other technology companies,
including "LightSurf Technologies," the originators of the camera cell
phone. No doubt, a great deal of his money is now safely stashed
beneath the sidewalks of Zurich, where Philippe gained his impressive
education.

Finally, we cannot leave the subject of IT advertising without
visiting those high-spending practitioners of the dark arts of IT consulting. There are dozens of them spread around the globe, but for
now, we'll concentrate on the eight-hundred-pound gorillas of
Accenture, EDS, Bearing Point, Deloite Touché, and the uber-mon-
ster of them all, IBM Global Business Services. These are the guys
who can walk into the Boeings, GMs, GEs, national, state, and city
governments of this world and walk out with multimillion dollar contracts for the instillation and upkeep of giant, sophisticated systems.
But one of the best kept secrets of this highly lucrative business is that

after having been paid millions to install these new state of the art applications and procedures, it's often found that they don't work with the old systems which have been humming along nicely for years. So, the consultant is paid many more millions to rip out the new stuff and make sure the old stuff keeps chugging along the way it always did. Sounds like another one of those wonderful licenses to print money to me!

Agencies love to pick up these IT consultancy accounts. Not only because they spend huge chunks of money, but also because, it's virtually impossible to describe in an ad just what it is they actually do. Which explains why the ads for Accenture feature Tiger Woods playing golf. Not just because they pay him several million dollars a year to wear their logo on his clothes, along with all the other sponsors who pay him millions to also wear their logo on the same shirt. Even more importantly, it's because the directors of Accenture, plus the CEO of their ad agency, get to play nine holes of golf with Tiger once a year. It's OK guys, we understand you have to put your shareholders money to good use. Wink, wink, nudge, nudge! But as most consultants' advertising is like most other consultant's advertising, just as most of the advertising for banks, or stockbrokers, or hospitals, or even undertakers for God's sake, is the same as everyone else's, why not use Tiger Woods so you can boast about how you crushed him at Augusta last year.

Just as many professions have a specialized language containing words specific to their trade or expertise, IT people have actually invented their own particular vocabulary, which is 10 percent logic and 90 percent bullshit, and which they insist on their agencies using in their advertising. That's why when you attempt to read their media, internet and other forms of communication, you might be somewhat confused to realize that most of these companies stopped selling products years ago and now provide "solutions." But these solutions do not actually have a specific function such as calculating a spreadsheet or displaying an architectural rendering. Now they enable the users experience and optimize their abilities. They'll even make your passions and aspirations achievable. And they'll do it enterprise wide in real time. Paradigm shifts take place (I know I promised not to say that again... But it's an essential part of consultant chat), bandwidth abounds, synergy invariably happens and everything is scalable and robust. Whatever you cough up huge amounts of money for will be world class, best of breed, bleeding-edge and state of the art. There's no question, it's a win-win situation for all concerned!

What's even worse is if you think their advertising is bad; check out their Web sites or annual reports. Consultants in particular are the world champions in turgid language. Here for instance is the "Mission Statement" from BearingPoint:

> Bearing Point, Inc. (NYSE:BE) is the leading global management and technology consulting firm, providing strategic consulting, application services, technology solutions and managed services to Global 2000 companies and government organizations. We help customers achieve results by identifying mission critical issues and implementing innovative and customized solutions designed to generate revenue, reduce costs and access the right information at the right time. Our proprietary research institute, the BearingPoint Institute, demonstrates the firm's commitment to analyzing and responding to issues with a thoroughly researched and informed perspective. Based in McLean, Virginia, BearingPoint has been named as one of Fortune's Most Admired Companies in America for three consecutive years.

All I can say is, keep that by your bedside, read it a couple of times and you'll never need to buy sleeping pills again.

IT advertising has made great leaps since the early eighties, both in terms of its content and that amount of money the big companies spend. Now smart companies don't cram their advertising with masses of information which rightly belongs in the technical literature. Now the purpose of most media advertising is to drive prospective customers to the company's Web site. IBM has hundreds of thousands of pages on its site, and it's architected in such a way you can virtually find any specific information within minutes. Dell, the masters of direct marketing sell the majority of their systems directly from their Web site which is also directly linked to their telephone sales force. Now broadly known as e-commerce, the Internet has revolutionized how many companies do business, but without question the technology companies themselves have been the ones to benefit most, to the point where many ad agencies are playing catch up. Although paying lip service to the potential of new media, only a small percentage has actually "got it."

As an example of one of the few who do "get it," Ogilvy has done a magnificent job of organizing, managing and creating advertising for IBM over the last ten or years ago. When Lou Gerstner took over as CEO of IBM, he discovered that the company was using more than eighty agencies, worldwide. There was no central coordination to make sure there was a continuity of message in the hundreds of markets that "Big Blue" addressed. As you can imagine, not only was the ROI on this chaotic situation pathetic, the resulting work was sub-standard and unrelated to any corporate master plan, primarily because there wasn't one, and every division and global territory was doing its own thing. Gerstner put IBM's entire account into Ogilvy, close to one billion dollars in billings at the time, and the result has been a constant flow of work that has a universally high standard and effectiveness. As mentioned earlier, Chiat Day does consistently great work for Apple, and has done for a very long period of time, apart from the aberration of the BBDO days. The third agency that "gets it" is Goodby, Silverstein and Partners with their work for Hewlett-Packard and Adobe amongst others. Other than that, even for some very large and well known clients, the general level of work produced for IT companies is mediocre.

In my opinion this is because most BDAs are not prepared to invest the time and money required to not only get up to speed on a technology account, but also to maintain the level of knowledge necessary to produce effective communications in one of the world's most rapidly changing business environments. It's far easier for them to manage a package goods, automobile, or travel account. You can't staff up an account that requires a deep knowledge of IT, and the market for it, with people who the week before were working on disposable diapers.

As I said at the beginning of this chapter, working with the CEOs of many IT companies brings you in contact with some of the biggest egos in the known universe. It also makes you aware of how many serially rich people there are in technology. Yes we all know about Bill Gates and Larry Ellison, as well as the new kids on the block, Sergey Brin and Larry Page, founders of Google, who've both become multibillionaires within a couple of years of going public. But these guys have done it by founding and running a single company. There are others who have leapfrogged from company to company, picking up millions in bonuses, stock options and golden parachutes along the way. Judith Estrin, who cofounded Bridge Communications twenty years ago and has since founded or been part of senior management of another five or six, has collected millions along the way. Mike Capellas has also made millions within the management ranks of at least half a dozen companies. What I never seem able to fathom out is how much is enough? How much money can you and your children spend in a lifetime? But then you have to remember what Larry Ellison said when he was asked by a reporter why he was driven to make so much money. "Because it isn't about making money" he replied. "It's about keeping score!"

My favorite story about the rich of Silicon Valley, one which is absolutely true, concerns one of Silicon Valley's first millionaires. Dennis Barnhart, the founder of Eagle Computer of Los Gatos, California, which was an early microcomputer manufacturing company. It sold a line of popular desktop computers which were highly regarded in the late seventies. After the IBM PC was launched in 1981, Eagle produced the 1600 series, running MS-DOS, but they weren't true IBM clones. When the market dictated that it wanted actual clones of the IBM PC, even if a non-clone had better features, Eagle responded with a line of clones, including a well regarded portable. The company prospered, and on June 8, 1983, the day of Eagle's IPO, Dennis Barnhart, picked up his brand new Ferrari and drove it up to Palo Alto to have lunch with a yacht broker who would help him spend some of the millions he had come into that very day. After several bottles of very good, very expensive wine, Dennis jumped into his Ferrari and sped off back to San Jose. Unfortunately, he crashed and was killed on the way.

But when you think about it, life is inevitably a series of ups and downs. Most of us we are never quite sure which will happen next. Dennis didn't, but was probably at one of the highest points of his life, and I would like to believe that he died a happy man. Anyway, you have to admit, it's a helluva way to go!

chapter ELEVEN. *all* **POLITICS** *are* **AS ADVERTISED**

Fifty years ago Vance Packard wrote about the ever increasing influence and effect of advertising on the political process. Today, its expense and impact is many times greater than it was back then. We explore the current state of political advertising and what awfulness we can expect in the future.

In *The Hidden Persuaders*, Vance Packard devotes an entire chapter to the way politics in the fifties was being increasingly influenced by advertising. As he points out, manipulation of the electorate is nothing new, from the "bread and circuses" approach of those seeking office in ancient Rome, to Napoleon's creation of a press office, which he called the Bureau of Public Opinion, politicians have never been shy about molding favorable opinions of themselves and their policies through mass communication.

It wasn't until the beginning of the fifties that political parties started to bring in advertising agencies and consultants. *The New York World Telegram*, a long since defunct paper, describing the 1950 Congressional campaign, ran a headline, "THE HUCKSTERS TAKE OVER THE GOP CAMPAIGN." It then went on to disparagingly explain that politicians were now increasingly using the same techniques employed to sell autos, bath salts, and lawn mowers.

Things were about to change drastically from the last old style election, the presidential race of 1948. Thomas Dewey was expected to win in a landslide. In a poll, fifty out of fifty top political pundits predicted Truman going down in defeat. This only goes to prove how full of shit both polls and pundits can be. But "Give 'em Hell, Harry" took to the rails to cross the country on an aggressive campaign whistle stop tour. He traveled over thirty thousand miles, speaking in person before more than fifteen million people. His re-election ranks as possibly the greatest upset in American political history and in many ways served as the last hurrah for a style of campaigning that no longer exists on a national scale. Interestingly, Rosser Reeves, he of flaming stomachs and hammers in the head fame, tried to persuade Dewey to make some TV spots, but Dewey refused, considering this to be far too undignified. He must be spinning in his grave if he's had a chance to check out the current state of political campaigning and advertising!

Reeves finally got his way when he worked on the 1952 Eisenhower presidential campaign. His "Eisenhower Answers America" effort is the first example of the really significant use of TV advertising in a political campaign. He wrote a series of sixty-second spots featuring a bevy of people identified as "men on the street" (in those days, for political purposes, men on the street outweighed women on the street by about ten to one) asking a series of "pablumesque" questions to the candidate. These had been prerecorded to make sure Reeves got exactly the questions he wanted. He then took a reluctant Eisenhower (who is reputed to have said, "To think an old soldier would come to this") into the studio to crash out obvious, and equally well scripted answers. Which when you consider the

uber-scripted town hall meetings in front of carefully screened sup-
portive audiences we are forced to watch as part of today's campaigns,
you have to consider perhaps the only thing that has changed is the
quality of the TV picture. Because in terms of the content of today's
debates, you would be correct in thinking it has taken a significant
turn for the worse.

As usual, Packard was obsessed with Ernst Dichter's take on
the whole situation and how the minds of the unwashed masses of
America were having their brains severely screwed over. The
Obersturmbannfuhrer doctor was convinced everything could be laid
at the doorstep of Pavlov and his theory of conditioned reflexes, Freud
and his sublimated sexual mother and father images, and Riesman
and his confusing concepts of Americans as some kind of split personality, spectator consumers. In the twisted mind of the evil Dr. Dichter,
it was inevitably all about bad potty training, or penis envy. And, you
know what? When you look at many of today's politicians, he may
have had a point.

The most dramatic shift in political advertising that occurred
during this period was the realization that most people weren't really
interested in issues; they were more interested in personalities. Even
today, many people who voted for George W. Bush gave as their primary reason that he was the kind of guy they could happily have a
beer with. The fact that he is a reformed alcoholic and hasn't touched
a drop in twenty years seems to make no difference. Although, if like
me, you rely for your world news on furtively reading the *National
Enquirer* at the supermarket checkout, I have it on good authority he
smashes back a fifth of "Jack" every night before kicking the crap out
of Barnie, then trashing the furniture in the Lincoln Bedroom.

As the famous *Rolling Stone* ad campaign put it so well for so
many years, "Perception is reality." And, the best demonstration of
this would have to be the televised 1960 presidential debate between
Richard Nixon and John F. Kennedy. This has long been accepted as
the perfect demonstration of how to shoot yourself in the foot when
taking part in a TV debate. Nixon's refusal to wear make up, his
heavy seven-o-clock shadow, and sweaty upper lip all served to have
Kennedy, by comparison, come across as much more youthful,

relaxed, and in control. Yet, in subsequent polls, people who listened to the debate on the radio overwhelmingly gave Nixon as the clear winner. This is further proof of the power of the visual medium and the fact that over the years, we've gradually been moving towards a situation were it matters little what you say, its how you say it, and above all, how good you look when you are saying it!

When we look at the savage, swift boating, rip the competition's entrails out, political advertising we are forced to watch ad nauseum these days, it's worth remembering, if you are old enough, there was once a time when politicians didn't treat you like the village idiot and they actually acknowledged voters might be blessed with a modicum of intelligence. This was demonstrated back in 1964, when the Democrats were smart enough to hire the best agency in America at that time, Doyle, Dane, Bernbach. Instead of taking the Rosser Reeves approach, "Let's beat the crap out of the viewer's brains" with repetitive, soporific slogans, what DDB did was make an emotional appeal ideally suited to Lyndon Johnson's campaign. It reminded voters of the administration's work fighting poverty and providing Medicare, while capitalizing on fear that LBJ's Republican opponent, Barry Goldwater, would seriously consider fighting the cold war with nuclear weapons. This Democratic effort is regarded as one of the best political campaigns ever, and included the famous "Daisy" TV ad, where the visual of a little girl counting flower petals is accompanied by a voice over countdown ending in an atomic mushroom cloud. And, it's worth considering that not only did the commercial never mention Barry Goldwater, it also received hours of free airtime via the news media coverage it engendered.

Having said that, even the best political campaign can only take a candidate so far; the rest is up to them. I have personal experience of this, having worked on the reelection campaign for John Lindsay when he ran for a second term as Mayor of New York in the late sixties. In his first four years, he'd really screwed up. There were strikes by teachers and sanitation workers, resulting in the famous pictures of mountains of rat-infested garbage lining the city's streets. There was even a strike by the union that maintained the many bridges connecting Manhattan to the mainland. This resulted in the drawbridges over the Harlem River being locked in the "up" position, barring access by cars and trucks, while striking sanitation workers let hundreds of thousands of gallons of raw sewage flow into the Hudson and East Rivers. Lindsay's first term was marked by one catastrophe after another, ending with the infamous "Hard Hat Riot" on Wall Street. So we decided the best thing for Lindsay to do was run TV spots in which he would admit that he'd screwed up (he actually said "mistakes were made"), but that he had learned from the experience and would do a better job if the electorate gave him another chance at "the second toughest job in America." So, they did. Against all the odds, John Lindsay got voted in for a second term. And guess what? He screwed up even worse. Politicians. What can I tell ya?

In the seventies, following Nixon's resignation, Jimmy Carter's campaign took advantage of the bitterness caused by Gerald Ford's pardon of "Tricky Dicky," but even more effectively by presenting himself as a Washington outsider, appearing in TV spots wearing a denim work shirt on his Georgia peanut farm. "You know, everybody from Congress that's running for president is a lawyer," he laconically says in his deep southern accent. Interestingly enough, this is when the ascendancy of state governors began. Since Carter, with the exception of the first President Bush, all the holders of the nation's number one office have been a state governor. But by the time you're reading this, we'll have a President who came up through the Senate.

Reagan ushered in the era of the performer. As an ex-movie star, he had a natural, easy-going presence that appealed to the voters; an increasingly desirable attribute which was demonstrated during the Vietnam War period, when a poll showed the most electable and trustworthy person in the U.S. was TV newscaster, Walter Cronkite. Even as I began writing this, one of the front runners for the Republican nomination was one of the stars of a popular TV series, *Law & Order*'s, Fred Thompson, who was also a senator, before taking up his acting career. He campaigned on the premise that he'd be another Reagan. However, Thompson flamed out early, primarily because his debate performances looked like he was auditioning for the lead in a zombie movie.

By the late eighties things were starting to get nasty. In the 1988 presidential campaign, George H. W. Bush was running against Michael Dukakis and his campaign communications consultant, Roger Ailes, who now heads up Fox News, was furiously throwing shit against the Dukakis wall to see how much of it would stick. It turned out, there was plenty. When Dukakis was filmed by the media riding around in a tank with what looked like a chamber pot on his head, Ailes used the embarrassing footage in TV spots that negatively compared Dukakis to bone fide war hero, Bush the elder - not to be confused with Texas Air National Guard hero, Bush junior. He used film of severely polluted Boston harbor to hammer Dukakis's environmental record as Governor of Massachusetts. But the archetypal "slime ad," since surpassed by even slimier efforts, was the "Willie Horton" TV spot. Using a very menacing police mug shot of an African American criminal and a long line of shadowy figures going through a revolving door, again all African American, the ad talked about how this convicted killer received ten weekend passes while serving a life sentence. On one of these weekends, he kidnapped a couple, stabbing the man and raping the woman. The purpose of the ad was twofold, to present Dukakis as "soft on crime," and to play on the racial fears of the electorate. This single TV spot is widely credited with costing Dukakis the Presidency. Unfortunately, since then, things have only gotten worse.

The eighties also heralded the increasing use of political ads not paid for and produced by the contender's campaign. Instead, political action committees (PACs) started to make an impact on the political advertising scene. Thanks to an amendment to the Federal Election Campaign Act allowing private individuals and PACs to spend unlimited amounts of money on behalf of candidates, this has now become common practice. Candidates love this, as it allows them to run vicious, pit bull attacks on their opponents and then claim, somewhat disingenuously, they had nothing to do with it and would never stoop to using such methods.

For one single campaign in the nineties, there was a brief throwback to the style of the fifties, when multimillionaire Ross Perot spent sixty-five million dollars of his own money buying thirty-minute segments of time on network TV to run a series of infomercials that went into great depth and detail describing what he would do for the nations economy and how he would tackle deficit reduction. These quirky half hour programs featured Perot himself giving a lecture on fiscal responsibility accompanied with schoolroom visual aids. The ads consistently drew bigger audiences than most of the evening sitcoms, with one October screening pulling nearly eleven million viewers. At last it seemed here was a politician who didn't dumb everything down into ten-second sound bites and treated his audience with respect. Unfortunately, his campaign imploded when he accused Republican operatives of trying to sabotage his daughter's wedding by flooding the media with compromising digitally altered photographs. Explaining that he wanted to save her embarrassment, he pulled out of the race, then after a couple of weeks, jumped back in. The end result was he lost a great deal of support and ended up being regarded by many as a something of a fruitcake. But at the end of the day he still got 20 percent of the vote. It was the highest turnout ever for a third-party candidate.

Which brings us to the abysmal state of political advertising today. Compared to the relatively simple era of the late fifties that Packard describes in his book, we now live in a world of nonstop political campaigning and its associated advertising. Starting many months, even years, before the primaries and then continuing without let up to the very day of the elections, there is no respite from it, and the vast majority of it now is negative. This in spite of the fact that everyone running for office, swears at the beginning of their campaign they will never stoop to running a negative campaign with its associated advertising, but they invariably do, particularly when falling behind in the polls.

Why do politicians increasingly use negative advertising? Do they think this is the most effective way to persuade voters during the course of the campaign, hopefully enabling them to win the election? There have been a great many studies on this subject, and the results are inconsistent. Yet nearly all politicians and the consultants responsible for creating their advertising instinctively believe attack ads work because their perception is that they have in the past, so when things get desperate, they fall back on what they do best. This is no different from many mainstream advertisers, particularly marketers of package goods, who as I have pointed out in earlier chapters invariably fall back on focus group, tested, me-too campaigns, because they are less risky, while failing to acknowledge that they are also less effective.

Personally, I believe attack ads work, but only against those inclined to believe them in the first place. Meaning they serve to incentivise the base, which is that group of people who would vote for you anyway, if only you can get them off their ass and to the polling station. Never forget, in the greatest democracy in the world, the majority of the American population doesn't vote. So, the key to getting elected is not spending untold millions of dollars trying to persuade those of another party to switch allegiance and vote for you. It isn't even in spending millions of dollars on the so called "undecided's" trying to get them to make up their minds. No, the real key, one which has been played so masterfully by people like Roger Ailes, Lee Atwater, and Karl Rove, is to get your base fired up. Because, if you do it right, you can get that hardcore, those who believe in your policies and point of view, to literally run to the polling station on election day, hopefully dragging every other voting member of their family with them.

Successful attack ads work against the base because they play on the prejudices and stereotypes that already exist in the viewer's minds - virtually all attack ads use the medium of TV. They also create a ripple effect when they are reported on and repeatedly rebroadcast by the news media, who by providing all this extra coverage, inherently reinforce the negative message of the ads. Perhaps the best example of this was the "Swiftboating" of John Kerry in the 2004 presidential campaign. Here was a decorated Vietnam War hero running against a guy who used family connections to get him in the Texas Air National Guard to ensure he wouldn't have to serve in combat in Vietnam. It should have been a no-brainer for Kerry. But a PAC created a TV campaign using some fellow swift boaters, who didn't actually serve with Kerry, but had carried a grudge against him ever since he'd joined the anti-war movement on returning from Vietnam.

The campaign unashamedly accused Kerry of lying and cowardice, claiming he didn't deserve his decorations. Kerry made the naïve mistake of initially taking the high road and chose to ignore the campaign. When the mainstream news media seized on the story and, by endlessly running it on their news programs provided the swift boaters with many hours of free air time, Kerry finally mounted a counter attack, using some of his ex-shipmates to defend his record. But it was too late, Kerry had let what was palpably an untrue story spin out of control, which also served to reinforce the image the Bush campaign had been painting of him as indecisive and a flip-flopper.

What also worked against Kerry was the nonstop characterization of him by the Bush campaign as an east coast, Chardonnay-swilling, French-speaking, and cheese-eating effete who was completely out of touch with Middle America - often referred to in the media as "Joe six pack." On the other hand, Bush was presented as a "good old boy" from Texas who'd pulled himself up by his boot straps in the rough and tumble of the oil business. In truth, Bush was born (with a silver foot in his mouth as Ann Richards once said) in a multimillion dollar, ocean-side home in Greenwich, Connecticut, one of the richest communities in America. He went to private schools and ended up at Yale. His business career in the oil business was a disaster, resulting in him being baled out of many bad business decisions by his father's friends. But, through the masterful handling of his political consultants, he became a living example of the *Rolling Stone* campaign I have mentioned previously; "Perception is reality." And when your political base *wants* to believe that perception, it does indeed become reality.

Such is the power of imagery over substance. By the very nature of TV ads, which are rarely over thirty seconds in length, it's obviously impossible to cover any public policy issue in a meaningful way. Candidates are persuaded by their handlers to rely on sound bites that are merely shortened versions of the already brief stump speeches they make on their endless swings through those areas of their constituencies where they feel they have the most chance of winning. These sound bites are arrived at through a continual process of polling, focus groups, testing, and honing of the three or four key messages the consultants have determined will resonate best with the electorate; not the electorate in general, but, as I have already mentioned, with the candidate's base. Because, before you can run for office, you have to win your parties nomination through the primaries. This is a uniquely American experience, as far as I know, and if I am wrong, I'm sure someone will be kind enough to correct me. No other country has a political system where you spend a ton of money, exist on three hours of sleep a night for months, kiss dozens of snotfaced babies, and eat whatever strange ethnic food is shoved in your face, just to get the nomination that guarantees you will have to go through the whole debilitating experience all over again when you actually run for office.

This unique process means that anyone running for a major political office in the U.S. must raise humungous amounts of money, which puts them in debt to the people and organizations they raised the money from. That however, is the subject of another book, one which has already been written dozens of times. My concern is the reason why politicians need all this money. And that can be summed up in one word: television.

As recently as 2004, the presidential campaign, from the New Hampshire primary to the general election in November, was described by the *New York Times* as "the Eight Month Election." As I started to write this book in August of 2007, twelve people were competing for the Republican nomination and about the same number were chasing the Democratic prize. And, it seemed to me as if they'd been running since the War of Independence. Fifteen months out from the November elections, the money was already flowing like water. One of the candidates for the Republican nomination had just spent three million dollars, mostly on TV ads, to win the Iowa Straw Poll, which is not even a primary, but seems to be a unique occasion where a couple of hundred Iowans get together in a field and eat free food while casting a vote for one of the half dozen candidates who bothered to show up. That's right, Mitt Romney spent three million dollars to win this particular exercise in democracy, and so, you can you imagine what kind of money he spent on the real primaries. Romney is coincidentally, a multi-millionaire, as are a great many of the candidates of both parties. The days of someone rising "from paperboy to president" are long gone. In fact, current opinion from those in the know is that the Republican and Democratic contenders for the presidency will need to spend five hundred million dollars each by the time they're done, and if you factor in what the couple of dozen contenders for each party's nomination must have spent while chasing the nomination, the 2008 presidential election will have cost two billion dollars. And, as for the 2008 congressional campaigns, the mind boggles. Then consider that within weeks of taking office, all of these people will immediately be running hard for reelection in a few years. No wonder "the eight month campaign," has become "the permanent campaign!"

Political advertising through the extensive use of TV campaigns, actually serves as a perfect metaphor for what *The Ubiquitous Persuaders* is primarily concerned with. That advertising now costs an arm and a leg, there's altogether too much of it, and it's increasingly becoming less and less effective. Which is certainly true as far as political advertising is concerned. As many states are now bringing their primaries forward in order to be the first out of the blocks to influence the final choice of candidates, the campaign season has doubled from just four years ago, and certainly tripled from a dozen years ago. I sometimes wonder whatever happened to political conventions. Wasn't that where candidates were supposedly selected by a roll call of states? Or am I getting confused with smoke-filled rooms here? Either way, it has become patently obvious the conventions of both major parties have degenerated into little more than a flag waving occasion to energize the core constituency and reward the party faithful by giving them a photo-op with the anointed nominee. Then everyone goes home to work their arses off for the same opportunity four years hence.

In the upcoming 2008 presidential election (a month away as I write this), the victor will end up spending more than half a billion dollars, with the biggest chunk going on TV advertising. Some of these ads will be based on issues, but as I have said, the content will be little more than sound bites wordsmithed to appeal to the broadest consensus of the viewing audience; some will be centered on thinly veiled references to their opponent's character, or more often, lack of it. A great deal of it will focus on the opponents voting record if they were previously in the house or the senate. And, if they were a governor, it will reference their legislative record. All the facts will be spun to create maximum damage to the opponent, implying they are against Mum, apple pie, and the flag, which will be waved incessantly throughout the campaign season. Every candidate worth their salt will have the stars and stripes behind them, in front of them, dressing the podium, on their Web sites, on their motorcades, and on their lapels. This unabashed flaunting of the stars and stripes will take place while delivering their standard stump speech about protecting American jobs, whilst oblivious to the irony that virtually all of the flags they are using as theatrical props will have been made in China.

In addition to the hundreds of millions of dollars the candidates will spend, tens of millions more will be spent in the form of "soft money," which since the Bipartisan Campaign Reform Act (BRCA) of 2002, has been funneled through PACs for so-called "issue advocacy." And, because they are not officially part of the candidate's organization, they can spend, say, and do whatever the hell they want. This is why they are often responsible for the worst kind of attack advertising a candidate will claim they had nothing to do with. These groups are responsible for the "Swift Boating" of Kerry mentioned above. One, the Club for Growth, a conservative, anti-tax organization sponsored anti-Howard Dean TV ads that ran prior to the 2004 Iowa caucus showing an Iowa couple saying, "Dean should take his tax-hiking, government-expanding, latte-drinking, sushi-eating, Volvo-driving, *New York Times*-reading…body-piercing, Hollywood-loving, left-wing freak show back to Vermont, where it belongs." Another group was responsible for the campaign that unseated Max Cleland, a much decorated Vietnam veteran, who had lost both legs and an arm in combat. A vicious TV campaign compared Senator Cleland to Osama Bin Laden and Saddam Hussein and questioned his patriotism. He lost his seat in the senate to a guy who had sat out the Vietnam War with multiple deferments.

Interestingly, by law, these campaigns are not supposed to advocate the election of a candidate, or the defeat of an incumbent.

They are supposedly to deal only in issues. The Supreme Court has dictated these ads must not contain, what are known informally in political circles as the "magic words." In legalese, this means they should not express any form of outright partisanship. For example, *vote for; elect; support; cast your ballot for; Candidate X for Congress; vote against; defeat; and reject.* The Supreme Court stated that by not using these words of "express advocacy" the ad was not subject to regulation because it was simply an issue ad. Amazingly, the ads may explicitly target candidates and attack that candidate's policies, but as long as the creator of them stays away from the "magic words" they are not subject to the strict regulation an individual candidate's ads are.

As increasing amounts of money are poured into these "issue advocacy" ads, the content of them becomes ever more vicious, and candidates increasingly rely on them, the question has to be asked, does this prove negative advertising works? The answer is that sometimes it does. But this can also be claimed for more substantive ads which focus on issues, rather than personalities. There was a study done during the 1976 presidential campaign showing both the Nixon and McGovern TV commercials spent far more time discussing foreign policy, inflation, taxes, military spending and corruption in government than did all the network news channels combined. A study conducted twenty years later (1996) concluded that voters are more likely to remember a candidate's position on issues by watching TV commercials than by watching TV news. In addition, the study found that ads help voters evaluate candidates and decide who to vote for. "Although many political analysts denigrate political ads," the authors noted, "...we find that they likely contribute to accurate information about the issues, as well as active use of issues in candidate evaluations." In the same year, another study argued, as I have done earlier in this chapter, that most political advertising merely reinforces existing views, rarely changing the viewers mind, or entrenched beliefs. This is why Conservative talk radio is so effective. The vast majority of people, who listen to Rush Limbaugh, share his views. The chances of a liberal Democrat somehow tuning in to his program by mistake and an hour later being reborn as a rabid, conservative zealot are exactly zero.

The biggest single fault with most political advertising is that, with the exception of the attack ads, it is often generic and rarely takes a hard stance on a single issue. This is particularly true when presidential candidates have slogged their way through the primaries and succeeded in becoming the nominee of their party. Then, they can no longer afford to simply court their base, whether it be on the left or the right. Now, they have to find some kind of middle ground which will appeal to the party faithful, whilst at the same time hopefully reaching out to that Holy Grail of politics, the Independents and uncommitted. PACs and special interest groups, such as trade unions and environmental organizations can still produce ads specifically aimed at their constituents, but the nominees must be extremely careful not to come across to potential voters as ideologues. Further compounding the difficulty facing most people who run for office is the general disenchantment of the public with politicians in general. We constantly pride ourselves on our unequaled and hard fought for democracy, yet we consistently have the lowest voter turnouts for elections of any Western country.

At the time of writing, the President of the United States is at an approval rating well below 30 percent, while Congress is enjoying an all-time abysmal approval rating of 12 percent. Yet, as I have said, more money is being spent on political advertising than ever before. Advertising which will increasingly having little or no effect on the audience it's aimed at. In fact, because advertising is now so pervasive in our daily lives, it has become for most people nothing more than wallpaper and background noise. As I write this in the late summer of 2008, for more than the last two years, the population of the United States has been bombarded by incessant political advertising repetitiously hammering away at the same narrow palette of themes. All of which will have been covered ad nauseum on news broadcasts, talk shows and televised debates. Normally, I would expect this to result in the usual low voter turnout in the upcoming general election. But the signs are that this will not be so. Thanks to extensive voter registration programs by the Obama campaign, indications are that the 2008 elections will enjoy an unusual level of participation.

Another major concern to those who spend huge sums of money on political advertising is whether they are ahead of the competition, or playing catch up. In early 2007, at the beginning of the Democratic race for the party's nomination, even though early polls showed Hillary Clinton was in the lead, much was made of the fact that Barrack Obama was level pegging her in raising money. This was almost a full year out from the first primary, yet this news was splashed across the media as if it was a true test of who would be best qualified to lead the nation in two years time. And, in a way it was, because money buys air time, and lots of money buys lots of air time, and air time is expensive. Which is why you might be asking yourselves, why don't these candidates get smart and jump on the new media bandwagon? To which the answer is, they already have. Every candidate has an incredibly badly designed Web site; some even have MySpace or Facebook pages. All come complete with the requisite flags and bunting. The really adventurous ones go viral with videos on YouTube. The problem is most of these sites, blogs, and videos are pathetic attempts at being cool, leaving the overwhelmingly young and increasingly cynical new media audience wondering what these old farts think they're playing at. The virals that get the biggest audiences and consequent PR benefits from the mainstream media, are the spoofs, such as the "Hillary 1984" video, or "Obama Girl" and its feeble "Giuliani Girl" rip off. Plus, it's worth considering many of the young people who are the most prolific users of new media are those least likely to vote. On the other hand, if there's one section of society guaranteed to get out, come rain or shine, and cast their vote, it's the old geezers who will watch your TV campaign as it runs alongside the "laxative with stool softener" ads on primetime news, or while nurturing a cup of hot chocolate watching reruns of *The Lawrence Welk Show* on late night TV. The consultants know this. It's why they plow so much money into network and cable TV. Traditionally, the people guaranteed most likely to go out and vote on a cold and blustery November day are the one's who watch, and get their news, entertainment and information from TV, not from an iPod. However, there are strong indications that in 2008, it just might be different.

Much of the above reinforces what I have emphasized throughout this book. The advertising business is conservative by nature, and with virtually all major agencies now belonging to one or other of the conglomerates, it is becoming even more conservative. Compounding this situation is the fact that virtually all political advertising is now produced by political consultants, who may be independent, or be part of an agency specializing in handling only political and advocacy accounts. The days when Doyle, Dane, Bernbach produced the memorable campaign for Johnson in the early sixties are long gone. What we have now is formulaic advertising based on rigidly tested and wordsmithed concepts that hammer away at one or two points the consultants have decided will have the most effect on the target audience. Most of the TV spots are either archived video clips of the candidate delivering a twenty second version of his/her two-minute-stump speech, clips of the candidate's opponent with running titles showing how he/she voted to bring back slavery, or increase taxes by 2,000 percent, or fake "concerned citizens" discussing how the candidate's opponent will vote for "socialized medicine," which means they'll have to wait ten years for their Botox injections and boob jobs. As with most forms of advertising, I am continually amazed how many agencies and their clients, or in this case politicians and their consultants, seem to go to extraordinary lengths to create advertising that's a carbon copy of what their competition is running. Which means it's nothing more than a carbon copy of really shitty advertising.

But, in truth, very few regular ad agencies now seek the accounts of political candidates, as they are usually the most difficult clients you could possibly wish to deal with. Apart from the fact that you have to work with, and get sign offs, from just about everyone on their staff, 99 percent of the people who run for major public office are insufferable, raging egomaniacs. I mean think about it, why would anyone who wasn't full of their own self-importance want to put themselves, and their family, through the rigors of years of campaigning. Political ads also require ridiculous turn around times for TV and print ads, particularly when the candidate you are unfortunate enough to be working for needs an immediate response to some ad their opponent has just run. But perhaps one of the major reasons mainstream agencies shy away from political accounts is that if the candidate you are working for fails to win the election, there's a pretty good chance, you're not going to get paid. This is why virtually all media companies who run political advertising expect to get paid upfront; otherwise, they won't run the ad.

And so, a final story on the vagaries of political advertising. When I started writing this book, one of the front runners for the 2008 Republican presidential nomination was Rudy Giuliani, the ex mayor of New York, who since 9/11 has milked every possible association with New York and his record as mayor of that city. From curbing crime, to lowering taxes, to his crowning glory on September 11, 2001 when he became known in the national press as "America's mayor." While stomping the country on his quest for the nomination, he took every opportunity to remind his audience of everything he has done for New York City and how proud he was to have had the stewardship of that great city. So, what did he do when it came time to pick his high powered ad team to manage his multimillion dollar advertising effort? You would expect an agency located on or near Madison Avenue, New York City, the very epicenter of the advertising world, right? Wrong! America's mayor decided he wanted to work with the usual collection of Republican consultant, attack-dog agencies, based in Dallas, Philadelphia, Pittsburgh, and Virginia. The same slime merchants who threw advertising, ripe with racial and sexual innuendos at African American Democratic senate candidate Harold Ford Jr. when he ran in 2006. But, I guess I shouldn't be surprised that Rudy is speaking out of both sides of his mouth. What else can you expect from a guy who claims he spent more time at ground zero than the police and firefighters? Yet according to a recent article in the *New York Times*, apparently during that period, he actually spent twice as much time attending Yankees baseball games. On top of that, he's a politician. Which is probably the ugliest thing you can say about anyone, short of accusing them of being a used car salesman, or working in advertising.

When I started writing this particular chapter (early 2008) we'd just had the Iowa Caucus. An event about which, I have to be honest with you, I'm not quite sure I understand what the hell was going on there. Being a Brit originally, American political primaries in general are hard enough for me to understand, but caucuses obviously belong in the Bermuda Triangle or Area 51 in New Mexico. Anyway, moving on. The most amazing thing is that a few hundred thousand people, which is a small percentage of Iowans, and is actually overshadowed by the multitudes of media people that had been camped out in Iowa for months, spend hours in cold schoolrooms or abandoned mine shafts deciding who they want to represent them as their Democratic or Republican party nominee. Prior to the event, the amount of money spent on advertising to influence these three hundred thousand people or so is staggering. Close to fifty million dollars on TV alone, throw in radio, print, billboards, and the odd guy in a gorilla suit and you're talking serious money here. As I mentioned earlier, Republican, Mitt Romney, who ended up a poor second, outspent the winner, Mike Huckabee by a ratio of more than ten to one. Obama won on the Democratic side, after spending a ton of money, but Hillary Clinton, who weeks before the event, seemed to be coasting to victory, was pushed into third place by John Edwards, who she had massively outspent. All of which goes to prove one of the oldest truisms in the business. You can spend a fortune and advertise your brains out, but if people don't like what you are selling them, or the way you are doing it. It won't do you any good.

And as I stress throughout this book, when advertising becomes ubiquitous, particularly when its purpose is to get you to vote for some bozo you know won't give you the time of the day once they've been elected, it becomes a waste of time, effort, and money. And invariably, that means lots and lots of money.

chapter TWELVE.

GREEN is
GOOD

To paraphrase the immortal words of Gordon Gecko in the movie, Wall Street, Green is good, really good to Madison Avenue these days. The Adverati have climbed aboard the environmental band wagon with a vengeance. Whether it's on behalf of PCB dumping toxic polluters, miners leaching cyanide into once pristine mountain streams, or Big Oil claiming to be guardians of the planets future... We can save it together. Providing you have an ad budget big enough!

As I've pointed out in previous chapters, after the decline of cigarette and booze advertising, the Adverati were saved by the boom in IT advertising. Then the dot com explosion happened, and everyone was convinced they could become instant millionaires flogging dog food over the Internet. Finally, the manna delivered from heaven which would allow them to continually suck on the giant, never-to-run-dry teat of healthcare, health insurance, and DTC drug advertising; 99 percent of which is still hammering away at the increasingly fatigued brain cells of the American consumer, even though there have recently been hints that as far as the DTC advertising of drugs is concerned, some form of control may be introduced to temper its more egregious forms. But rest assured armies of lobbyists and their always open coffers will make sure Washington, irrespective of which party is in power, will continue to look favorably on their efforts. However, just in case there may be some cutbacks, Madison Avenue in its never-ceasing concern for the well being of the American consumer, has already jumped on the next bandwagon. Namely, saving planet Earth by encouraging us all to go "green," and shrink our "carbon footprint." Oh yes, that's just what we need, a bunch of corporate spokes-hacks telling us what we should do to save the planet, which is a touch ironic, when you consider they represent the same people who've been despoiling the planet and bloating their bottom line since man discovered fire and invented the wheel! In fact, they're probably pursuing intellectual property claims on behalf of the "Acme Fire & Wheel Company" in federal court right now.

It's somewhat funny that terms such as "green, carbon footprint, Organic, biodegradable" and many others, after wandering around on the semi-lunatic fringes of corporate America for years, have now developed an, I can be holier than thou, strident life of their own. To the point were it is becoming impossible to escape them on TV, in the newspapers, on the Internet, and increasingly in advertising. Whether it's the latest "Save the wolves" campaign on behalf of McDonalds "WolfBurgers," or Exxon claiming they are all about clean shell fish and fresh salmon, in spite of their multibillion dollar oil spill many years ago in Alaska. The consequences of which they have fought in the courts for years in a successful effort to reduce the damages awarded from billions of dollars to mere millions. Now, of course, Exxon is claiming they are, cross my heart and hope to die, an environmentally conscious company, swearing on their honor they will never fuck up again and be true custodians of the environment, for ever and ever. Or at least, until the next time they do.

It's a fact that in 2007, U.S. companies and the people who shop with them spent fifty-four million dollars on carbon offset credits. It's also a fact that very few people have any idea where a substantial portion of that money actually went. Major corporations such as Dell, Continental Airlines, and Volkswagen initiated various offset programs, but they handed them off to other companies to be run and administered. Many of these programs promise to plant trees in remote parts of the country, yet rarely are the exact locations and results of these efforts revealed. In fact, there is no general consensus over the effect tree planting has on the reduction of carbon dioxide in the atmosphere. But as I have said so many times, "Perception is reality."

For anyone who's ever lived and worked in New York, a severe case of firmly planting one's tongue in one's cheek has to be the campaign the New York Metropolitan Transportation Authority is currently running under the somewhat confusing umbrella slogan of "Ecolution." This is obviously, something a bunch of twenty year old agency creatives and overly-precious, uber-planners came up with late one night after a Peruvian marching powder, Grey Goose fuelled, "let's just fucking wing it," creative gang bang. The essential message of this pathetic tour de force is that the unfortunate riders of the subway should be congratulated for doing their part in reducing their carbon footprint by sitting or standing in a noisy, sweaty, smelly and crowded seventh circle of Hell, mode of transport. What the Adverati, as usual, seems to have misunderstood, is that the majority of New York subway riders have little choice other than this mode of transport. Unlike the people who created this campaign, they are not in the fortunate position of stroking their company paid for, cool iPhone, and summoning up a limo to drive them from their Soho loft to their Mies Van Der Roe furnished, twenty-fourth floor office in midtown Manhattan. No, the unfortunates riding the subway are people getting paid pathetic amounts of money to work long hours in a pizza joint, or deal with a bunch of drunks or overdosed crazies in the ER of a Manhattan hospital at two in the morning. But, as I have pointed out in my books, blogs, and magazine articles over the years, the most egregious and unforgivable sin repeatedly committed by most of the Adverati is that they have completely lost touch with the people they are paid obscene amounts of money to communicate with.

With the "greening" of Madison Avenue, even the arch villain of retailing has jumped on the bandwagon. Wal-Mart has recently announced it would be asking all its suppliers to not only lower their carbon footprints, but also offer some kind of guarantee they would maintain these practices in the future. To ensure this commitment is adhered to, and that "greenness" will be one of its guiding principles while selling really cheap and nasty Chinese manufactured plastic tchotchkes that will live forever in the nation's landfills, they have created a middle management position with the rather grandiose title of sustainability officer. The lucky holder of this title will be henceforth known as the senior VP of sustainability. The fact that this particular department is running lean, with less than ten people reporting directly to the Obersturmbannfuerer der Grün will not deter Wal-Mart's spokes-hacks from announcing they are irrevocably committed to reducing their carbon footprint. No doubt the billionaire members of the Walton family share the same values and goals as they sit in their 50,000 square foot, centrally air conditioned, Arkansas mansions.

Even BP, one of the world's largest petroleum companies, now features a carbon footprint calculator on the home page of its Web site, side by side with links that will allow you to read about why they consider "Global Warming" to be nothing more than some kind of communist plot to destroy the free enterprise system that has made America what it is today. Although I have a nasty suspicion that by the time this book is published, they may want to rethink that particular hypothesis.

Some companies even invent an "environmentally safe" seal of approval for their own products. S.C. Johnson and company, one of the world's largest manufacturers of highly toxic cleaning products has introduced, and features heavily in their advertising, their "Greenlist" label, which appears on everything from Windex window cleaner, to Raid insecticide, to Scrubbing Bubbles bathroom cleaner. As their Web site claims, "When you pick up any S.C. Johnson product, you can trust that the raw materials have been evaluated for health, safety and environmental impact through our Greenlist process." What they don't tell you is that the evaluations are made by

S.C. Johnson employees working in S.C. Johnson laboratories. So, in effect, when you see a Greenlist label on an S.C. Johnson product, there is absolutely no independent corroboration about whether or not it might do you and the environment harm. As one critic put it so well, "S.C. Johnson seems to think that by making harmful products slightly less harmful, they magically become healthy."

General Electric recently joined the "guardians of the earth" chorus, and because for many years this has been one of the most famous and most trusted U.S. companies, enjoying a reputation for high standards of ethical and financial performance, along with an ability to deliver bumper returns to investors, it soon became a flag bearer for the greening of corporate America. It should be noted that a great part of General Electric's prior reputation was due to Wall Street's unstinting love affair with the company's former chief executive, Jack Welsh, otherwise known as "Neutron Jack." A "nom de guerre" earned because this was the guy who never failed to deliver generous quarterly numbers that met or exceeded analyst's expectations, thanks to his unfailing ability to jump through hoops delivering results, which he seemed able to pull out of his arse if necessary, quarter after quarter. Wall Street seemingly didn't pay much heed to the fact that one of the ways he was able to consistently make these numbers was his propensity to lay off 10 percent of GE's workforce, annually. Even when he dumped his wife of many years to take up with a much younger lady from *Harvard Business Press* few blinked. After all, this is little more than standard practice for captains of industry when they have reached a certain stage in their careers and the shine has gone off acquiring yet another yacht. And if you have enough loot stashed offshore you can make sure the "ex" goes quietly with a few million and the ski lodge in Aspen. Unfortunately for "Neutron Jack" the "ex" refused to go quietly, demanding a more than hefty share of the loot. So, things turned nasty and thanks to the wonders of the "blogosphere" and the "ex's" army of divorce lawyers, it turned out that GE shareholders had not only been footing the bill for "Neutron Jack's" potentate-like lifestyle for years, the board of directors (many of whom had been recommended by him) had signed off on a huge retirement package for Welsh that had all the many perks he'd been enjoying while running GE. These included the unlimited use of company jets, limos, several country club memberships, box seats at the Met, Knicks, Shea, Yankees, Olympics etc., a Central Park West apartment complete with chef and housekeeper that, even though he only stayed in it a few nights a month, had a monthly flower bill that ran into thousands of dollars. And get this; the retirement package even included free vitamins! Still, I guess when your new wife is half your age; it's more than possible they consider Viagra to be an essential vitamin.

Anyway, "Neutron Jack's" successor, Jeffrey Immelt, decided it was time to steer the ship in a different direction after years of being top of the environmentalists' most-hated list. In 2005 the company launched a multimillion dollar TV campaign titled, "Ecomagination." Thanks to the wonders of CGI (computer graphics) and seemingly unlimited amounts of cash for their agency, BBDO, to play with, we were treated to elephants dancing through the jungle to the strains of "Singin in the Rain," with a tag line, "Technology that's right in step with nature." Another spot sported hard-hat-wearing, hard-bodied models in a coal mine wielding pick axes to the accompaniment of Merle Travis' "Sixteen Tons." The tag line for this particular epic was, "Harnessing the power of coal is looking more beautiful every day." I don't know how successful the program was, but within a year it was replaced by a new campaign sporting the theme, "Imagination." The "eco" lives on as part of GE's Web site, but it seems to have dropped out of the mainstream advertising. You can however, sign up for a General Electric platinum credit card, which, instead of offering the usual cash back or frequent flyer miles, promises to help consumers fight global warming. Even though it's described as Platinum, the card is only available in shades of green. That should help your carbon footprint while you're destroying your bank account.

It's no surprise then that in a recent study seven in ten Americans either strongly or somewhat agree that when companies call a product green, implying it's better for the environment, they know that it's more often than not, just a marketing tactic. No wonder consumers are becoming increasingly wary of companies who label their products as green or environmentally friendly without offering any real proof as to the validity of the claim. This whole emphasis by companies in the marketing of products and services as green is described by environmental activists as "greenwashing." Or, as a writer on design and architecture put it so well, "Has green advertising nuked the fridge with its pervasive imagery and feel good message?" It would seem so, to the point were the Federal Trade Commission even has a page on its consumer protection section titled, "Sorting out Green" advertising claims. Unfortunately, when the government gets involved, you know it's almost too late to do anything about it.

In addition to every BDA claiming to have drunk the green Kool-Aid, there are now an ever increasing number of specialist green marketing consultants and advertising agencies, all swearing to be dedicated to increasing their client's profits while recreating the Garden of Eden. One such company is GreenOrder, a marketing consultancy that according to its Web site, which is suitably covered in images of blue skies, crystal clear water, and green forests, has "a diverse, proven expertise in business strategy, environmental science, and marketing that allows us to produce results that are credible and compelling for the broadest range of internal and external stakeholders." Too bad they can't do something about "greening" their boilerplate corporate speak, which to my mind is responsible for as much pollution as any companies ever expanding carbon footprint. Interestingly enough, their impressive client list of some of the world's major historical polluters, includes General Electric, for which they claim to have played a key role in developing "GE's groundbreaking, multibillion dollar Ecomagination initiative, providing high-level strategy, conducting in-depth empirical analysis of products and their environmental benefits, and advising on marketing and communications." Well, that certainly sounds impressive, until you realize that in common with most other highly publicized corporate programs aimed at cutting greenhouse gases to a certain percentage by a specified target date, these reductions are based on current levels of pollution, rather than the increased levels expected in the years ahead. So, even if the programs are 100 percent successful, they will do little more than maintain current levels of pollution. As for trading carbon credits, I confess to being completely baffled by a scheme that apparently allows major polluters of the atmosphere to continue their evil ways if they simply buy credits from companies that pollute less. But then again, I never understood what Enron was about, either!

Even the direct mail industry is jumping on the green bandwagon, with the Direct Marketing Association (DMA) featuring an Environmental Resource Center on their Web site that talks about their "Green 15" environmental protection program. But, not satisfied with that, a group of direct marketing agencies and their clients have formed yet another industry group, the Green Marketing Coalition, offering its members a series of best-practices guidelines in an effort to give the impression that an inherently unsustainable business model is actually socially conscious. Which when you consider the millions of trees destined to end up in your mail box as junk mail, is a yet another wonderful example of Greenwashing. The United States Postal Service is also getting in on the act and has trademarked the name "environMAIList" as part of a program that encourages direct marketers to become more eco-friendly. As you would expect, the USPS Web site proudly displays a green mission statement: "As one of the nation's leading corporate citizens, the U.S. Postal Service is committed to environmental stewardship. USPS empowers consumers to "go green" through a comprehensive approach to mail production, delivery and recycling that enhances sustainability, meeting the needs of the present without compromising the future." There must be a PowerPoint template somewhere for a mission statement that comes with the obligatory words, "committed, empowers, enhances, and stewardship." Doubtless, it was created by an MBA.

But neither the Green Marketing Coalition, nor the USPS have actually set definite goals or timetables for their respective initiatives, or as Todd J. Paglia, executive director of ForestEthics, an activist group for the protection of forests puts it so well, "The idea of greening junk mail is a bit like putting lipstick on a pig!" (With apologies to a certain Northern governor, there.) And when you consider that discarded direct mail comprises nearly 3 percent of the garbage in our rapidly filling landfills, you have to hope that one day it will be entirely delivered in a digital format. Which unfortunately means that on top of all those e-mails from Nigerian bank managers anxious to deposit millions of dollars in your bank account, you can look forward to even more exciting offers for flushing twenty pounds of unimaginable detritus out of your colon, and how to save 50 percent on the price of your next hearing aid. All I can say is, you'd better invest in a mainframe sized storage drive for your computer.

At the time of writing, the shrinking economy, and the thought that America's motorists are ready to storm Washington because they are being forced to pay for gas almost 50 percent of what European drivers have been paying for years, is certainly having an effect on the population's perception of what is environmentally acceptable in terms of transportation. Hence the move towards smaller, more fuel efficient vehicles, plus the increasing use of public transport, discounting of course, the unfortunate "Ecolutioneers" who have little choice but to ride the New York subway. And it goes without saying that if the price of gas should drop back to more acceptable levels; everyone would soon be back in their monster trucks and SUVs. The decline in the economy is also starting to have an effect on the organic and sustainable food industry, whose flagship success story has been the rise and dominance of Whole Foods Inc. A seven billion dollar chain of supermarkets that has built its business on a "price no object" platform of offering only the finest and freshest in groceries and produce. This has led to the somewhat derogatory moniker "Whole Paycheck." A description well deserved, as I have personally stood behind people at the Whole Foods checkout who have willingly spent obscene amounts of money on Albanian hand-milled pretzels and Mongolian Yak cheese. If you really need to know, I was there for the Transylvanian organic beer.

In spite of the benevolence of its stated mission of bringing the finest and most wholesome foods to American consumers, the same cannot be said for Whole Food's aggressive attitude towards its competitors. They scored a major coup in 2007 by acquiring their largest rival, Wild Oats, for 565 million dollars after allegedly pricing the smaller company out of the organic-food business. One of the stranger aspects of this takeover came to light when it was revealed that Whole Food's founder and CEO, John Mackey, had posted numerous weird and Pollyannaish messages on a Yahoo financial forum under the username "rahodeb." All of these were extremely positive in the way they painted a very bright future for the Whole Foods organization, while downplaying the threat posed by competitors. There was much talk that Mackey may have violated the law in his postings, thereby raising several thorny legal questions. As a result of this the SEC began an examination of whether Mackey had contradicted what the company had previously said about the current state of the business, and was making overly optimistic posts about the firm's financial performance. But, to be fair, in early 2008, Mackey was cleared of all charges; however, there's no question, it's left an unfortunate impression of the CEO of a company who over the years has gone out of his way to publicly declare, market, and advertise the company as a fair, conscientious, and environmentally sensitive business. Anyway, with a certain amount of poetic justice, it would seem that the rapidly shrinking economy is kicking the crap out of Mackey's rosy forecasts. Most analysts had been expecting growth of up to 30 percent in fiscal 2008. In reality in the third quarter of 2008 the company reported profits of $33.9 million, a 31 percent decline from the previous year. Sales growth at stores open more than one year slowed to 2.6 percent, down from 6.7 percent, the lowest in the company's history. It also plans to reduce the number of new store openings (which has been on an aggressive pace for years) by nearly 50 percent and suspend its twenty cent quarterly dividend. They further suggested that 2009 revenue growth would be down to 6–10 percent. And you can probably take that optimism with a grain of organic salt.

However, The National Marketing Institute is still estimating that consumers with environmental concerns represent more than 230 billion dollars in spending power at the time of writing in the second half of 2008. The problem with this rosy outlook is that it presupposes consumer incomes will remain at present levels. If, as seems likely, with the present and future state of the economy, they shrink, there will obviously be a move to less esoteric and costly foodstuffs and everyday household items. Overlay this with the results of a recent survey of more than six thousand adult Web users, who when asked, almost half recalled seeing ads that had some kind of green or environmental protection claim. Yet even though they could recall the ads, they didn't feel inclined to trust them. Twenty percent never believed these claims, while 60 percent say they sometimes believed them. In another study, two thirds of the respondents claimed to understand what was meant by green advertising. Yet, upon further questioning, it turned out that only one in five understood that the use of the term green usually means less harmful than before rather than positively good for the planet.

This inevitably reinforces the commonly held perception that many companies and their ad agencies are engaged in greenwashing. Environmental activists are more than ready to leap on any suggestion that companies are purposely fudging the gap between consumer expectations and company manipulation, and with the instant communication achievable through the Internet, virtually all of these activists can immediately share information online about the environmental impact of a particular product and the advertising created to support it.

So, now we have the ultimate catch twenty-two situation where the giant food/drug/energy corporations unfailingly stress their devotion to protecting the environment and reducing their carbon footprint. They also claim not to exploit the indigenous people they employ at subsistence wages in the sweatshops where the goods are made that they eventually sell on Fifth Avenue, or Bond Street, or Rodeo Drive, for a 10,000 percent mark-up. Yet, because of the tightening economy, the majority of consumers, even if they are truly concerned about being environmentally conscious when it comes to their purchases, are driven to buy products that by no stretch of the imagination can be considered as environmentally friendly.

Meantime, the Adverati of Madison Avenue is jumping on the bandwagon of "green" as fast as their gold snaffled Gucci slip-ons will allow. The problem is that when you read about their various efforts, it all comes out as the same mind-numbing, corporate bullshit we've heard over the years regarding their past efforts to be regarded as champions of equal rights, openness, accountability, or whatever happens to be the politically correct movement of the moment. In fact, most ad agencies seem more committed to reducing their own, individual carbon footprint rather than jeopardizing existing client relationships by suggesting they might be ready to do something about theirs. This is a pity, when you consider agencies actually have an opportunity to influence their clients to do something with their advertising which might actually make a difference. Having said that, I'm the first to own up to the seldom acknowledged fact that the vast majority of advertising makes not a scintilla of difference to most people exposed to it. But, wouldn't it be nice if they at least made the effort?

Interestingly, in a recent "Green Marketing 2008" feature in *AdAge*, twenty-one agencies were profiled concerning their efforts to help clients improve the environment. As expected, all stressed their commitment to working with companies to further their green initiatives and sustainability programs. But, I have to admit that after reading the piece, I was not surprised to discover that the ecco-conscious efforts of the vast majority of these agencies, fifteen out of the twenty-one, seemed to be concentrated on making themselves appear to be "green," rather than the clients they were representing. Their pathetic efforts ran the gamut from the recycling of paper and glass, green cleaners for the floor and windows (no doubt carrying the S.C. Johnson Greenlist label) issuing bagless vacuum cleaners to the janitorial staff, and making sure that any left over pizza and other junk food remaining in the morning after pulling an all-night creative gang bang, gets donated to homeless and senior programs. As expected, they all have energy conservation programs, which include the obligatory replacement of incandescent light bulbs with the fluorescent ones guaranteed to make you look like The Joker in a Batman movie, turning off the lights and air conditioning in rooms not in use, and switching off computers over the weekend. I know that every little bit counts, but it seems to me this is a rather pathetic list of "green" initiatives from some of the major advertising agencies in America.

There are, however, a couple of notable agency exceptions who are attempting to change attitudes amongst consumers regarding sustainability issues on a global scale:

Leo Burnet Worldwide: Instituted a global program for the World Wildlife Campaign to increase awareness of global warming, it kicked off with an event in Australia on the last Saturday in March, 2007, called Earth Hour. Expanded globally in 2008, it asked households and businesses to turn off non-essential lights and electrical appliances for one hour to raise understanding of the need to take action on climate change. Many major cities throughout the world took part, and even Google's home page used a black background from midday on March 29, 2008 until the end of Earth Hour. The tagline on the page read, "We've turned the lights out. Now it's your turn - Earth Hour."

Droga5: These guys came up with a totally unique, in fact, a revolutionary way of tapping into both the consciousness, and conscience of people in virtually every state in America for a program to run during Unicef's World Water Week aimed at bringing potable, disease free water to millions of children in less fortunate parts of the world. Called the "Tap Project," it's based on a very simple premise. When you go out to eat at a participating restaurant (and over 2,350 have signed up so far), you agree to donate to the program a minimum of one dollar for the tap water the restaurant normally provides you for free. As Droga5 says in some of the materials they have created for the "Tap Project." For every dollar raised, a child in need will have forty days of clean drinking water. Droga5 then asked other agencies across America, including large mainstream shops, such as Saatchi & Saatchi, Hill Holliday and Goodby, Silverstein & Partners to volunteer and create city-centric creative campaigns to promote World Water Week. The whole "Tap Project" was a truly remarkable idea, in that it took what had always been perceived as a free, readily available commodity that most people never gave a second thought to, and turn it into a global brand. Even better, it encouraged consumers to donate to a worthwhile cause, while thinking better of themselves.

Unfortunately, I am driven to the conclusion that with the exception of the couple of examples quoted above, many agencies institute green programs which are little more than greenwashing programs, because, as I said at the beginning of this chapter, the Adverati have climbed aboard the environmental band wagon with a vengeance. They even go so far as to head up their programs and initiatives with middle management hacks, who luxuriate under such exalted titles as, chief sustainability officer, or the even more grandiose, vice president, global sustainability. After all, we are trying to save the entire planet here! Presumably, when the bottom drops out of green marketing (or the funds dry up) the ad biz will find the next bandwagon to jump on. They always have.

Perhaps it's been put best in the words of my favorite *New York Times* editorial observer, Verlyn Klinkenberg: "The two things we do most instinctively are manipulating language and creating markets, and these two instincts converge when it comes to carbon footprints. Creating a market in moral carbon. (I love that, why the hell couldn't I have come up with that brilliant descriptor? Moral Carbon, indeed!) Offsets that counter our energy-rich life style, which feels a little like Rotisserie baseball. Which is more illusion than reality."

Perhaps that's why I continue to despair at the way the ad biz never fails to revert to its bad habits, particularly in terms of the way it seizes every chance to address major societal and humanitarian problems as yet one more opportunity to suck on the teat of corporate America, whilst at the same time piously shrouding itself in some kind of holy cloak representation of itself as a concerned citizen of the world. But then again, who am I kidding here. Why would I expect it to ever change for the better?

chapter THIRTEEN. *my, but those*

METEORS
ARE PRETTY

Just as millions of years ago the dinosaurs gazed in awe at the meteors rushing towards them, today's big dumb advertising agencies talk up a storm about new opportunities yet blithely ignore new dangers. All are convinced they can reinvent themselves. So, what kind of advertising can we expect when celebrating the fiftieth anniversary of The Ubiquitous Persuaders? Will the practitioners of the world's second oldest profession have steered the Exxon Valdez of Madison Avenue away from the rocks of irrelevancy?

Fifty years ago, Vance Packard finished *The Hidden Persuaders* with a chapter discussing the morality of the methods used by the practitioners of advertising he'd investigated and discussed throughout the book. Standing atop his soapbox he warned society to beware of the way "so many powerfully influential people were taking such a manipulative attitude towards our society." These persuaders, as he called them, shared an attitude that man existed to be manipulated.

Remember, he is making these claims in 1957 when the American public was exposed to a fraction of the advertising they are now. You have to wonder what he would think of the nonstop, ever increasing bombardment of ads consumers face today. Yet even then he hinted that the public was already becoming skeptical enough of advertising that their psyche was not being damaged by its various assaults. He did caution though, this was a major reason why "Ad Men" (the great majority of "Ad Women" in those days, typed letters, brought coffee, and made sure their charges were sober enough to get the 5.27 back to Chappaquiddick after their three martini lunches,) were turning to subconscious appeals because they wanted to bypass our conscious guard. Enter Dr. Dichter and his dark army of mind manipulators, who through the use of their insidious Freudian methods, claimed they were able to convince women that the cigarette they were lasciviously flaunting over their evening cocktail or three, was indeed a penis.

These arguments continue today, not so much about your cigarette being a substitute penis, but about the morality of advertising in general. In earlier chapters, I've touched on this, particularly with reference to advertising aimed at children, or the bonanza healthcare and prescription drug advertising has brought to both the media and ad agencies in the last ten years at the expense of the general public's peace of mind and pocketbook. But in reality, most people would recognize the futility of arguing about the worth or value of any kind of advertising, because it's a subject which can never be resolved, particularly if you choose to live in a capitalist society. After all, the only way you could achieve 100 percent morally correct advertising would be through the institution of some form of draconian regulation, or by completely banning it. However, I hasten to add, questioning the morality or ethics of advertisers and their ad agencies is not really what The Ubiquitous Persuaders is about. All I am endeavoring to do is give an overview of where advertising was fifty years ago, where is today, and hopefully, some insights into where it might end up in the future. And rest assured, I would not presume to forecast the state of the advertising business fifty years from now. With its continuing state of flux, five years or so is ambitious enough.

There is no question that with a combination of the growth of new media, and the conglomeratization of the major agencies into one or other of the four largest holding companies, the business will never again resemble that which Vance Packard wrote about fifty years ago. Reinforcing this will be the increasing ability of consumers to screen out the ever-growing amounts of advertising being directed at them throughout their waking hours. Although I'm sure that one day advertising will have finally become a 24-7-365 nonstop, wallpaper operation, as some clever bugger will have come up with a way to get at you in the middle of your sleep to inform you of the benefits of their revolutionary new drug/credit card/weight-loss aid/whatever.

And yet, most agencies are still reluctant to accept that advertising is merely another form of communication through which we expect consumers to be influenced to change their purchasing preferences after learning the supposedly superior benefits of whatever it is that's being offered. Unfortunately, most advertisers and their agencies seem incapable of realizing the stunningly obvious fact that virtually everyone filters everything they see and hear, then chooses to ignore those parts that don't excite, enthuse, inform, or have relevance to them. This ultimately determines the effectiveness of any advertising, whatever shape or form it is dished up in, irrespective of the medium used to deliver it. And yes, even though I have likened Big Dumb Agencies to the dinosaurs standing up to their armpits in ooze admiring the meteors that were about to destroy them, this unflattering description of the current state of affairs, can equally be applied to many Big Dumb Clients.

We are increasingly hearing that many advertisers are waking up to the realization they may no longer be well advised to shovel all their marketing dollars into a single agency, even if it purports to offer every kind and combination of communication and marketing skills. More and more are considering they might, in fact, be better served shopping around for individual specialist companies with proven expertise in the areas of digital, guerilla, word-of-mouth, viral, or whatever happens to be the marketing flavor of the month. And yet, the irony of this state of affairs is that if they follow through on this suggestion, because the conglomerates are buying up specialist companies at a frenzied rate, most of these advertisers will still end up putting all their eggs in the Omnicom, WPP, IPG, and Publicis baskets. Meaning they will still be locked into a relationship that on the agency side continues to demand the quarterly reporting, make the numbers, keep the shareholders and analysts happy attitude, which has served their clients so badly in the past. But to paraphrase someone much wiser than I, the majority of Big Dumb Clients are destined to ignore the lessons of history.

For years studies conducted on behalf of the Association of National Advertisers have presented evidence that, yes, if you pump enough money into it, advertising can increase short term sales, but it does absolutely nothing to boost long term market share or profits. Yet this is exactly the drum the Big Dumb Agencies continue to beat when persuading their clients to invest umpteen millions of dollars into such esoteric exercises as brand creation, or delivering brand value, or 360 degree branding, or whatever the particular brand cliché of the month is. As I've discussed in previous books, there are many factors that can contribute to successful marketing, from pricing, distribution, promotion, beefing up the sales force, even giving the delivery trucks a new coat of paint, which inescapably leads you to the conclusion that advertising might often be the least effective, and certainly the least quantifiable part of most marketing programs. Yet, here we are on the threshold of the third millennium, and we still haven't the faintest glimmer of an idea of what works and what does not. As I have said before, it's no different from screenwriter William Goldman's wonderful definition of movie making, "In Hollywood, nobody knows anything." I sincerely believe this also applies to Madison Avenue!

And yet, the advertising profession continues to claim that because it has some kind of Ouija board, or Magic 8 ball, it is able to see where we shall be in the future. At the beginning of 2007, the Institute of Practitioners in Advertising (IPA), which is the UK equivalent of the American Association of Advertising Agencies, published a sixty-page study, titled *The Future of Advertising and Agencies*, which claimed to answer the following five questions:

1. What will advertising mean in 2016?

2. How big will the advertising market be?

3. How will the competitive set change?

4. What will agencies look like?

5. How will agencies be paid?

Even I wouldn't have the temerity to suggest I have the faintest idea where the ad biz will be in ten years, yet the IPA, in conjunction with "The Future Foundation," a think tank sporting one of the more grandiose names I've heard in quite a while, will slip you this sixty-page report for a mere six hundred dollars. That works out to exactly ten dollars a page, and, I'll guarantee they will be filled with the same stultifyingly boring PowerPoint charts and bullet point summaries you always find in these so-called "studies." Even worse, I'm sure it will make soporific generalizations you could have come up with after an hour in the pub, and for the price of a couple of pints, let alone six hundred dollars. And no, I haven't read it, but I did sneak a look at a couple of reviews and was not surprised to read *"The report indicates that by 2016 traditional advertising will shrink at the expense of consumer-influenced content and brand–influenced editorial so agencies will need to both innovate and evolve into new territory. New freedoms in the delivery of content, data and channels will provide new business opportunities whilst still maintaining the overriding focus on brand creation and development."* Well, if you think I'm going to shell out six hundred dollars for boilerplate bullshit like that, you definitely owe me the price of a couple of pints.

The problem I have with all these pundits and pontificators is that they never stop talking about where they think we shall be in the future, and how, by following their advice, we'll be able to prepare ourselves to work and prosper in this new world. I was recently asked to review a book which claimed to educate the reader into discerning, what was "cool," thereby enabling them to identify future trends and shifts in consumer attitudes. But anyone with a modicum of intelligence realizes that the whole premise of such a book is total crap, because by the time you've read it in a book, it's no longer "cool," and it has certainly ceased to be a trend. Few of these advertising and marketing experts actually address the serious problems the ad industry is facing right now, most of which are due to the dramatic changes brought about by the growth of new media and the increasing stranglehold of the conglomerates. Not to mention the amazing hubris Madison Avenue has suffered from for many years in continuing to believe the good times would roll forever. With new media offering advertisers a growing choice of inexpensive ways to reach consumers, and the conglomerate's domination of the agency business dramatically changing the structure, staffing, and economic performance of their constituent agencies, it should come as no surprise a recent study by Sapient Consulting, covering more than one hundred chief marketing officers of major companies in the U.S. and the UK, showed 52 percent of them believed BDAs were unfit to meet their online marketing needs, while a full 49 percent considered BDAs as having difficulty thinking beyond traditional TV and print media via expected creative models. While this is obviously a bummer for BDAs right now, it will be a ball-buster of a problem for them in the future, particularly when you consider just how many consumers, especially younger ones, are getting most of their 24-7-365 communications, information and entertainment services through digital channels.

At the same time, we've been hearing for years that the days of the thirty-second TV commercial are over, particularly since the proliferation of the DVR and the "great commercial destroyer" Tivo. Yet advertisers continue to spend significant amounts of money on "bog standard" traditional TV campaigns that are usually ineffective, and more often than not, impossible to measure in terms of the value they deliver. However, all is not lost, thanks to the eight-hundred-pound gorilla always lurking in the wings, namely, Google, we may be about to see a renaissance of the thirty-second spot we have learned to love and put up with over the years. This long enjoyed advertising cornucopia will continue liposuctioning massive amounts of dollars from advertisers, big and small, thanks to the efforts of a dedicated team of Googlerati working away deep in the bowels of the silicon mine at the beating heart of the GooglePlex. These are the Jolt-slurping, pizza-eating, work-round-the-clock guys who will one day make sure that whenever you do a Google search to find out what you can do about that serious ass itch you get every time you indulge in a Rat Vindaloo, the minute you turn on your Wal-Mart, Chinese made, seventy-four-inch plasma TV, you'll be bombarded with non-stop ads for your local "Ass Itch Research Center." This will ensure you can never escape from advertising for the rest of your life! You should also consider that while this will benefit clients smart enough to jump on the Google bandwagon, it will, cause serious grief for BDAs who will now be cut out of the loop when it comes to immersing their snouts in the previously overflowing trough of TV commercial creation, media planning, and buying. Moreover, they'll never, ever, get back in.

At the moment of writing this (early 2008) Google's preliminary aim has been to change the way the way TV advertising time slots are merchandized. It currently has a partnership with EchoStar which allows it to automate the way TV ads are bought and sold. Even more dramatically for the impact it may have on a BDAs ability to continue selling its clients the effect of branding, it changes the way a commercials effectiveness is measured by studying the second-by-second logs from millions of set-top boxes and what immediate effect this has on sales. In contrast, the set-top boxes you are currently provided with from your cable or satellite TV companies are nothing more than the simplest of computers, reminiscent of those available in the early eighties. Their functionality is crippled, because they are loaded with a few simple applications—a program guide, DVR menu, customer-service messaging, and not much else. They are completely closed boxes, not too far removed from the early Macs! And just like Apple used to believe, the cable and satellite TV companies still think they can control everything, and even more unrealistically, they think they can control it forever. This, as we all know, is dumb, because nothing lasts forever. Right now, it's a dead certainty that Google will expand into almost every conceivable form of media and entertainment. This means that by the middle of the next decade they will be an all-encompassing communications network capable of delivering content that can reach you at any time of the day or night, wherever you are, whatever you might be doing. Whether it is via television, cable, satellite, radio stations, cell phones, movies, games, ATMs, books, magazines, newspapers, etc., you will be reached, and you will not be able to escape. Remember the 2012 Los Angeles of Ridley Scott's Blade Runner? Apart from the fact that it seemed to be dark and raining all the time, and everyone in the movie ate nothing other than soba noodles at sidewalk stalls, they were continually bombarded with flying billboards and holograms featuring ads relentlessly entreating the soaking wet citizens of LA to sign up for a tour of the "outer worlds." Well, now you know what your future will be like, courtesy of Google!

Just as Queen Victoria once said, "If rape is inevitable, relax and enjoy it," both consumers and the BDAs currently targeting them, will have to come to the realization that wherever there is any kind of digital platform, when it comes to advertising, even though their corporate slogan is "Do no harm!" Google will eventually rape you. So, even though you may not enjoy it at the time, you had better work out some way you can relax while enduring it. Because there will not be a damn thing you'll be able to do to avoid it!

The thing you really have to admire about the Google advertising business model, particularly if you are an MBA-wielding douchenozzle whose only concern is extracting the major amount of personal income out of any business situation, is that they don't have to spend big-bucks developing much original content for their digital platforms. All they need is their phenomenally successful search/ad model and they can lie back and relax as dumpster loads of money come pouring in, because they are the creators and owners of the tollgates everyone traveling the Yellow Brick Road of the Google Universe has to pass through.

Even better, local auto/carpet/roofing dealers, feng shui experts, tattoo artists, or hot rock massage parlors can now afford to have highly targeted TV commercials aimed at their prospective customers for less than the price of paying off their local sheriff with doughnuts and coffee. This will obviously be to the detriment of local newspapers. But hey, isn't that what makes capitalism great? Unless you happen to be a local newspaper. The important thing to recognize here is that by beginning to create what will very likely end up being the dominant advertising platform of the future across the entire digital spectrum, Google will have unmatchable power and leverage in how they deal with Advertisers and their Big Dumb Agencies in the future. And because it's no secret Google is already staffing up with experienced TV creatives and producers in order to offer advertisers a complete suit of services, Big Dumb Agencies will undoubtedly lose most, if not all, of their profitable creation of content business.

But, disregarding the argument of whether or not the thirty-second television commercial is dead, a more fundamental question is being asked by those aware that things are rapidly changing and will never be the same again. Marketers are continually developing and improving ways to deliver the right commercial messages at the right time and to the right people by isolating those communities where their target groups are to be found, then through the use of increasingly sophisticated data they are able to tailor their message to have the most impact. But, let's face it, it's still advertising, and it's still interruptive. Just because the message is more relevant to the target, aren't they still going to get pissed off when they have your ad constantly shoved in their face? And don't kid yourselves you can semi-disguise it as an informational message. That's like trying to pretend those dreadful thirty-minute TV infomercials featuring the guy with the bad wig and false beard screaming at the top of his lungs about the miracle scouring powers of Scamo Clean are not really TV commercials. To repeat myself, yet again, the two long dead ad guys said it best: David Ogilvy: "The consumer isn't stupid, she's your wife!" And Howard Gossage: "People don't read advertising, they read what interests them, and sometimes, it's an ad!" The point being that no matter how clever you think you are after spending a fortune on research, insights, datametrics, psychometrics, and endless other expensive mental crutches, at the end of the day, it's all about content. So, why take the chance of making your audience mad by insulting them?

Another example of how the mainstream agency business has been losing its way is the growth of agency search consultants over the last few years. These are companies who on behalf of a major advertiser, and sometimes for surprisingly small ones, will help find them their next advertising agency. They obviously do this for a suitably outrageous fee. Yes, they do a certain amount of weeding out of the chaff from the wheat, in terms of compiling a list of a half dozen or so agencies they consider most suitable to handle the clients account, who will then go through a series of presentations, usually winnowing the list down to three finalists who fight to the death, while expending ridiculous amounts of money for the one in three chance of winning the account. There are at least a couple of things wrong with this state of affairs. Firstly, shouldn't that be the job of the client's marketing and advertising managers? Why are they not aware of who is currently doing good work out there, particularly in their specific markets? Secondly, after expending all that money to win the account, the odds are that within eighteen months, the winning agency will lose it, long before recovering the cost of the pitch. And both these problems have the same root cause: Accountability. As I've mentioned before, the agency and its clients each have to make their quarterly numbers, if the client doesn't, they often blame the agency, eventually firing them. In the pre-search consultant days, that would have reflected badly on the middle management advertising and marketing directors who chose the agency. Now with the buffer of the search consultant, they can offload the blame. As for the unfortunate agency that gets fired after its brief eighteen month honeymoon, it just has to keep pounding away on that new business treadmill. This way they can pacify the bean counters at the conglomerate headquarters for a while, hopefully putting off the day when their corporate masters finally realize that virtually all of their BDAs are expending greater and greater efforts for less and less reward.

However, we are now beginning to see the development of a number of agencies prepared to work outside the constraints of the traditional model. Some are headed and managed by people who've spent years working inside BDAs before coming to the realization that the business model which has existed since the primordial days of *The Hidden Persuaders* is now irrevocably broken. Then again, others have come from non-traditional advertising backgrounds such as music, film/video, and publishing. There are now an increasing number of these new kinds of ad agencies, many of which even refuse to call themselves ad agencies, popping up on both sides of the Atlantic. What most of them have in common is they expect a commitment on the part of clients to be considered as full partners in the creation of branding, marketing and promotional programs. Which is a hell of a shift (not paradigm, I promised, remember?) from meekly playing the expected "servant" role in the "master-servant" relationship that has been the norm between clients and agencies for many years. There are increasing numbers of these new kinds of agencies, but a representative sample would include Naked, which started in London and now has offices in New York. Anomaly, which started in New York and now has offices in London. Droga5 in New York. AnalogFolk in London. IrisNation, which seems to be increasingly all over the place, including the U.S., the U.K, and Singapore, and TeamNoesis, which is currently in California, but which I confidently expect to very soon bust out of the confines of the La La state. I'm sure all of them have plans for global domination in the future. What they all have in common is that they are being careful not to lose the sense of individuality and entrepreneurship which caused them to create something other than the traditional model of an ad agency in the first place. They certainly seem to have taken to heart the insightful words of the late, great, Jay Chiat, who once said, "I can't wait to see how big we get before we turn to shit." Perhaps in response to that inspiring thought, at the end of 2007, Anomaly created "Another Anomaly," which was basically a stand-alone clone of the original Anomaly. Why? Because Anomaly's founders were smart enough to have arrived at the conclusion that sixty employees was the optimal number of people anyone needed to produce good work for their clients. After achieving that level of staffing, most regular agencies create lard-like layers of ineffective churls whose major function is to "manage the process." This requires filling in of lots and lots of timesheets with lots and lots of billable hours, rather than producing anything of actual value. Think of it like being a lawyer in a large malpractice office.

The very name Anomaly was purposely chosen to indicate this would be a new kind of communications business deviating from the norm or the expected. As they say on their Web site the company was created because they recognized that traditional advertising solutions were becoming less and less effective, and what was needed was not the compartmentalization typical of the BDAs, but a mindset that would enable them to deliver complete branded marketing solutions as opposed to branded advertising concepts. This is a method of working that would have been completely alien to the world of *The Hidden Persuaders* fifty years ago. As I have pointed out in earlier chapters, the dinosaur like BDAs are structurally and financially unable to disengage themselves from a business model based on a series of silo like departments operating under a common roof. This, they proudly proclaim, allows them to offer clients a "one from column A, B, or C, Chinese menu approach" for everything a client could possibly want, including creating and producing ads, design, direct marketing, media planning and buying, digital, event planning, etc., etc. The problem is that all these silos are usually run as separate profit centers with their own financial targets and goals, and all are committed to a single end: making the quarterly numbers that will keep their conglomerate masters happy. This invariably results in work that is rarely integrated, in spite of the BDA's claims to the contrary, but is cobbled together with the always-expected, ultra-expensive branding TV campaign sitting at the top of the pyramid with all the other "integrated" components bolted on like some Rube Goldberg creation. Most of these new kinds of agencies do not work on that principle. Instead, they attempt to break down the barriers between the traditional disciplines of advertising, marketing and business solutions, and they don't create solutions via rigidly structured teams assigned to specific accounts. Above all, most of them refuse to bill hours or sell time. Quite simply, they develop intellectual property, for both their clients and themselves. This means that they work in partnership with their clients, and in so doing, share the rewards.

A good example of this is the way New York agency, Droga5, has entered the branded entertainment space via the launch of its dedicated Web channel, "Honeyshed," which I discussed in detail in chapter eight. Even though it's early days yet (at the time of writing the channel had been in operation for less than a year), as Andrew Essex, CEO of Droga5 puts it, "This is about multiple brands getting strength from other brands, like a mall. The emphasis will be on pre-commerce not e-commerce. A lot of times when you go to a mall you don't have a transaction, sometimes it's about learning about what the brands you discover there have to offer. This complete re-evaluation of what it is an agency can do for its clients, leads me to believe that, even though some may fail, many of these new kinds of ad agencies have a good chance of outperforming and taking substantial business from existing agencies. I believe this will happen because they are prepared to break with the traditional methods of doing business. This is demonstrated by their willingness to negotiate deals with clients that if their work doesn't produce agreed upon results, they do not expect to be rewarded. Not only is this a revolutionary method of working and remuneration that undoubtedly sends cold shivers up the spine of BDAs, it is also extremely appealing to clients who are becoming increasingly disenchanted with their existing agencies.

Another of the six I have chosen as examples of companies that are breaking the traditional BDA mold is a recently created agency in London, "AnalogFolk, which takes an even more extreme view of advertising and marketing communications. Their position is that agencies and clients need to be thinking of communications as a product rather than something that has a finite value which decreases over time. They also refuse to be categorized as traditional, digital, guerilla, word-of-mouth, or whatever happens to be the current mot du jour. Their primary positioning is that they create a marriage between digital technology and real-world interaction. Hence the use of the word "analog" in the company name is support for their argument that consumers react to both cerebral and physical stimuli when it comes to making choices. As Ed Ling, one of the agency's principals puts it, "The agency will create new currency for brands, things that people will seek out, use, play with and share."

Another interesting operation that refuses to be categorized by any of the traditional labels is "Noesis," operating out of Los Angeles. Founder Lynn Casey has created a marketing company which like "AnalogFolk," believes consumers are no longer merely users of brands, but are increasingly taking over the ownership of these brands, a fact rarely acknowledged by traditional advertisers and their agencies. Noesis is very much a research focused company, yet it takes a unique approach to the research most of their work is based on. Unlike others that rely on formulaic focus groups, Noesis has created clusters of niche specific consumer panels, comprised of people of all ages, from two to sixty two, or "noe-it-alls" as the company so eloquently refers to them. These panel members are encouraged to share their current and constantly changing beliefs, attitudes and preferences with Noesis on a continual basis. This allows TeamNoesis to track not just the buying habits of thousands of Americans from their pre-teen years, to early adulthood, through to maturity, but more importantly, to get meaningful insights into what social, economic and environmental issues are driving their thinking and life styles. With these continually updated insights, Noesis creates marketing programs and solutions for their clients that are based on current reality and future possibilities, rather than the "boiler plate" outdated and expected campaigns BDA's have force fed their clients for years. Equally important is the way Noesis is able to continually modify their methodology to meet changing market environments.

Proof of how successful the new kind of advertising agencies can be if they are flexible enough to avoid becoming bogged down in traditional thinking, would be the rapidly growing Iris network headquartered in London with a global presence on five continents. Even though their basic philosophy sounds simple, "Media Anything - Ideas Everything," unlike the vacuous claims made by most BDA's, Iris is proving on a daily basis that you can achieve total integration, media neutrality and effectiveness through the creation of meaningful content, executed through the most suitable channels to get the job done. Their growth over the nine years since their foundation has been phenomenal. In my opinion, the major reasons for this have been their maintenance of standards, their openness to new ideas, and above all, staying out of the grasping hands of any of the giant ad conglomerates.

This is just a small representation of the many new kinds of agencies flowering in the current ad agency environment. There will be many more by the time you are reading this. What they all have in common is recognition that the old model is broken. Unlike the BDA's they are not sitting around waiting for the economic climate to reverse to the good old days. They are doing something about it.

Perhaps the best illustration of why so many BDAs simply go through the motions when they talk about reinventing themselves to better cope with the challenges of new media, not to mention fighting off the realization by many of their clients that the old agency model is broken, is illustrated by the recent relevancy efforts of J. Walter Thompson, one of America's oldest and largest agencies. Which in the interests of full disclosure, I must say I have worked for both as a freelancer, and on staff, over a period of many years, and in the process of doing so, been fortunate enough to make a boatload of money! However, in 2005, they decided to revitalize, if not rebrand themselves by changing their logo and corporate identity. So, how did they set about achieving this? By spending several million dollars to change their name from J. Walter Thompson to JWT. Which is what everyone had been calling them for years! They also announced a new "mission statement." I have often thought that if you have to tell the world what your mission is via a statement, rather than simply getting on with it, perhaps you need to re-think your mission. JWT's proudly stated that from now on they would believe in, "Being Anthropologists First - Advertising People Second." Wow, that's pretty heavy shit, particularly if you're a potential client actually in the market for an ad agency, rather than wanting to know who first developed the use of hand tools. If however, you are looking for that kind of esoteric expertise, you might be better off going uptown to Columbia University. The agency also declared that "Time is the new currency. Our job is to ensure more people spend more time with our clients' brands. We need to create ideas that people want to spend more time with. The better the idea the more time people will spend with it." Apart from saying "more time" many more times than was actually necessary, did you notice how they managed to sneak their favorite word "brand" in there? And, for the icing on the cake, it was reported that all JWT employees would now sign a "creative partnership contract," and no doubt will now be required to recite the JWT pledge of allegiance at morning assembly after having first sung the "All Praise Sir Martin" anthem and done ten minutes of mass calisthenics. In the words of JWT management, *"This will reiterate the need to stop interrupting what people are interested in and be what people are interested in. Because this will symbolize a personal commitment and accountability to improving the creative product as well as shape the agency's future. This fresh way of thinking will fundamentally alter how our company operates and how it is perceived. It addresses an ever-changing media landscape and an increasingly savvy consumer, returning JWT to our pioneering roots of defining the future rather than chasing it."* Note to management: I have absolutely no fucking idea what you are saying. Please remember, you are in the communications business, plain English always beats the shit out of management babble! But no, I'll give them the benefit of the doubt; I think they were actually trying to say what I said earlier in the book. *Create stuff that interests people.* Now that wasn't too hard, was it?

Having said that, because they have been so good to me over the years and because they are no different than all the other BDAs out there, I ask forgiveness of JWT for using them as an example. I know, in future, don't call me, we'll call you! But JWT in common with all BDAs cannot help themselves from selling the same old snake oil. OK, every now and again, they attempt to dress it up in new clothes, but, in common with used car salesmen, lawyers and politicians, they are hard wired to keep spouting the same hoary, lichen encrusted clichés accompanied by the incessant banging of that good old brand mantra. Don't believe me? Here are some current samples taken from the various Web sites of a representative sample of BDAs:

Y&R: *BrandAsset Valuator.*

Ogilvy: *360 Degree Brand Stewards.*

Grey: *Brand Acceleration.*

JWT: *Brand Storytelling.*

DDB: *Positioning brands to compete.*

EuroRSCG: *Maximizing the relationship between consumers and brands.*

Even current "Hot Shop Du Jour" Crispin, Porter + Bogusky, declares that *they make branded creative content.* Think I'm making this stuff up? Simply go to any BDA Web site and check out their "mission statement." And the saddest thing of all? These guys are supposedly in the business of communicating to their client's current and future customers why they should choose to spend their hard earned money on their product, rather than the competitions.

However, even though many BDAs hide behind the cloak of branding, and can therefore claim they are spending millions of their client's dollars to build brand awareness, enhance brand value, increase share of mind, or customer acceptance, which, coincidentally, are all things that cannot be definitively measured, particularly as regards how they relate to sales, I am coming to the sad conclusion that many of the new guys on the block are starting to get up to similar tricks. OK, they may not be blowing gazillions of their client's dollars on grandiose and often ineffectual TV campaigns, but they will claim their "cool" viral campaign, using a one minute video of the clients widget being eaten by a boa constrictor, which for some unknown reason is wearing a Darth Vador helmet, got a million hits on YouTube, while blithely ignoring this is no guarantee it will sell a million widgets.

Many of the behemoths will survive through a process of

self-preservation and pseudo-reinvention by their continuing acquisition of smaller, specialist companies. But, in spite of these efforts and their desperate hyping of the great results each ineffectual take over will produce, they will eventually atrophy in the same way dwarf stars finally burn out when they have absorbed nearby suns, sucked out their energy, and eventually collapsed within themselves to create a black hole! OK, I know that's a bit over the top, but I'm trying to make a point here.

So, let me have a stab at describing what I think the agency of the future will look like. But please, don't hold me to this and come back in a couple of years telling me I am full of crap 'cos I didn't get it right. It's just a half-assed, semi-educated guess on my part based on more than thirty years in the trenches of Madison Avenue, which considering the current state of the ad biz, qualifies me as knowing nothing. But, what the hell, here goes. Let's start off by assuming the Adverati can somehow get it right for a change and convince their clients they might get a better ROI on their marketing dollars if they allowed their agency to act as a true, equal partner, rather than a vendor. If this happens, then here are what I would consider to be the four essential ingredients necessary for a successful and rewarding relationship.

1. The agency of the future should avoid becoming part of a conglomerate. In the case of a startup this means it must have an unabashed commitment to never sell out. Forget the usual bullshit of how by doing this, you will be able to expand globally, call on greater resources, and benefit from the synergistic relationship with other companies within the conglomerate. Rest assured, apart from making the principals rich, this will almost certainly, after a period of time, destroy the company. The original desire of the founders to create great work, that piss and vinegar attitude they meticulously cultivated, because they wanted to do it their way, will gradually lose out to the overarching need to make the numbers every three months. To achieve this grubby end, the bean counters at corporate headquarters will make the agency management's life hell. They will suffer, the clients will become disaffected and the work will inevitably suck.

The last thing any self-respecting ad agency, which sees itself as more than a money-making meat grinder should be part of, is an organization traded on the stock exchange. Without doubt, the great agencies of the future will be independent.

2. The agency of the future will be structured and organized around a central core competency: creating great work, which simply means delivering unique ideas and original content to clients. Yes, I know, every agency in Christendom currently claims to do that. But that's sheer, unadulterated bullshit. Thirty percent of the stuff ad agencies produce today is mediocre, 30 percent is awful, and 30 percent is absolute shit. That leaves 10 percent which is hopefully worthwhile and not a direct insult to the consumer's intelligence. Can you honestly think of any other business with such an abysmal level of productivity or effectiveness?

3. The agency of the future will execute the core competency. This means making sure all their original ideas and wonderful content should be translatable into any media. Not just the traditional, or even the new, but media we haven't yet begun to imagine. It will also be able to execute in non-media environments, because it will be fearless enough to recommend that clients shouldn't necessarily spend their money in traditional ways. Instead of the expected TV campaign, the client should perhaps have all its employees learn Mandarin Chinese, or setup and manage sidewalk stalls. Better yet, take every single employee and their families on a Caribbean cruise. The return on this would far outweigh the effectiveness of most advertising currently produced!

4. The agency of the future will make its money in radically different ways than was possible, or accepted, in the era of *The Hidden Persuaders*. Yes, we know the days of the 15 percent media commission and the 20 percent mark up on all various forms of production are long gone, and we know that fees in lieu of commissions have been with us for a considerable time and will probably continue to be. In fact, at the time of writing WPP has negotiated with the Dell Computer Company an exclusive deal to handle all its business on a global basis through a dedicated in-house agency. The business is reputed to be worth eight hundred million dollars (which is still based on the anachronistic metric of how the client would blow its ad

budget if it was still spending it in traditional media). So you have to know that as part of his argument to win the business, the fee negotiated by Sir Martin will provide WPP, at best, a razor thin margin of profitability. And because the agency will revolve around a single client who is providing all its income, any pretence at objectivity will be laughable. The new guys on the block I have discussed earlier in this chapter claim they will make their money selling "Intellectual Property," and by being paid purely on a results/rewards basis. Which sounds great, until you realize it's almost impossible to correlate spending and results with most advertising, whether it is of the new or old variety. With the single exception of direct marketing, where you can measure a campaigns effectiveness from the sales directly generated by a special offer, promotion or ad campaign, virtually all other forms of advertising, whether you call it brand building, viral, guerilla, word-of-mouth, sponsorship, event marketing, product placement, or whatever is currently in vogue, are impossible to nail down when it comes to identifying the activities ROI.

Perhaps that's why advertising never has been, and never will be a precise, let alone quantifiable, way to promote a company or sell its products or services. This has nothing to do with the claimed subconscious manipulation of consumers which sent Vance Packard into such a tizzy fifty years ago when he penned *The Hidden Persuaders*. It has even less to do with the fact we are increasingly bombarded by ever proliferating messages in the age of *The Ubiquitous Persuaders*. The consumer is smart enough to tune out whatever they aren't interested in, increasingly so with the aid of current and future technology. Yet in spite of this, the Adverati continue to claim they have the all the answers. But their clients realize they now have an increasing variety of options that offer not only different and far more sensible ways to approach how their marketing and advertising is created and managed, but an indisputably more effective way to pay for and measure its effectiveness.

Perhaps fifty years from now someone will write an update to *The Ubiquitous Persuaders*. I won't be around to read it, but I'll hazard a guess that as the world's second oldest profession, advertising will still be here, the people in it will still be dispensing snake oil and the public will be even less influenced by it. Billions of dollars will be spent creating it, and the vast majority of the results will still be used to wrap tomorrow's fish.

Because it's such a bloody good story, and a perfect way to end this rant, I'll repeat something from an earlier chapter. As David Ogilvy said forty five years ago at the end of his must-read book, *Confessions of an Advertising Man*, in answer to his sister's suggestion that advertising should be abolished. "No, my darling sister, advertising should not be abolished. But it must be reformed."

Ah David, you always did have a wonderful way with words.

post-
SCRIPT

It's not as bad as you think it is… It's a hell of a lot worse.

The Ubiquitous Persuaders is finished, edited and designed. And yet, I am driven to add this postscript, not because I want to subject you to even more of my Cassandra like prophesy's, but because several of the ones I've made, particularly in the final chapter, seem to be coming true at a pace even I didn't expect. In the last months of 2008, the shit has hit the fan with a vengeance. Highly paid economists have finally come to the conclusion we've been in a recession for over a year, something everyone else had been aware of for well over a year. Gas jumped to over $4.50 a gallon leading the unfortunate owners of Hummers and other giant gas guzzlers to experience severe palpitations of the pocketbook. Yes, gas has since fallen to about $1.50 a gallon, but as the ranks of the unemployed continue to swell, many drivers of these behemoths have decided they'd rather make one more mortgage payment than slake the thirst of their mechanical beasts. America's "Big Three" auto companies are begging for government handouts. Which basically means taxpayer dollars. Auto ad accounts, for both domestic and imports, which have traditionally represented rich pickings are being ruthlessly slashed.

So, the days of milk and honey for the Adverati are rapidly drawing to a close. Omnicom has announced they are laying off five percent of their workforce, a total of three thousand five hundred people. WPP instituted a hiring freeze, which within weeks transmogrified into mass layoffs. Interpublic continues to sink without a trace whilst issuing pink slips to increasing numbers of its unfortunate employees. Publicis has loudly proclaimed they wouldn't consider laying anyone off, which everyone knows is merde de vache, but what can you expect from the cheese eating, Chablis swilling French?

With the Super Bowl just a couple of weeks off as I write this, NBC has announced twenty percent of its commercial inventory remains unsold. An occurrence which has never happened within living memory of most of today's media planners and buyers. We can therefore, expect a fire sale of the remaining slots as game day gets closer. This will, undoubtedly, leave those BDA's who had earlier committed to blowing $3 million of their client's money for a single thirty second spot with large quantities of egg on their Botoxed faces. Staying with sports, the International Olympic Committee has just announced that many of its "TOP" sponsors, a select group of companies dumb enough to pay between $80 million to $100 million for a four year sponsorship cycle are pulling out. Meaning the TV coverage of the 2010 Winter Games in Vancouver, and the 2012 Summer Games in London, will be interrupted by amateurish commercials featuring used car dealerships and your friendly neighborhood acupuncturist. Media is rapidly becoming such a commodity product that advertisers are increasingly realizing they no longer need a third party to plan, negotiate or book most forms of traditional media for exorbitant fees and commissions.

Another significant sign of the times is the number of outfits springing up who have ceased to refer to themselves as advertising agencies, but as creators of IP, or intellectual property, a subject I touched on in my final chapter. However, some are going even further, not merely expecting a share of the income and profits their particular communication brainwave will deliver, they are moving into the business of actually producing products of their own. In London, ad agency BBH, has created a spin-off with the somewhat expected title, "Zag!" And if I have to explain the reason for the name, then it won't have served its purpose. Amongst the products they are creating are a range of vegetarian meals selling in supermarkets and a range of personal alarms that emit a painfully loud woman's scream when the user finds herself in a difficult situation. Zag, has just opened a New York office and is involved in a fashion start up, "Mrs-O," that will be offering a range of "First Lady" fashions, kicking off with designer tee shirts. Yes, that's exactly what America needs in the middle of a depression, more tee shirts. Or, as the CEO of Zag breathlessly puts it… "It's exciting, it's unpredictable, it's all the things you'd expect from an entrepreneurial business trying to find its way." Oh dear.

At the same time, The Brooklyn Brothers, an agency in New York has created a range of organic chocolate candy by the name of "Fat Pig." These are described as, are you ready for this? "Oinkganic." They also have a product, "Premcal," a vitamin/mineral medication to relieve the symptoms of PMS. You have to take your hat off to these guys; they've certainly covered all the bases. Ad Agency product creation will be an activity you can expect to see a lot more of as traditional forms of advertising are increasingly starved of money.

But as long as the economy remains depressed, I can guarantee that as ad budgets diminish, clients will increasingly demand the delivery of quantifiable results. This will be accompanied by what Jeff Zucker, of NBC, has described as the conversion of analog advertising dollars into digital advertising pennies, a situation that will put further pressure on BDA's to slash costs and reduce overhead. Only a couple of weeks ago, a senior executive of Interpublic gave a speech in which he promised clients they could now expect "hard sell advertising for hard times." He went on to say that clients should look forward to increased sales as a result of this new emphasis on no-frills, hard-nosed advertising. Which, if I was one of their clients, would make me wonder why they would only offer me this wonderfully effective method of driving sales during hard times, rather than all the time? For the next couple of years, you will see branding taking a back seat to advertising programs their creators claim will actually sell stuff. And I guarantee that an inspection of many BDA Web sites will see the replacement of much abused, "branding" with the increasingly in vogue, "selling." The end results will not be pretty, both in the esthetic quality of the work, and the less opulent life style of those producing it.

I'm sure David Ogilvy will be laughing his sides out as he spins six feet down in the grounds of the Chateau de Touffou.

about the
AUTHOR

George Parker has spent more than thirty five years in the Madison Avenue salt mines with such major agencies as Ogilvy & Mather, Young & Rubicam, Chiat Day. J. Walter Thompson and many others. He's worked in New York, San Francisco, London, Paris Stockholm and anywhere else were they would pay him obscene amounts of money and give him an AmEx platinum card with no questions asked. In the course of his career he's won Cannes Lions, CLIOs, EFFIES, the David Ogilvy Award and several hundred other bits of tin and plastic. His blog AdScam.Typepad.com, which was named as one of the four best ad blogs in the world by *Campaign Magazine*, is required reading for those looking for a piss & vinegar view of the world's second oldest profession.

Made in the USA